D1343973

WHEN WILL I BE FAMOUS?

Martin Kelner

Published by BBC Worldwide Ltd,
80 Wood Lane, London W12 0TT

ISBN 0563 48777 1

Commissioning Editor: Ben Dunn
Project Editor: Sarah Emsley
Copy Editor: Judith Scott
Book Designer: DW Design, London
Production Controller: Arlene Alexander

Set in Sabon
Printed and bound in Great Britain by Mackays of Chatham plc, Kent

DEDICATION

*To Janet, who understood when I said I could not
celebrate our anniversary because I was going to see
a Freddie Mercury tribute act in Halifax.*

ACKNOWLEDGEMENTS

Thanks:

to my agent Roger Davis for wising me up to certain aspects of show business, for always returning my calls, and for the gig he got me four years ago...

to all the acts who hung around in dismal dressing rooms while I questioned their very existence...

and to my friend Paul Reizin for some rather good jokes.

CONTENTS

INTRODUCTION

Old joke: A man in a pub is complaining about his job, which is to follow behind the elephant as the circus parades through town, shovelling up the droppings. As a result, he constantly smells of elephant shit and finds it impossible to make friends or get dates. 'So why don't you quit?' asks the barman. 'What?' he replies, outraged. 'And leave show business?'

I had an elephant shit moment once. I used to present a late-night show every Saturday on BBC Radio 2 on a freelance presenter's contract, one of those rock-solid agreements which ensured that the only circumstances in which they could possibly get rid of me was if they wanted to. It's the kind of contract that fellow light entertainers will be familiar with. Contract, schmontract, as it is sometimes known.

Anyway, around this time I was approached by an advertising agency for whom I had scripted some videos and presentations, and offered a real job; with money – tons of it – a car, private health insurance, a proper contract, and lots of grown-up stuff like that. I pondered the offer for maybe six and a half seconds before deciding to persist with my career in show business, which I felt was going rather well. I mean, any day soon I expected to make it round to the *front* of the elephant.

If I may be allowed to stretch this metaphor just a little further, most people in show business are more or less *behind* the elephant. The entertainers you see on TV are the exception. There are thousands more, possibly hundreds of thousands, who dream of breaking into the big time – for half a lifetime in some cases – although privately they must realize they have about as much chance as Michael Winner has of being named rear of the year.

There are others who have actually enjoyed their moment in the sun and are now hanging on for dear life. People in show business never die, you see. They just get worse gigs. Shorter contracts.

This somewhat discouraging thought occurred to me – surprise, surprise – as I turned fifty (biologically, that is, for my showbiz age still hovered hopefully around the mid-forties). I had just agreed to part with Jazz FM – I think they decided they wanted someone taller or something – and was pondering writing a newspaper feature about my colleague Tony Blackburn.

Tony, it seemed to me, had been right at the front of the parade: the Radio 1 *Breakfast Show*, Carnegie Hall for disc jockeys in his day. But his career was now approaching the fade, where the grooves begin their headlong rush towards the hole in the middle of the record. He was presenting a soul show on Jazz FM, some oldies' shows on radio in London, and spending the rest of his time working his nuts off driving up and down the country doing a parody of his old act. Making a good living, sure, but a little undignified for a man of his age. Surely Tony must realize his glory, glory days are behind him, nationwide fame a distant memory.

Shows what I know. At a dismal gig in Newcastle, Tony mentioned casually that he had been approached to do a reality TV show where they planned to ditch some 'celebrities' in a remote jungle somewhere – a popular move in my view, although I gathered there were plans to bring them back as well – and sort of see what happened. The whole thing struck me as vaguely preposterous, and I got the distinct impression Tony might not have been the programme's absolute first choice. But what can I say? The guy's a trouper. He did it, won it, and as a result, at fifty-nine years old, he is on the TV every time you switch on: *The Weakest Link, GMTV, Ready Steady Cook, Newsnight with Tony Blackburn*, everything.

It is stories like Tony's, actually, that keep some of us going. Whenever I got depressed about the biological clock ticking so much faster than the showbiz clock, I always used to think of the great comic actress Irene Handl, who did so much exceptional work with Peter Sellers. She never made it until she was fifty-eight. From now on, though, Tony will be my inspiration.

And what exactly is meant by making it? Why, becoming famous, of course. Forget the money, the houses, the passport into the finest bedrooms in the nation. Fame is the spur.

For the past two years, television has been awash with youngsters of uncertain talent – *Pop Idols, Fame Academy, Popstars: the Rivals, Big Brother* – saying: 'Broken marriages? Drug problems? Reporters going through my dustbin? Body in the swimming pool? Bring them all on. You know what I want.'

Fame! Like the song says, they want to live forever. And who wouldn't? My dictionary defines famous as well known; celebrated; renowned. Its second meaning is great; glorious, as in *a famous victory*. The thesaurus, meanwhile, offers such synonyms as acclaimed; legendary; remarkable; illustrious. The three miserable antonyms it provides are unheard-of; unknown; obscure. Hands up who wants to be unheard-of and obscure, when you can be celebrated and legendary.

Problem is, for those who miss out on reality TV's short cut to fame, the journey can be long and uncertain. Years, decades even, of pounding the road to thankless gigs in working men's clubs, or mystifying evenings providing background colour for a bunch of pissed-up insurance brokers at their annual shindig. That Austin Allegro better be regularly serviced and you better get used to chicken sandwiches from the BP Shop.

The strange thing is that, amid all the so-called reality TV shows purporting to tell us something about the entertainment business, the only programme to get anywhere near the truth is *Phoenix Nights*, a fictional comedy series on Channel 4. I would never have thought of Peter Kay's brilliant programme as a documentary had I not picked up a copy of *Showcall*, the annual index of artistes and attractions published by the *Stage*, the performers' weekly bible. *Showcall* is chock-full of artistes and attractions, all available – ever so available – for work. Very few of them, you feel, would look out of place on cabaret night at the Phoenix.

This great doorstop of a book – nearly 1,000 pages – became my source material as I sought to discover who all these people were, out there on the road, and who it is exactly that they are entertaining. It is a fantastic read and I recommend it to you. There is a subtext to nearly every entry. Take the contact details, for instance. Where an act is enjoying a modicum of success, you will get just one phone number, their agent's. Other less celebrated, more available performers, however, will offer home, mobile and fax numbers, email addresses and mum's mobile number, plus if you want you can leave a message with the grocery shop on the corner, so there is absolutely no chance they will miss out on a gig. 'Twenty-four-hour answerphone' is a favourite – very handy should you need a comedy hypnotist at three in the morning.

Then there are entries like the one for Adger Brown: 'Complete comedy entertainer and after-dinner speaker.' This bears the information, 'Formerly just Adger.' What thought processes, you wonder, informed the change from just Adger to Adger Brown? 'Well, Adger, this could be the year you make it,' you can imagine his manager announcing. 'We're changing your name from Adger to Adger Brown. All that single name stuff is just so passé these days. Look at Sting and Madonna. No, it's Adger Brown from now on for you, my lad. Go home and prepare for fame.'

I have been getting *Showcall* for four years now and there is just one change I have noticed that *Phoenix Nights* has failed to take account of, and that is the gradual disappearance of novelty acts. Those strange turns – the sad animal acts, the chap spinning on a wheel singing 'Space Oddity', the woman whose dove flies into the air conditioning – auditioning over the final credits, have largely been supplanted by lookalike acts, as I discovered on my travels. You can still find them, though. Among the fine entertainers we encounter in this book are a woman in Benidorm who entertains with her front bottom and a chap in Macclesfield with equivalent talents round the back.

What drives these people on? Where, and for whom, do they perform? Not just them, but the Abba soundalikes, pub and club comedians, the cruise ship entertainers, the whole army of performers crowding the pages of *Showcall*. That was what I set out to discover.

Some of you, of course, will have spotted the hint of a double meaning in the title of this book. Am I asking the question on behalf of other people or do I really mean: 'When will *I* be famous?' Frankly, that is a question I stopped asking some years ago, but then the more I immersed myself in the show business world, the more I itched to stick my head above the parapet and have a try. So I did and, having performed stand-up before a few dozen people in a London pub, I can confirm that the (limited) laughter of a live audience is a powerful drug. (As indeed is cocaine, as many of our top comedians will testify.)

Nevertheless, it took several days of feverish preparation and caused me agonies. The effort it must entail to be halfway decent would surely call for abnormal dedication, and probably a degree of psychological dysfunction as well. Entertainers at the very top of the tree are clearly either barking, have struck a deal with the Devil, or have been extremely lucky.

So, no, fame no longer motivates me. I am not sure it ever did, actually. You probably have to want it, really want it. Like one or two of the performers I met, I was always quite happy to have found a job that allowed me to stay in bed and watch daytime television.

For this reason, I am lost in admiration for those who choose show business for a living; out there on the road, behind the elephant, eating those sandwiches, working on the act, adding or dropping surnames, waiting for the phone call that might mean the big break, and smiling, smiling, always smiling.

Some people might find this laughable or sad – worth a giggle in *Phoenix Nights*, but not a life. Having dabbled ever so slightly in show business myself, though, I must say I find it rather heroic.

1

HELLO NEWCASTLE

Is there a sadder sight in the world than a fifty-eight-year-old man alone in a nightclub? I am downstairs at a club in Newcastle-upon-Tyne called Nice at the Playrooms – which to be honest is not very nice at all – and there is a fifty-eight-year-old man in here. His name is Tony Blackburn.

I am not claiming any chronological high ground as I am not so much younger myself, but my excuse is I am gathering material for a book exploring the outer suburbs of the entertainment world; and suburbs do not come much more outer than these.

Because of my age, and the fact that I am jotting things down in a little notebook, people assume I am something to do with the management of the club and keep coming up to me to ask where the toilet is. Resisting the temptation to say, 'You're in it,' I try to direct them, although it is not easy to make yourself understood at one in the morning when everybody else is under the influence and you aren't.

Let me explain what is going on. It is a fortnight before Christmas, and Newcastle is in what is popularly known as carnival mood. Everybody is out for the night, weaving between the clubs and bars, wearing almost nothing despite the sub-zero temperatures, as is the Saturday night custom in this part of England. An intense battle for the pounds in these punters' pockets is being waged by the town's nightspots – or 'nitespots' as it is often spelt.

As it happens, that is an awful lot of pounds. Although most economic indicators place the northeast of England down amongst the wines and spirits, there is more cash sloshing around in these pockets than you will find in buttoned-up Croydon or Wilmslow or any of the supposedly more prosperous towns in Britain. People's money is not tied up in their houses here. They like to go out and spend it. When your home was worth £75,000 last year, and £77,000 this, it hardly seems worthwhile staying at home and throwing a dinner party to talk about it.

There are geographical and historical reasons for the spend, spend, spend mentality, too. Stuck out here on the cold northeast coast, there is something of a frontier town atmosphere. Also, Newcastle, with its tradition in heavy industry, has been built on the weekly wage packet rather than the monthly salary. Without getting too heavily into social science, the upshot is that at Christmas time there are an awful lot of people in their party clothes filling the streets, looking for somewhere to spend their money.

Nice at the Playrooms is a rave club, playing music which to the uninitiated sounds like a car alarm, occasionally interrupted by some idiot with a whistle. But the kiddies love it and I am assured that the DJs who make a very handsome living playing it are as skilled as any music producer in mixing and matching tracks in a way that will keep people dancing until the chemicals wear off.

I was told a rather shocking story recently by a BBC sound engineer who accompanies some of the big-name DJs to Radio 1 promotions in Ibiza and Ayia Napa. He says that some of their mixing is done in advance in the calm of recording studios and with the assistance of the latest in digital editing facilities, with the results being dubbed onto mini-discs to be played – under the counter, as it were – while the superstar DJ merely goes through the motions of rocking the old twelve-inchers back and forth. All smoke and mirrors.

Be that as it may, tonight's star turn is one Lisa Loud, spinning the platters in the cavernous upstairs room that looks rather more cavernous than it should. I have seen those programmes like *Ibiza Uncovered* that they put on TV late at night to refresh the jaded palates of middle-aged channel surfers, and it seems to me that the norm for these dance venues is that there should be barely enough room to slide a cigarette paper between you and the person jigging up and down next to you.

Ominously, there is enough space here for the dancers to express themselves in the style we were encouraged to follow at primary school when Miss Alderson played the piano and told us to pretend to be lambs gambolling in the fields. I appear to have picked one of those nights – and my own experience as an occasional light entertainer tells me they are many – when not everything is running as smoothly as it might.

Lisa, who is well known and much admired by people who know and admire her kind of performer, should have drawn a much bigger crowd, but Sacha, an even better known DJ, is spinning discs at the nearby Telewest Arena and the town has been flooded with free tickets. Also, I learn, 'There has been some kind of cock-up with the advertising.'

None of this is good news for Tony, whose booking is a rather extravagant add-on to the evening's line-up. He is to appear in the club's 'chill-out zone', a dank downstairs room to which dancers retreat when they need respite from the relentless activity upstairs.

It is some years since I have been in a basement nightclub, but this could be the Continental Club, Manchester, circa 1978. The toilets, the way your feet stick to what is left of the carpet, and that distinctive smell – tobacco, beer, cheap perfume and the promise of sex. I sense this is not a good venue for Tony's particular talents.

As the mothers and grandmothers of tonight's clientele could confirm, Tony Blackburn was briefly one of the most famous men in Britain. Had you stopped anyone in the street in the late sixties or early seventies and mentioned his name, you would have got an immediate response. In the days when Britain had only one radio station playing pop music – when pop music meant the Beatles, the Stones and Tamla Motown – Tony was the man playing it.

It is Tony as much as anybody we have to thank, or blame, for introducing belatedly into Britain the essentially American art of the disc jockey, 'the wriggling ponces of the spoken word' as Orson Welles called them – which always seemed to me fair comment, if a little hurtful.

When Tony presented the BBC Radio 1 *Breakfast Show* he had 21 million listeners. Before him, the BBC employed announcers rather than disc jockeys; perfectly spoken chaps in dinner jackets introducing gramophone records by Miss Alma Cogan. If you listen to archive clips of those early record shows it is difficult to discern much difference in tone between them and Neville Chamberlain announcing 'Peace in our time'.

You would never confuse Tony with the Prime Minister, though. He told awful jokes – Tony, that is, not the PM – had a sound effects dog called Arnold, and used to sign off with, 'Have lots of fun, be good' – in a comedy deep voice – 'and bye for now.' Not much, I know, but for those of us who were part of Britain's post-war baby boom, Tony's show was the soundtrack to our childhood and adolescence. What we fell in love with most of all, I suspect, was the fact that he seemed to take the same cheerful joy in cheap music that we did. Still does, in fact. A television producer friend once told me that Tony 'could bore for Britain', which turns out to be hugely unfair. I know what he meant, though. Tony is obsessed with the vaguely ridiculous business of introducing music on the radio. It is almost his sole topic of conversation. It is a subject that interests me, too, having done quite a bit of it, but even I feel myself going when he starts enthusing about all the stations he can receive on his digital radio.

Tony's love of radio and pop music may be what has held his career back a little. Not that he has been unsuccessful, but you have to wonder why he is doing a gig in Newcastle while Noel Edmunds is circling his country estate in a helicopter, tossing empty champagne bottles into his lake. Sure, Tony is probably not as clever as Edmunds, but he may also have been just a little too enthused by what he was doing. It is not a good career move for disc jockeys to become too interested in music.

Tony is enjoying a late flowering, though. Just when he might have expected his career to be sinking into that twilight zone inhabited by sixties pop bands like the Bachelors or the Searchers, or old cabaret turns like Nookie Bear, he is in greater demand than ever. For the past two years he has been flown out to Ibiza each summer to perform at Eden, one of the biggest and most famous rave clubs in Europe where, in the midst of the frenzy, he does his 'Tony Blackburn' act. He wears a glitter suit, with a big, comedy, gold medallion, about six inches in diameter, which he swings around in a vaguely suggestive manner, while playing seventies floor fillers and party records from the Bee Gees and Kool and the Gang, the kind of songs he would have played years ago without irony.

He invites the crowd to join in with the tunes, singing along, or shaping the letters for 'YMCA', and has a dancing competition where the winners are awarded gold-style medallions, slightly smaller than his own. And that is about it. He is on stage for roughly an hour. To kids who have danced themselves almost to a standstill, it is a welcome interlude. I suspect also that some of the strong melodies of those seventies disco classics are quite welcome, given that most modern dance music shuns melody in favour of the prescribed number of beats per minute. Whatever the reason, I am assured that Tony's ironic act goes down a storm.

In freshers' week you will find him at university unions the length and breadth of Britain and he is a popular draw at corporate gigs as well, being wheeled in to sweeten the pill after the workforce has suffered a weekend of 'motivation'. Tony's act works on two levels: as nostalgia for older employees, and as post-modern irony – or indeed something out of which to take the piss – for the younger element.

Tonight in Newcastle his act does not even work on one level. So flat does it fall that he telephones me the morning after to apologize, in the manner of someone who has failed to perform as advertised in the boudoir department, insisting: 'This doesn't normally happen.'

Not that we were without warning. The evening, from the time I met Tony at the airport at around nine o'clock until he went on stage at half past midnight, conformed absolutely to the cock-up theory of showbiz. For a start, nobody but me recognized Tony at the airport. The two young boys in comedy flared trousers and training shoes who had been dispatched by the club to fetch the veteran record spinner walked straight past him to welcome another passenger off the plane. Unbeknown to Tony, alongside the raddled businessmen with whom he shared the last flight out of London was one of the new stars in the DJ firmament.

Lisa Loud is about thirty, hair in a fashionable short blonde bob. She steps off the plane wearing what I take to be sportswear but is probably extremely expensive 'chilling out' gear. As her website says, she 'combines glamour, elegance, and sophistication on the decks, and is devastatingly fashionable and most devastatingly loud'.

I strongly suspect Lisa Loud is not her baptismal name, especially as she often shares a stage with Nancy Noise. (What happened to the supply of imaginative stage names? Did the seam get exhausted after Judy Garland and Joan Crawford, or Madonna?) Whatever the name, despite ostensibly being a colleague, Tony has absolutely no idea who Lisa is. There is no point of contact. It is as if some brilliantined sportsman of the past like Stanley Matthews were suddenly to find himself playing alongside Beckham or Paolo DiCanio.

Once I had pointed Tony out to the two boys – Gaz and Daz, I think they were called – they crammed him and Lisa into the back of a rather small car, but one with go-faster stripes and alloy wheel trim, and drove them to the Malmaison Hotel on Newcastle's Quayside to wait for the gig.

Newcastle is very proud of its tarted-up docks area, as it is of Ponteland Airport. (I like to refer to northern airports by their traditional names, like Ponteland, or Yeadon in Leeds, and Speke in Liverpool, to undermine their pretensions.) If you really want to know what the North is all about these days, sit around one of these puffed-up bus stations for an hour or two. Newcastle International indeed.

For a couple of months in the summer, the place is bustling, hosting the exodus from the cold North to the Mediterranean – a procession of dubious leisurewear and over-stimulated children moving through the departure lounge and emerging a fortnight later through the arrival doors, as if on some human baggage carousel, but now burnished and mosquito-bitten and clinking litre bottles of cut-price vodka.

Most of the time, though, Ponteland is used by captains, or more likely lieutenants, of industry, flying closer to the centre of Europe, from which Newcastle seems ever more remote, to business meetings in London, Paris or Frankfurt.

Tony had been fairly vague about what time he might arrive at the airport, so I turned up at 7.30 p.m on a bitterly cold evening to find the place spotless, gleaming and empty. Not a-few-people-milling-around empty but post-nuclear empty. The last flight from London was delayed, leaving me a lavish two hours to explore the airport, which I could not help seeing as representative of what I like to call the cappuccinification of the North.

If you want more of this, go to the Quayside, or to the docks area of Liverpool, Manchester, Hull or Leeds. Actually, you don't even need to go. Telephone the council and pretend you represent a financial institution thinking of relocating to the North and you will receive by return of post a small forest of brochures with pictures of 'exclusive developments' where penthouse flats command stunning views of where they used to build the ships and where in the basement you're never more than a minute away from an exercise bike.

Down the road from your secure apartment building you will find vodka bars and Japanese restaurants, reassuringly run by the same chains that own the ones you're thinking of leaving behind in Harrow or Highgate. Rest assured: the North is no longer a stranger to shaved Parmesan. Virgin olive oil, we spit on you. Give us extra virgin or nothing.

But it takes more than a little suckling on the corporate tit to squeeze the life out of Newcastle-upon-Tyne. The most famous characters ever to come from Newcastle are probably cartoon figures: Andy Kapp, an unreconstructed northern working man, who drank, smoked, backed horses, treated his wife like a doormat and whose adventures appeared every day in the *Daily Mirror*; and two girls called Tracy and Sandra, the 'Fat Slags' of the scabrous 'adult' comic *Viz*, produced in an old warehouse in Newcastle city centre. Tray and San's favourite things are sex and kebabs, not necessarily in that particular order, and occasionally simultaneously. Outrageous and damaging stereotypes, of course, as any representative of Newcastle Council will tell you, but not without a grain of truth. What characterizes the city is the capacity of its residents for cheerful, unselfconscious, effortless enjoyment.

I have been to Belfast, Dublin and Edinburgh and had fun, but in those towns there is almost a political element to it. You have fun by becoming one of the gang, an honorary Celt. None of those cities in my view holds a candle to Newcastle as a party town. Adolf Hitler could have fun in Newcastle.

I freely admit – and I am probably some kind of pervert who ought to be locked up – that I find the sight of a gang of plump young girls giggling their way from one bar to another, in little black party frocks about three sizes too small for them, lifts my spirits. I like the way they signal a really interesting story or express outrage by beginning the sentence with an intake of breath and a falsetto 'Eeee …'

The centre of Newcastle on a Saturday evening, especially the old town (on streets called Bigg Market, Cloth Market and Groat Market where, presumably, cloth, groats, and biggs were once traded) is full of these girls, eyeing up, none too surreptitiously, young lads with gelled hair, wearing T-shirts in the middle of winter.

The Malmaison, of course, is another world. In Tony's room all the four-star accoutrements are in place: trouser press, complimentary soaps and hair conditioners, and a bed at least three times as big as needed to accommodate a disc jockey barely five feet six inches tall.

It is interesting how many disc jockeys – entertainers of all sorts, actually – are small. Tom Cruise, I believe, could fit comfortably onto a charm bracelet. A popular theory is that exerting control over an audience is a unique chance for the little man to exercise power. And power, of course, is a great aphrodisiac, which is why those ultimate controllers, the stand-up comedians, even the least prepossessing ones, manage to sustain an interesting and varied sex life. That is the theory, anyway, and until somebody comes up with something better it provides a possible explanation for the Woody/Diane/Mia/Soon-yi conundrum.

(And, if I might digress within a digression, is it not richly ironic that these showbiz Napoleons criss-crossing the world to entertain us are sleeping in the unnecessarily large beds that four- and five-star hotels feel they have to provide, while six-foot security guards and chartered accountants have to squeeze into normal size ones? The smallest people get the biggest beds. And they say capitalism works.)

Tony definitely likes to be in control. He tells me that it is written into his contract that he has to perform in the disco equivalent of a proscenium arch, a raised stage, which directly faces the audience and allows him plenty of room to 'dance about'. The Lisa Louds of this world will happily operate from a DJ booth, headphones on, mixing music intently, with the crowd at either side, or even behind them. Theatre in the round.

Tony is not too sure about the Newcastle gig, which has come in at the last minute, and he is right to worry. As we sit in the gloom of his hotel room – with the very heavy curtaining that is obligatory in hotels charging over £100 a night – drinking the free bottle of red wine provided, the telephone rings, and it is Tony's one and only conversation with the mysterious Skev.

Skev was the name given to Tony as a contact, but not only was he not at the airport, he failed to make an appearance all evening. I could only hear one side of the conversation, but it sounded like Tony's fears were being realized.

'Is there a stage?' he asked. 'I need to face the audience ... A podium? What do you mean by podium? I am not sure I can work on a podium ... Well, how big is it?' (Long pause.) 'Big enough for what? You know, I need to be able to jump around a bit. I do a lot of dancing ... Well, is it a stage or is it a podium? Will I be facing the audience? Good, the audience has got to be in front of me ... No, no, I couldn't do that.'

'There's no stage. He says it's a podium,' Tony says to me somewhat unnecessarily when he comes off the phone. 'He says it's quite a big podium,' then a pause and a sigh, before, 'but it's not a stage ... What do you understand by a podium? How big is that going to be? And he wants me to turn up at half ten and have some drinks at the bar with the customers. I am not going to do that.'

Tony is extremely easygoing but he is not stupid. He is acutely aware of the dangers of appearing a sad bastard and turns down no end of TV and press if he thinks that might be the outcome. He will change into the garb of irony at the club. If all goes to plan, no one will see Tony Blackburn, only 'Tony Blackburn'.

No worries on that score, say Gaz and Daz when they arrive to take us to the club. We are to go in through a back door and they drive us through some dimly lit back streets in what I take to be the warehouse district of Newcastle, deserted save for those involved in alfresco micturation or fornication, whom you would not expect to be on the lookout for passing broadcasting legends.

Tony actually started out as a singer. While still at Bournemouth College, he appeared with dance bands in the seaside town's hotels. In 1964, at the age of twenty-one, he answered an advert in the *New Musical Express* for disc jockeys to work on a pirate radio ship, but only because he thought it might be a short cut to a recording contract. Pretty soon, though, he realized that his future was more likely to depend on a natural gift for wriggling poncery than any vocal talent. His voice, though not unpleasant, was not a strong one, a little wimpy and too Home Counties, prompting the cruel thought that, if he had really worked on the singing, Tony could have been another Andrew Ridgeley. Instead, he started playing other people's records for a living. 'My wages were £27 a week, but in those days, remember, you could buy an E-type Jag for £2,000.'

Interesting example. Cars and birds have always been key ingredients of the DJ lifestyle. Tony had his share of both through the sixties and seventies when he was a star of the Radio 1 *Roadshow*, an 'entertainment' that involved wearing shorts and a suntan and exhorting thousands of teenagers to shout out a 'great big hi from Weymouth'. In the evenings, Tony could earn himself a handy wedge of cash for doing something fairly similar in discos or dance halls, with the addition of vaguely suggestive party games, mostly involving balloons.

Around this time he was married briefly to a pretty blonde actress called Tessa Wyatt. When their marriage broke up, so did Tony, live on air, ditching Wonderful Radio 1's snap-crackle-and-pop in favour of lachrymose tunes he dedicated to his baby son, Simon, and Tessa, who, the newspapers usefully informed us, was involved with one of her co-stars in a TV sitcom.

Tony's on-air breakdown has always made him more interesting than most of his contemporaries but it was not exactly what was called for in those days, at least not on the station-of-the-nation's bright 'n' breezy morning show, so he was shunted into ever lower profile slots, before drifting onto London's local stations. He has never wanted for work, though. His dance band experience, his facility with pseudo-erotic balloon games, and his name, which retains a high recognition factor even when his ratings slip, make him an attractive prospect to proprietors of provincial dance venues wishing to make a bit of noise in town.

'Funny way to make a living,' I say to Tony, as we jostle for space in the back of Gaz and Daz's little car. I mean, there he is, a middle-aged man in the back of a small car in one of the less attractive parts of Newcastle in the dead of night, while his wife and young daughter sleep back home in London. On his knee is a glitter suit in a bag and in his hand a small attaché case containing his CDs and 'gold' medallions.

We get out of the car and ascend three flights of a fire escape like thieves in the night, only to find a padlocked door. Gaz and Daz curse a little and bang on the door. We end up walking through an alleyway and into the club through the front door. But Tony, despite his still boyish appearance and mysteriously unchanging hairstyle, is recognized by no one as the radio star of their childhood.

The great stage/podium debate continues when we are ushered into the manager's 'office', a chaotic jumble of wires, clapped-out speakers and yellowing papers in a room with cardboard walls and dirty windows. The manager, slightly older than Gaz and Daz, and possibly called Baz, is a cheerful, balding scally with a Manchester accent. He breaks into a broad grin when he sees Tony. 'Tony Blackburn,' he says, shaking his head in mock disbelief. 'Tony Blackburn's in the house.'

There is no dressing room but he offers to vacate his office so that Tony can don his sequins. 'Is there any kind of a stage?' asks Tony. 'I need to move around a bit.' 'Well, it's more of a podium,' replies Baz, 'but it's quite big. You'll be fine.' 'And the audience will be in front of me?' asks Tony. 'Most of them,' says Baz.

'It's definitely more of a podium than a stage,' says the house DJ, who enters the room at this point along with his sidekick, turning it into more of a scene from a Marx Brothers movie than the prelude to an evening's quality entertainment. 'But there's plenty of room. What are those things they have on ships? You walk down one of them and then you get onto the podium. Well, it's more sort of an area.' 'Yeah, it's stage-ish,' says Baz. 'You'll be fine.' 'Oh yeah, there's plenty of room to move about,' says the DJ. 'We sometimes have strippers.'

Tony's other concern is security. He wants an assurance that no one can get on to his podium/stage/area while he is performing. 'No worries,' says Baz. 'It's sort of fenced-in. Nobody's ever had a go at the strippers.'

Ten minutes later we are in the cellar and the house DJ is wrestling a young rather drunk blonde girl off the catwalk. There is a low railing around Tony's performance area, where he is doing his best to do some kind of sub-John Travolta routine. But the restricted space he has to work in gives him the appearance of a caged animal and he is visibly uncomfortable.

There are around 100 people in the room, of whom possibly a dozen are showing any interest. One, a bespectacled woman in her mid-forties, is standing by the railing gazing abstractedly at him but does not look particularly impressed. Demonstrably not a raver, she has come along with work colleagues out of curiosity to have a look at the famous disc jockey, in much the way you might slow down to peer at a road accident.

There are space hoppers scattered around the room to underline the ironic/nostalgic nature of the entertainment (or something) and some young chaps necking bottles of lager are kicking them around. They are wondering, no doubt, what the point is of a Smashie and Nicey act with no jokes, not realizing that Tony was doing this kind of thing long before the Smashie and Nicey spoof was even thought of.

'Shite' is the verdict of one of these young men and I feel it is only the natural affability of the Geordie, and the general loved-up nature of the nightclub crowd at the fag end of the evening, that prevents the atmosphere from turning nasty. It has been a classic bad night out.

It happens from time to time, says Tony. On other occasions, he assures me, the problem is that the crowd can get too enthusiastic. 'I had a problem with some sex-starved women down in Kent recently, trying to get at me,' he tells me. In his Radio 1 *Roadshow* days, of course, that would not have been a problem at all. There were lots of girls. Even years after that, he still projected himself, with varying degrees of irony, as something of a 'lurve god', as this extract from his modestly titled 1984 autobiography, *The Living Legend*, demonstrates:

I invite all the ladies in my life to the same Italian restaurant in west London where the waiters understand how to create the mood of love. As I take a girl's hand in mine, the lighting is lowered by an attentive waiter to cast a seductive glow ... if she agrees to come home with me it's not long before we are climbing the stairs to my king-size bed.

Fair enough. Being a disc jockey has always been a good way to meet girls for someone with neither the talent nor the capacity for drugs to be a rock star. When I was a single man with a late-night show on commercial radio in Sheffield, I was amazed how many women there were 'out there in radioland', as we used to like to say, who were prepared to form fleeting attachments on no sounder basis than the fact that I had a nice voice and played records they liked. Very thin divorcees mostly, or rather plump nurses.

Meeting girls cannot be overestimated as a motivation for entering such a ridiculous business. But beyond a certain age – boyish looks, unchanging hairstyle notwithstanding – there is a danger you become a figure of pity or ridicule rather than one of lust. Friends of Tony say he was in danger of slipping into that deeply sad state when he was rescued at the age of fifty-two by Debbie, the theatrical agent who became his second wife, and saved him.

So why is he still on the road? The money, probably around £2,000 (exact figures are rather hard to come by in this area), obviously comes in handy. But if he had spent Saturday night in London with Debbie and his little daughter Victoria, instead of in the Malmaison Hotel, no one would have gone hungry in the Blackburn household.

My view is that Tony, and other entertainers of his vintage, have to carry on. If they stop, they will ossify. Performing is something to do instead of dying. Also, I think he is having fun. He's been on the road for 37 years now – occasionally, in his younger days, doing three shows a night – and he can't let go. Tony still drives to most of his gigs, thousands of miles a month. He gets terribly excited telling me about the satellite navigation system he has had installed in his car, which guides him right to the doorstep of each venue. 'It's fab'lous,' he says, just like he used to say it on the radio, when he played the 'fab'lous Temptations', a group I heard for the first time on his *Breakfast Show*, or the 'fab'lous Four Tops'.

As a teenager, I loved his show, and wanted to do what he did – even before I perceived it to be a good way to meet girls. This, however, was an ambition that dared not speak its name. In an aspirant Jewish family, recently decamped from inner city Salford to suburban north Manchester, hopes for Number One Son tended to centre on respectable professions like dentistry or the law, or at the very least running a small rainwear factory. If they had caught me with my elder sister's Grundig tape recorder, holding the tinny little microphone up to the speakers of the family gramophone, while I taped myself introducing the records, they would have been horrified.

Maybe this is why I have chosen to follow entertainers around Britain. They have lived – are living – the dream. Their in-built satellite navigation systems help them negotiate all sorts of indignities and setbacks. Growing old, for instance. Who could ever have predicted that was going to happen? Being of limited talent. There is another one they never saw coming.

I don't think I could cope. I am not sure whether it is fear of rejection or fear of appearing ridiculous, but faced with the kind of indifference that met Tony in Newcastle, I am fairly sure I would crumble. I do gigs from time to time but normally as a genial host or compere or as an after-dinner speaker. Getting up on a stage – or even a podium – is a different matter.

Every night there are in Britain, by my very conservative estimate, around 2,000 entertainers of some sort driving home after gigs – musicians, disc jockeys, comedians, jugglers, strippers, women who have knives thrown at them. (A friend of mine, a pharmaceutical rep, wants to be an actress, so she does amateur drama, and in the evening she's a knife-thrower's assistant in working men's clubs.)

Several of them will have little or no discernible talent. Some will be better than artistes you see every day on your television but will have been badly advised. Others will have already had a career as award-winning, chart-topping artistes but will have remained on the road because what's the alternative?

All of them, criss-crossing our little island, stopping only for petrol and a service station chicken sandwich, driven on by the belief that a break is going to come. All of them, even those who know for definite that it absolutely, positively is not. As someone who could never quite conjure up that level of faith, I feel the least I can do is join them.

2

GOING UNDER

Let me try an experiment. Hold your arms out in front of you and clasp your hands together. Now push them against one another as hard as you can. You are pushing harder and harder. Your hands are clasped together so firmly you could not separate them if you tried. You are pushing so hard that your arms begin to shake uncontrollably.

Now, if I wanted to hypnotize you, those of you with your inseparable hands held out in front of you, shaking, I could. You don't believe me? Well, now your head feels heavy. Your heavy, heavy head slumps forward, and you are falling into a deep, wonderfully relaxing sleep. And sleep.

When I click my fingers you will wake, you will feel refreshed, and be seized by an uncontrollable desire to go to amazon.com, buy four copies of this book, and post a review saying it is the finest volume it has ever been your privilege to read.

Ha, ha, my little joke. Of course it is not going to work, but the point about hypnotism is that it is a trick, and one that is not actually all that difficult to master. Andrew Newton, one of Britain's leading stage hypnotists, reckons he could teach it to me in a fortnight. 'Easy, but you would recognize its limitations as well. Hypnotism is much closer to our daily lives than people realize. The difference between being hypnotized and not being hypnotized is minute.'

Andrew tells me to 'forget all that Vincent Price bullshit, where you see a huge close-up of a doorknob turning and the next thing you know some guy in a trance is murdering some poor bastard. It's not like that.' Fair point. Getting someone to bark like a seal or imagine they're riding a horse in the Grand National is hardly the stuff of forties *film noir*. Still, the thought that the dividing line between being a normal human being with a Marks and Spencer's charge card and an opinion on who might win the test match, and being a home-baked fruitcake happy to charge round the stage like a racehorse, is so wafer thin is quite a spooky one in its own right, and profoundly depressing for those of us with any faith in human reason and logic.

I first saw Andrew Newton around 20 years ago, when I went along somewhat reluctantly with a bunch of work colleagues to one of his shows. At that time, stage hypnotism had scarcely been seen on television but through word of mouth its popularity was growing, particularly in the north of England, and particularly Andrew's act. I was not sure it was something of which I approved. Maybe I am just one of those pinko liberal *Guardian*-reading softies who takes things too seriously but it seemed to me to be mucking about in people's heads in the cause of light entertainment.

In the event, I was simultaneously fascinated and appalled by Andrew; fascinated by the speed with which he hypnotized his volunteers but appalled at the mildly undignified acts he then got them to perform, to the obvious amusement of their companions. I seem to remember – and I may be wrong, it's certainly not in his act now – him getting his subjects to perform a burlesque 'sexy striptease' without actually removing any clothing.

There is, of course, a strong sexual element to hypnotism, it being a none too distant second cousin of seduction. Among the suggestions Andrew makes to his subjects, for instance, is that a pair of 'magic' glasses he puts on them will enable them to see everybody in the theatre naked. They gasp and squeal when they put the glasses on and look into the audience. Some of them go all coy, whereas others snigger about who is big and who is small. I know it is childish but you have to laugh. Another trick Andrew pulls is to suggest to a subject that on waking he or she will be irresistibly attracted to the person sitting next to them.

So – and excuse me while I regress into childhood for a moment – tell me, Andrew Newton, could you get any woman in the world to sleep with you? Could you, could you? Well, if she were, in the modern parlance, 'up for it', he probably could. But, if she were up for it, what would be the point in hypnotizing her?

Hypnotism, says Andrew, who loves to talk about what he does (his downfall, as we will discover later), is what he calls 'a numbers game'. He will start a show with the hand-clasping routine in order to find out who is particularly suggestible, 'up for it' if you like. Only a limited number of those in the audience who clasp their hands together will begin to shake and it is these people who may prove suitable subjects, or victims.

Once they are on stage, and put to sleep, some will appear less suggestible than others, failing to stay under or to perform specified tasks. In a further selection process they will be weeded out, leaving the hypnotist with probably the half-dozen most suggestible people out of an audience of maybe 1,000. The people who are undeniably, incontrovertibly, up for it.

Could we, I wonder, have hit here upon the secret of the multi-squillion-dollar self-improvement industry; the Anthony Robbinses of this world, the hypnotherapists, the authors of all those manuals with titles like *How to Fuck Everyone Over and Feel Really Good About It*?

Maybe they are all playing the numbers game. Maybe the secret is not mind control, nor that women are from Venus, nor any of that stuff. Maybe the secret lies simply in finding those people who are up for it, flogging them whatever you have to flog, and scarpering. That is certainly Andrew's view. He reminds me irresistibly of the market traders I used to come across that time I helped my father's friend Ralph. Ralph sold dress lengths and curtaining at various markets in the north of England, and one summer, when I was back home in Manchester from Uni and at a loose end for a few months, I schlepped and drove for him.

Schlepping involved turning up at Ralph's shop at 5.30 a.m. and helping the other schleppers – the goyim – load rolls of cloth into his 'fleet of vehicles'. Both schlepping and driving were activities that were beyond Ralph himself, who was a shape I had only ever seen before in illustrated versions of *The Pickwick Papers*: small hands, small feet, small head, and then this gargantuan bit in the middle. I never actually measured his equator of a waist – the situation just never cropped up – but it must have been 80 inches if it was an inch.

Ralph's fleet management policy was an interesting one: to buy a couple of fifteen-hundredweight Transit vans, overload them with rolls of heavy brocade curtaining so that the floor of the vans almost touched the road, and then persuade them they never needed an oil change. Driving these vehicles was always a challenge because you never knew if the brakes would be a going concern that day, and which of the gears would be available for selection. Once we had made it to Fleetwood, or Bakewell, or Liverpool, though, had unloaded the cloth onto our stall, and had a sausage sandwich and a mug of tea, we had fun pretty well all day.

We were wise guys from Manchester and the customers were the bumpkins who would eat out of our hand, and it really was the most tremendous fun: pulling tricks on the punters, doing a little pitching to draw a crowd, laughing and joking with some of the other traders. It was a kind of showbiz, I suppose, and also probably the only area other than showbiz itself where someone like Ralph, who in his 'casual' clothes looked like an explosion in an Oxfam shop, would be considered remotely employable.

Ralph, by the way, for all his eccentricity, must have been very good at what he did because he always had heaps of money, with which he was very generous. When we schleppers arrived back at the shop, his wife Stella – who, with her rosy cheeks, curly black hair and general corpulence could have been a character from Dickens herself if Dickens had ever written any half-decent Jews – had usually laid on a lavish buffet, from which the concept of portion control was a notable absentee. 'Isn't Ralph going to eat with us?' I asked one evening. 'No,' she said. 'He has his in a trough in the backyard.'

Ralph and Stella were an odd couple but clearly in love. She used to glow with pride when she spoke of his heroism during the war. He didn't actually encounter the enemy as such but once, when he heard one of his fellow soldiers making an anti-Semitic remark, he threw him through a window.

Maybe it is the fact that Andrew is a Mancunian that makes him so reminiscent of the schleppers and traders whose company I enjoyed so much. It is also, though, his breezy attitude to what he does, his quick wit and the sharp put-downs he has for the poor saps who volunteer for public humiliation. He warns them not to wander too close to the edge of the stage because if they fall off 'there's mountains of paperwork afterwards, a nightmare'. He asks Mick, one of the volunteers, where he's from. 'Great Harwood,' says Mick. 'This will all be new to you, then,' says Andrew. 'Curtains and electric lights and things.'

Andrew got into hypnotism, he says, simply as a way of earning some easy money. His start in showbiz was as a pianist and percussionist, playing while still in his teenage years with the Liverpool Philharmonic Orchestra, and Max Jaffa, among others. But when he saw a performer called Robert Halpern in Glasgow in the late seventies doing stage hypnotism – which in those days was all dressed up in top hats, cloaks, and mumbo-jumbo – he thought he could make it funnier and more contemporary, and this would be his escape route from his position behind the band.

He persuaded Halpern to teach him the tricks of the trade, something he now offers to do for me. I am tempted, and maybe I will take him up on his offer. Maybe, after I have travelled around the country and talked to some other turns about their life in showbiz, I will learn Andrew's tricks, because I am writing about show business and hypnotism is, in many ways, the perfect paradigm, being the ultimate exercise of power over audience by performer. And I am not entirely without experience in the use of the voice to connect with an audience, often in the most unexpected ways.

For 15 years I was a late-night disc jockey and I never ceased to be intrigued by how powerful a tool the voice is. I used to keep a 'weirdness' file, full of bizarre letters I had been sent over the years – people who thought I was passing on secret messages to them via the airwaves and so on – and details of odd encounters with listeners.

For eight years or so I was stalked, and I wrote a piece about it in the *Guardian*, my thesis being if you are a late-night DJ and you do *not* have a stalker, you are not doing your job properly. Chances are people are listening to the radio alone last thing at night, or in the early hours of the morning. If the sound of your voice does not connect with at least some of them, especially, in Elkie Brooks's famous phrase, the 'lost and the lonely', maybe you are in the wrong business.

This is not about me, though. I don't think I am quite ready for that yet. That is a drawer I may peek into once or twice but I don't want to pull the whole drawer out, lest all my socks fall on the floor, as it were.

Andrew Newton, meanwhile, who I am going to watch performing at a golf club social in Lancashire, has a pretty packed wardrobe of his own through which to rifle. As we begin an inventory of its contents, we are looked down upon by the contented bourgeois faces of 20 past lady-presidents of Rishton Golf Club, whose framed portraits decorate the walls of the ladies' lounge, which has been allocated to Andrew as a makeshift dressing room.

Every now and then a jovial Lancastrian pops his head round the door and asks Andrew what he requires in the way of sound and stage facilities and then cheerfully tells him why he can't have it, always concluding with an exhortation not to worry, and a breezy 'Be reet', the Lancashire version of '*Ça ne fait rien*'. It was not reet, of course, but then Andrew's avowed policy of 'Do the gig, get the money, go home' tends to exclude the possibility of displays of artistic temperament.

The clubhouse, where he performs to a capacity audience of around 200 people, is an ugly, single-storey, prefabricated building that has been slung up at the back of the car park – more working men's club than Royal Birkdale – but the course itself is quite pretty. It is high up so you can look down upon an almost Lowryesque scene of narrow streets – some still cobbled – of terraced houses clinging to the hillsides, and the mills down in the valleys, except these days they are not mills but discount shoe warehouses or arts and craft collectives.

Having left Andrew to his preparations and taken the opportunity to look around the town, I wander into the Rishton Arms for a quick drink before the show. Bad move. If you are inclined like me to feel self-conscious, something of an outsider, the very worst place you can walk into is an English local pub, especially one on a housing estate.

In the seventies, Sam Peckinpah made a film called *Straw Dogs*, in which a young American and his pretty wife, played by Dustin Hoffman and Susan George, move to an English village. When they walk into the local pub, the atmosphere of menace and hostility is tangible. Later Susan George is brutally raped by four of the local 'lads'. The film was criticized at the time as the overheated product of the grizzled old Yank's fevered imagination but it has always seemed to me to be perfectly plausible, almost a documentary.

So, sitting in the Rishton Arms, reading the *Guardian* – an act of defiance in itself – I can feel eyes burning into me and feel sure that on leaving I will be at the very least savagely beaten if not tied to a lamp-post and anally raped. The Rishton Arms strikes me as just the sort of place where those anal rapist chappies hang out.

It is a big, tatty pub, desperately needing a lick of paint. Inside, it has been refurbished – probably at around the time Abba were winning the Eurovision contest. Its seventies style decor – the careworn orange carpet with the geometrical pattern, the yellowing wallpaper with the 'contemporary' design – give it the appearance of a faded colour poster for a long ago *Daily Mail* Ideal Home Exhibition.

The Rishton Arms stands at the bottom of an unnecessarily wide boulevard called Station Road but the days when it could expect any passing trade are clearly long gone. Mine is the solitary vehicle in its huge car park. This does not really surprise me as the pub is quite literally at the end of the line. Beyond it nothing, except Rishton's railway station, which these days is little more than a glorified bus stop on the line between Burnley and Preston. All those vacant parking spaces are there either as a reminder of better times, or deliberately to spook me, like the 14 vacant cabins at the Bates Motel.

When I order my bottle of beer, I half expect someone to say, 'We don't get many strangers round these parts,' which would be fair comment, as everybody in the pub appears to know everybody else. However, the atmosphere at this stage of the evening, when not too much has been drunk, is benign, and I am sure that, as long as I do not establish eye contact with anybody's girlfriend, or look too hard at some chap's pint, my sphincter should be safe.

Coincidentally, I have recently finished reading *The Road to Nab End*, William Woodruff's vivid recollection of his childhood between the wars not far from here. As well as a personal memoir,

Woodruff's book is a social history, making the point that cotton ceased to be king round here some time in the twenties, and the area has been in a steady economic decline ever since.

Rishton was a weaving town. Around the time Woodruff was born, in 1916, there were 8,000 looms hard at work in the town, the last of which turned up its clogs in 1972. If you were to hazard a guess at the town's major industries now, on the basis of the evidence before your eyes, you might say hairdressing and takeaway curry.

You can buy a terraced house in Rishton for £35,000 in one of the tight Victorian streets with names like Brook Street and Cliff Street, where the mill workers used to live. Even in the Hawthorn Closes and Beech Avenues you could buy a seventies semi with garden and garage for well under £100,000, the kind of money that might just buy you a parking space in parts of London, with enough left over for a roasted sea bass and julienne of vegetables, if you are lucky.

One more thing about Rishton: its most famous former resident is Harry Allen. As Britain's chief executioner from 1956 until capital punishment was abolished in 1964, this son of Rishton dispatched James Hanratty for the so-called A6 murder, a case that is still the subject of newspaper articles from time to time. Recent DNA evidence seems to indicate that Hanratty was guilty of the murder of Michael Gregsten, and the rape of Gregsten's lover, Valerie Storrie, but when Allen died in 1992 at the age of eighty, he will have gone to his grave not knowing whether the twenty-five-year-old he hanged by the neck until dead on the morning of 4 April in 1962 was guilty of anything.

Interestingly, Allen's predecessor as chief executioner was Albert Pierrepoint, who kept a pub near where I was brought up, in Prestwich, north of Manchester. Allen actually died after contracting pneumonia at Pierrepoint's funeral, which is probably deeply ironic; but I am more taken with the remarkable thought that there have only ever been two hangmen in living memory and each was born and brought up in the same area of Lancashire, less than 20 miles apart.

They are trying to revive this area by building pointless roads, as a result of which I am able to drive into Rishton double quick on the M65, a motorway I had never heard of before. It certainly never features in the traffic news, and no wonder. Who uses it? It is a fast route into towns like Oswaldtwistle, Accrington and Haslingden, whose curry houses and hairstylists are probably no better than those in your own town.

I took a train once from Leeds to Preston, coincidentally on the same day Tony Blair made a speech saying there was no North–South divide. As I looked down from a viaduct onto Accrington below and noted how different it was from Kensington or even Wood Green, I formed my response to Blair's statement, which was roughly, 'Bollocks'. If there's no North–South divide, move the Department of the bloody Environment to Accrington.

Hypnotism has its own North–South divide. While Andrew Newton established it in a few select theatres in the north of England, like Leeds's City Varieties, where I saw his act in 1982, it was left to a Londoner to introduce stage hypnotism to a wider public.

Paul McKenna, or 'that fucker McKenna' as Andrew routinely refers to him, is, at thirty-seven, ten years younger than him and is the hypnotist most people in Britain will have heard of. He has had his own television series and cropped up on Ruby Wax's daytime show just the other day, doing a few stage hypnotism tricks and plugging his new thing, Neuro-Linguistic Programming seminars, 'using accelerated teaching models to make your life a more wonderful place to live'. Yeah, sure.

McKenna is in the happiness business now. My brother, who is a national newspaper editor and has no idea I am writing about McKenna, tells me he is to visit the miracle worker to see if he can help him quit smoking.

McKenna has been living in America of late and he was telling Ruby Wax how, in contrast to his American friends, we are all mired in negativity in Britain. He wants us all to start thinking positive thoughts. That could be a problem for Andrew, who, I am afraid, is prey to some rather negative thoughts about McKenna. When I telephone him to tell him his arch nemesis is on the Ruby Wax show, Andrew, who has a full head of lustrous brown hair, comments, 'Oh yes, there he is, the world's baldest hypnotist.'

Andrew's beef with McKenna is quite a simple one. He claims the younger man stole his act, about which I make no comment, other than to report what is not in dispute.

Some time in the late eighties, when McKenna was a disc jockey on Capital Radio in London, and Andrew, who had had some success with his act in provincial theatres and in seaside summer seasons, was trying to move into the West End, McKenna interviewed him on his radio show. After the interview, McKenna went to see Andrew's show several times and met him backstage. Soon after, he abandoned his radio career to become a stage hypnotist.

This, of course, proves nothing, and neither does the tape Andrew sends me a few days after our first meeting, comparing extracts from his stage show with McKenna's TV series and pointing to many striking similarities. The 'magic' glasses sequence is in there, as well as a routine where people are told they are the world's greatest liar and persuaded to spin outrageous yarns; these are just two of several bits that appear in both Andrew's and McKenna's act, with very little variation.

By the same token, though, most conjurers do a routine with a rabbit in a hat, or a piece of rope, which is probably why Andrew's legal action against McKenna never reached the courts. Andrew says he abandoned his legal claim because of the exposure 'the fucker' had given hypnotism on TV. 'When it was on TV every night, all of a sudden you got 200 hypnotists all over the country doing it and fucking it up,' he complained. 'After a while I think people got tired of it anyway, because it's basically a one-show joke.' Andrew decided the business was 'shagged' and that pursuing McKenna and his big-name lawyers through the courts would be like two bald men arguing over a comb.

So in 1997 Andrew sought new audiences in South Africa, where stage hypnotism was pretty well unheard-of. He stayed there for three and a half years, presenting his own TV series and travelling round the country to perform in theatres. While on the road, he says, he saw some villagers celebrate the arrival of the weekend by attacking a live cow with a chainsaw. I somehow feel this is not a story that Paul McKenna with all his positivity would casually toss into the conversation, which is why I instinctively side with Andrew.

On stage, there is little to choose between the two and certainly there seems no obvious reason why one rather than the other should have reached the Holy Grail of television first. Both rely on a slick line in patter and a certain amount of gentle mickey-taking of the poor saps who step up to take part in their act. I prefer Andrew, finding McKenna a little mechanical, like a smarmy quiz show host from central casting. Andrew's Mancunian accent gives him added warmth. He tells me he was, in fact, due to make a television show with Thames Television, around the time the company lost their franchise to Carlton TV, who promptly produced a similar show with McKenna. This has all the hallmarks of a classic show business hard-luck story. Every entertainer has one, in the same way that every angler can tell you of the big catch that narrowly evaded him, and there is not a gambler alive who has not at some time been just a whisker away from a life-changing win.

I love show business nearly-stories and the jealousies and bitterness invariably associated with them. It has always struck me that many entertainers appear younger than their years and I believe it is often a healthy dose of rancour that keeps them (us?) young, alongside, of course, the enduring belief that their big break is just around the corner and they will obviously need to look their best for it.

A quote from Mao Tse-tung (one of China's top turns for a number of years) goes something like: 'If you live long enough, you can sit by the river bank and watch the bodies of your enemies float past,' and it is this thought, I am sure, more than anything, that has a strengthening and rejuvenating effect on many turns. They want to make sure they stay fit enough to lift up the *Daily Telegraph* on the morning it includes the obituary of the slimy git who nicked all their jokes.

The secret is not to be consumed by the bitterness and certainly not to go on constantly about how you have been shafted – except to those of us writing books about show business. Fortunately, despite having suffered grievously at the hands of the poltroons who run the media, I myself am prey to no such feelings of resentment. As far as I am concerned, the bastards that fucked me over can just go and fuck themselves, which I think is the mature way to look at it.

I do have a peach of a near-miss story, though. Back in the eighties I met a talented young comedian and would-be actress called Caroline Aherne and paid her £15 a week to do an improvised comedy bit with me on my radio show each week as a character called Mrs Merton. After a few years of doing this, a friend and I, 'borrowing' studio time and equipment from Yorkshire Television, produced an amateur TV pilot in which Caroline interviewed various vaguely famous friends of mine – disc jockeys Andy and Liz Kershaw, and Chris Donald, editor of *Viz* – asking them impertinent questions in the character of Mrs Merton.

We tried, in a fairly half-arsed way, to interest various TV companies in the project without success and eventually gave the tape to Caroline, who met someone from Granada TV at a party, to whom she showed the tape, and the rest more or less is history.

Caroline, as we had tried in our naive manner to persuade the great and good of television – and we have the rejection letters to prove it – is one of our most talented writers and performers and all these years later when I see her get up at an awards ceremony and thank all the little people, I still feel an inner glow, as I issue foul-mouthed curses through clenched teeth.

I wonder which is healthier: my disdain for the entire television establishment or Andrew's single-minded hatred of Paul McKenna? I only ask because I think it important we get this negative energy working for us.

Andrew's show at the golf club is not brilliant. Playing the numbers game is difficult when there are only a couple of hundred people available in the audience, so some of Andrew's more elaborate stunts have to be jettisoned. The important thing is that the customers, middle-aged couples on a night out and the crowd from the Rishton Arms, seem to be having a good time. There is a group in from the NatWest bank, enjoying seeing their workmates acting stupid. The even more important thing is that the jovial Lancastrian has visited us in the ladies' lounge bearing Andrew's fee, a satisfying wedge in a little brown envelope.

After the show, there is a disco, which seems more lively than such events sometimes are. There is something about an evening of hypnotism that leads to a general lowering of inhibitions. You don't need to have been under yourself. Simply being present when the natural order of things is subverted, witnessing the fragility of the human mind, can be somehow, well, sexy.

Not everyone sees it like that. There are those who believe stage hypnotism is dangerous and should be banned. Their pressure led to a parliamentary inquiry, which tinkered with the licensing regulations a little but concluded that the entertainment was basically harmless. It is a subject I take up with Andrew, referring specifically to three well-publicized court cases over the past decade in which stage hypnotism found itself in the dock.

'There is absolutely no evidence that stage hypnotism does anybody any harm,' he insists. 'The problem is all the arseholes who came into the business after hypnotism was shown on TV, guys who were painters and decorators during the day and were doing an act in pubs at night. These guys just shit and move on.'

He is particularly scathing about a stage hypnotist who lost a high court damages action after a forty-year-old woman claimed his show led her to attempt suicide. The hypnotist had told her to imagine she was a child again, allegedly reawakening in her memories of sexual abuse as an eight-year-old and triggering depression. She was awarded £6,500 compensation and the judge criticized the performer – who had long since abandoned show business – for his 'cavalier attitude' to the woman's complaints.

Andrew also has strong feelings about this matter, although not quite in the same vein as His Honour. 'It's not the hypnotism that's at fault,' he says, 'it's the way these arseholes deal with problems. People come up and say, "Ooh, I had a terrible headache after your show." Yeah, sure you had a fucking headache. It could be something to do with the nightclub you went on to and the 12 pints you drank.' And he lights up another in a long line of Silk Cuts.

Ten minutes earlier he had been studying my voice recorder and wondering if he could buy a load of them wholesale for £20 each on which to knock out a self-contained hypnotherapy programme for smokers who want to quit. 'You're not much of an advertisement for the programme,' I suggest. 'What can I say?' he says, and he shrugs and smiles and I sense he is that close to saying it is all a load of nonsense anyway. Not hypnotism, that's not nonsense, exactly, but Andrew's view is that it suits some of his colleagues to gloss over its very real limitations.

A well-known, much-publicized and almost certainly untrue story about hypnotism is the one about the stage hypnotist who suggested to a subject that his belly button had been stolen, sending him on a hunt for the missing part through the audience, being persuaded at one point, to great hilarity, that his wife had taken it. Later that night, when his wife was sleeping at home, the story goes, the man took a carving knife and tried to extract retribution by cutting out his wife's navel. (The belly button routine or something like it is a staple for stage hypnotists, as illustrated by the following eye-catching newspaper headline over a report of one of Paul McKenna's court cases: 'Losing willy was pleasant experience.')

The belly button story has appeared in so-called American supermarket tabloid papers and was told to a round of applause on a British daytime television programme about hypnotism but there remains no evidence it ever actually happened. 'People believe it, though,' says Andrew, 'which is rather ironic, in that our whole business depends on people accepting outrageous suggestions. In this case, the instrument of our success is also the instrument of our downfall.'

There have been at least half a dozen daytime television discussions about stage hypnotism in the last ten years, most of which have featured Margaret Harper, founder of the Campaign Against Stage Hypnotism.

Margaret's twenty-four-year-old daughter, Sharron Tabarn, died in 1993 a few hours after being hypnotized in a stage show – by another pub turn. The inquest verdict was death by natural causes but Margaret claims her daughter's death was caused by post-hypnotic trauma.

I do not intend to go into details of Margaret Harper's allegations, as there is a 20-page paper on the subject on the internet, written by Dr Tracie O'Keefe, an Australian hypnotherapist. (Dr O'Keefe, interestingly, is a transsexual, who tried to force Westminster Register Office to allow her to marry her lesbian lover, Katrina, an actress, linguist and 'gossip columnist', on the grounds that she, the good doctor, was born a male and therefore the proposed marriage was to all intents and purposes a conventional one between a man and a woman. I add that piece of information without comment merely to illustrate that the more you delve into the world of stage hypnotism the more it resembles wandering into one of those fairground crazy-mirror houses. Professor Michael Heap of Sheffield University, who gave evidence to the parliamentary inquiry, said a study of hypnotists would be far more interesting and entertaining than a study of hypnosis.)

One further case that Andrew Newton and I discuss is that of his old rival Paul McKenna, sued for £200,000 damages in the high court in 1998 by Christopher Gates, a thirty-four-year-old French polisher, who claimed taking part in one of McKenna's shows turned him into an 'aggressive schizophrenic'. McKenna won but said the case had cost him £1 million in lost business and sponsorship.

Over the years, McKenna has spent a fair bit of time with his solicitors. He sued Tracie O'Keefe (incidentally, if you are changing from a man to a woman, why would you give yourself the name Tracie?) who had said she did not consider stage hypnotists sufficiently qualified to teach clinical hypnosis, but later withdrew his suit. Then Tracie sued him for the allegedly libellous comments he made about the first case, and won damages.

There was also Andrew's abortive legal claim to defend, leading you to wonder what it is with these hypnotists, always suing each other. Could they not just look into each other's eyes and try and get a result that way? You know, the first one to go under is the loser. Hey, duelling hypnotists. Sounds like another winning TV proposal.

Because Andrew's show has not been a significant success at Rishton Golf Club, and because I like him and wish to write well of him, I return to Leeds's City Varieties, where I first saw him.

The City Varieties is one of the joys of Leeds, not a big, posh theatre but a perfect, little, Victorian music hall, one of the few remaining in Britain. It was opened in 1865 and Houdini, Marie Lloyd and Charlie Chaplin are among the performers to have trodden its boards. In the seventies and eighties it was the venue for the popular TV show *The Good Old Days*, which recreated Victorian music hall with contemporary performers.

These days it gets by mostly on a diet of sad shows in which tribute bands recreate 'the golden days of rock 'n' roll' or pretend to be Abba, as well as some interesting touring stand-up comedians. It also hosts oddball shows like *An Evening With Freddie Trueman*, in which the famous old Yorkshire cricketer relates some mildly racist anecdotes and explains why today's cricketers are not as good as he was, evenings with clairvoyants, and Andrew's shows, which always attract healthy audiences despite minimal publicity.

The theatre is down a back street at the heart of Leeds's newly poshed-up shopping centre, called Swan Street, named after a famous old pub, the White Swan, where apparently as early as the eighteenth century you could enjoy rude entertainment and the occasional knifing. And Leeds still has its rough edges, despite the council's valiant efforts to turn it into the Barcelona of the North. There are still pubs like the Horse and Trumpet, round the corner from the Varieties, a rough-hewn drinkers' pub, welcoming every variety of drunk; and not just the frayed shirt collar, cardboard belt and shiny trouser type, with their hard luck stories, but also the slightly florid well-spoken ones, clearly over-educated, who wear their grey hair long, swept back, self-cut and none too recently washed. They will be smoking some brand of untipped cigarettes you thought they'd stopped making years ago and telling a wildly unlikely tale about Princess Margaret. I always wonder what their own story is. How they ended up in a pub in Leeds. *Great Drunks of Leeds*, I have always felt, would make an excellent picture book. Or possibly one of those Observers' books we used to have as kids, except instead of marking off British birds you would add classic drunks to your collection.

Andrew, meanwhile, entertains the wholesome, fun-loving comedy crowd: office parties, hen parties and the like. He has a bunch of people from Barclay's Bank who are in Leeds on a training course, some trainee managers from Burger King and, bizarrely, some families. I am not sure an evening of hypnotism is somewhere I should take a child. Andrew comments on the presence of children and asks for them not to join the volunteers on stage. 'It's not that there's a problem. It's just that I don't like kids,' he says.

The show itself is perfectly suitable for families. The fashion for hypnotism to stray into more outlandish and seedy areas died out in the eighties, according to Andrew. It was particularly popular in Liverpool, he says, where occasionally subjects were persuaded to strip down to their underwear and get into a bath full of baked beans.

Paul McKenna hypnotized a woman on shock jock Howard Stern's American TV show into either having an orgasm or faking an orgasm (don't ask me, I can't tell the difference), a tape of which was played to the judge in the Christopher Gates case – without convincing the judge that McKenna was doing anything in any way unethical or dangerous.

There are no orgasms or lost willies, however, in Andrew Newton's family show, which is surprisingly good fun. After the curtain has come down for the interval, he hypnotizes a couple of his subjects without the knowledge of the audience. When the show is ready to restart, these two march through the bars like sergeant majors rounding everybody up and ordering them back to their seats. It was funny, but I expect you had to be there.

Another bit I found quite uplifting. Andrew persuades his volunteers that he is invisible and then starts moving stuff around the stage in a spooky way. The subjects, understandably, get a little frightened, at which point a rather camp chap called Neil, who worked in IT, took charge of the situation and started looking after the others, hiding them in the wings and so on, bless him.

It was a better night out than either my talk with Andrew or his show at Rishton had prepared me for. Although he is proud enough of his stunts and little bits of business to tape them all now, and copyright them, I still get the impression he thinks it a rather unworthy way to make a living. 'I really just do it for the money,' he tells me.

He is in his mid-forties and lives alone in a city centre flat in Manchester. 'There is a lot of travelling and staying away from home. I'm on my own, which is how I prefer it.' And yet he quite clearly thinks there is more to life than travelling the world picking up little brown envelopes for persuading people they are Elvis Presley.

Before we met, his agent had sent me a videotape Andrew had produced in which he puts forward an outlandish conspiracy theory about the *Titanic*. According to him, the disaster was somehow an insurance scam, with another ship substituting on the fateful voyage for the famously unsinkable liner. He filmed the whole thing himself, cheaply in South Africa, in Cecil Rhodes's old house in Cape Town, and feels if he could get someone to stump up £25,000 he could turn it into a very saleable product.

For a while, he toyed with the idea of running a little private airline. He did 600 hours of flying, learned about gas turbines and so on, but then, when he went for a medical, he was denied a pilot's licence because of a leaking kidney. 'That was an unmitigated disaster,' he told me. 'When you're in your thirties you feel great. I never suspected it for a moment. I still feel great, actually.' After this there was a brief foray into the antiques business but always he returns to hypnotism. 'My life has been a story of looking for easy ways to make money. I leave a trail of failed businesses behind me but the hypnotism is something I can always go back to.'

Next time I phone him he is in Torquay, visiting the town hall and local theatres, asking about visitor numbers and seeing which venues might be available for a show or two in the summer. 'The six 'P's,' he explains, 'Prior Planning Prevents Piss-Poor Performance.' He might do one show a week there during the summer, he says, if he can find a suitable venue.

It is Andrew's role in life to be the second most successful stage hypnotist in Britain. Second in a field of one, really, but he is a solid professional, always worth his little brown envelope, because he gives value for money to people who want a good night out. Sure, he still hopes that the big break might come, maybe with the *Titanic* movie, but he has been around long enough to know that if show business teaches us anything, it is that the gap between major celebrity and middle-ranking professionalism is Marmite-thin, rather like the gap between the hypnotized and the non-hypnotized.

For some reason, I think of those Leeds drunks when I think of the future for Andrew, and possibly for myself. I am not suggesting for one moment that either of us is on the verge of alcoholism. Two small bottles of beer is all the jovial Lancastrian is summoned to bring into the ladies' lounge. No, it is just that the division between hopeless drunk and mild eccentric is another of those wafer-thin gaps. The wrong woman, the wrong parents, the wrong word at work. It does not take much when your existence is as precarious as ours.

So let us try once more. Your eyelids are closing, they feel incredibly heavy, you cannot keep your eyes open, now your head feels heavy. It is slumping forward. Feel your heavy, heavy head slump forward onto your chest. And sleep.

3

SHE FILLS THE STAGE
WITH FLAGS

It is odd – and also hugely irritating – how catchphrases sometimes seep out of the television, gradually as if from a slow leak at a nuclear reactor, until suddenly one morning everybody is using them at every possible opportunity. I am constantly surprised that more people are not bludgeoned to death and tossed into a shallow grave as a result of saying 'You are the weakest link, goodbye' or 'Can I phone a friend?' and then giggling as if they were the first person ever to think of it. It says a great deal for the tolerance of our great nation.

In the summer of 2002 everybody was saying 'my arse'. My arse this, my arse that. On the *Late Review* programme on BBC2, I think the poet Tom Paulin said, 'Objective correlative, my arse' in the course of an argument with Germaine Greer, while Her Majesty the Queen, I believe, said, 'Opening of Parliament, my arse.'

They were taking their lead from the character Jim Royle, played by Ricky Tomlinson, in Caroline Aherne's marvellous comedy show *The Royle Family*. The show was a kind of live action version of *The Simpsons*. The family lives on a Manchester estate – probably Wythenshawe where Aherne grew up – where they seem to do little but watch television and eat comfort food. They are tolerant of petty criminality and, like their American equivalents, they appear to be a dysfunctional family that functions perfectly.

If the Royles ever went on holiday, they would undoubtedly go to the Spanish resort of Benidorm, playground of what used to be called the British working classes. This would be remarkably handy, as they could stay in Ricky Tomlinson's caravan. Not the character, but the actor, whose advertising contracts alone would certainly buy him a secluded Continental hideaway, but who chooses instead to vacation with the hoi polloi in the home of bargain basement holidays. I saw Tomlinson on a TV chat show, talking about his caravan in Benidorm and, cynic that I am, assumed it was just a pose to retain working-class credibility. But no, because the next time I see him he is actually in Benidorm, in Steptoes Cabaret Bar, happily grinning for countless photographs with holidaying British TV viewers, drinking pints of mild and complying with constant demands for him to repeat his catchphrase.

Join us, then, in historic Benidorm, jewel of the Costa Blanca (the white coast), prey to invaders through 3,000 years of turbulent history. First settled by Iberians, Phoenicians and Greeks, who built important naval bases, it was later turned over to Rome. On the collapse of the Roman Empire it became the subject of fierce battles between the kingdoms of Aragon and Castile, before Alfonso the Wise conquered the city in 1246 for the Castilian crown.

But none of that, nor much of what followed, need concern us, until 1952, when a disastrous tuna fish haul persuades the city fathers that the future for their fishing village lies not in the nets but in tourism. Their far-sightedness laid the foundations for what Benidorm is today. And what Benidorm is today is best summed up by the fact that the town's most celebrated cabaret performer is an artiste known as Sticky Vicky, who is, for want of a better word, a vaginalist.

I am not sure the word actually exists but those chaps who can play tunes by compressing air between their hands to produce funny little farting noises call themselves manualists, so surely ladies using the more private parts of the body in the noble cause of entertainment should also be allowed the dignity of a proper title.

Admittedly, La Vicky does not actually produce music from her pudenda. How could she, when she is busy producing the flags of all nations, chickens' eggs, a family-size vibrator and, frighteningly, one metre of threaded razor blades? Maybe there are not enough artistes with Vicky's singular skills to qualify for a generic term, although friends of mine who have been out East and seen a thing or two tell me it is not unusual to find lady performers there whose show-stopper – their 'My Way', as it were – is to demonstrate the versatility of their lower body by propelling ping-pong balls across a Bangkok bar-room, for which they pick up tips. And when I say pick up, I mean … well, I think you know what I mean.

Vaginalist it is, then. Not that Vicky's surprisingly demure act has much in common with Thailand's table tennis temptresses. For one thing, Vicky is sixty-seven years old, about forty-five years past retirement age, I suspect, in Bangkok's dens of iniquity. If four Thai ladies were laid end to end – and if you have the money, I am sure that would not be a problem – their combined ages would still total less than Sticky Vicky's.

It was not my intention, I should add, to include Vicky's act in my review of Benidorm's nightlife. As a father of four, I think it is incumbent upon me to at least try and set some sort of an example. ('What did you do on your short break in Spain, Daddy?' 'Well, darling, Daddy went to a bar to see a naked lady pull bunches of flowers from her front bottom.') Also, my appetite for the sexually bizarre is strictly limited. I tend, for instance, to give a wide berth to those magazines chaps sometimes pass round when they come back from a stag weekend in Amsterdam and the kind of videos I like to watch are on open display in Blockbusters.

Having reached sexual maturity some time between the rampant sexism of the fifties and sixties and the new laddism of the nineties, I am uncomfortable with anything that treats women as sex objects. Like a lot of liberal men of my vintage – and, please forgive me, this does sound awfully wet – I suppose I am a feminist of sorts. Not exactly Germaine Greer, I grant you, but more committed than my friend who joined the National Union of Journalists' Feminism Working Party 'because it was a good place to pick up chicks'.

Only once before had I ever been to a striptease show and then I made my excuses and left early. It was in the late seventies, a clandestine affair, arranged by the programme controller of my first radio station as a sort of bonding exercise, what with the industry, in those days, being almost exclusively male. At one point in the evening a small, wiry stripper, who bore a regrettable resemblance to the boxer Barry McGuigan, grabbed some reluctant chap from the audience who was being propelled forward by his workmates and proceeded to strip him and perform on him an act more usually enjoyed by chaps alone in the privacy of their own reading room.

What made this display particularly offensive, quite apart from the obvious lack of joy on the faces of the participants, was the fact that the 'volunteer' climaxed while still only semi-erect – what my friends at *Viz* comic who have compiled a glossary of sexual slang tell me is known as a 'dob glob' – at which point I made for the door. I am told the entertainment got rather raunchy after I left.

I think, on balance, I prefer the modern version of bonding: a speech from a rugby international and an afternoon's paintballing. Just as pointless, but not quite as messy.

Anyway, 25 years later, here I am in Benidorm at 2.30 a.m. in an almost deserted Steptoes Cabaret Bar at my second striptease show. I have been watching late-night shows by comedians Crissy Rock and Danny Downing and they insist I stay for Vicky's act. 'Coming to Benidorm and not seeing Sticky Vicky would be like going to Blackpool and not seeing the lights,' says Crissy.

It is Sticky Vicky's fifth and penultimate show of the evening. At the height of the season, I am told, she may perform in as many as 15 bars like Steptoes in the course of an evening. She can do this because her act is all over in less than ten minutes and she has a reliable family saloon in which to drive around town.

Vicky slips into Steptoes almost unnoticed. She is a neat elfin figure, a little over five feet tall. As she clicks down the steps into the bar, carrying a small suitcase with her props in it, you could easily mistake her for a businesswoman going to her weekly sales conference, were she not wearing a satin dressing gown and sparkly high-heeled shoes. And businesslike is definitely the word to describe her. She walks quickly and confidently straight through the audience – which tonight is just Crissy, Danny, me and a few stragglers – smiling all the while. Despite the drunks and bad people you might expect to find in a seaside town at three in the morning, she travels alone. No security, as far as I could see. Mind you, who is going to try anything? She could be hiding a flick knife or a baseball bat.

As Benidorm's pluckiest pensioner approaches the performing area – no stage, just a space at the side of the DJ booth – the DJ announces 'the one and only Sticky Vicky' and puts on a tape of the standard illusionists' swishing and swooshing music, because that's what Vicky is, essentially: an illusionist. At least I hope that is what she is.

The lights dim and she sheds her dressing gown and presently her sequinned bikini. Anybody aroused by the sight of Vicky's naked body should seek help. She has two perfect little plastic tits, brand new by the look of them, small, pert and high up on her body; they are the breasts of a slim seventeen-year-old and stay absolutely static throughout the entire performance. Plastic surgery apart, Vicky is in phenomenal nick but with her smooth, immaculately shaven performance area, those polythene breasts and her neat little dancer's legs, she resembles one of your daughter's Barbie dolls with its clothes removed.

She never stops smiling for a second, from the moment she descends the stairs into Steptoes until she is at the top of the steps on the way out, fumbling for her car keys in her dressing gown pocket. As I left the club, I actually caught her without a smile on her face. I rounded the corner to walk back to my hotel and there she was, putting her suitcase into the boot of her car (and pulling it out again through the exhaust pipe, ha ha). Recognizing me from the audience, she seemed genuinely flustered to catch me catching her.

I almost ask for her autograph. Actually, I should have liked to have asked Vicky a lot of things, like how she first embarked on her strange career path, how she feels about performing all summer long for sniggering British tourists whose appreciation of her panache may be less than complete, and why when she produces the flags of all nations it's the Swedish flag that appears first. But, alas, she does not speak English, or at least claims not to. Crissy and Danny, who have been on the same bill as Vicky Leyton, as she calls herself, hundreds of times, say she 'seems very nice', but never talks to any of the other turns. They tell me she came to Benidorm from South America and has been doing her singular act in the town's bars and clubs for probably more than thirty years.

For some reason, the story of this elegant artiste, thousands of miles away from her homeland performing night after night for jaded, unappreciative audiences for all those years, brings to mind Humphrey Bogart in *Casablanca*. Silly, really, because there is no war on, I am sure Vicky is reasonably well rewarded for what she does, and besides, it is nice to see a pensioner with an interest. It cannot be all that bad anyway, because Vicky, I am told, has a daughter to whom she has taught the act, ensuring the family business stays in safe hands – if hands is the word I am looking for.

Final amazing Vicky fact is that her husband used to be Benidorm's chief of police, which presumably would have come in handy should anyone have been inclined to complain about the nature of Sticky Vicky's performance. I could not see that happening, though, because it really is a very sweet show. Each time Vicky produces something she does that little flourish that conjurers' assistants habitually do when the great man successfully saws someone in half or pulls a rabbit out of a hat, all the while wearing her fixed innocent smile.

After the flowers and flags, she gives new meaning to girl power by appearing to insert a light bulb into herself, causing it to light up, an interesting echo of Dusan Makavajev's film *WR: Mysteries of the Organism*, which dealt with Wilhelm Reich's controversial theories about harnessing the orgasmic power from down there. I get the impression some of her audiences may miss this reference. And if I hadn't seen the film, I would have as well. The string of razor blades she then produces must confuse spectators under the age of 30, as she uses Gillette safety razor blades of a type I have not seen for about 20 years, giving her show a delightfully retro appeal.

Sticky Vicky's *pièce de résistance* is to open a beer bottle in her own very individual way, reinforcing that well-known internet joke which lists All the Things a Woman Wants From a Man, like sensitivity, understanding and so on and then responds with All the Things a Man Wants From a Woman, which reads simply: 'Turn up naked, bring beer.' Great finale, and she is out of the door in seconds flat.

The 'one and only' Sticky Vicky, however, seems a less than adequate billing for the great pudendist. Back in the days of variety theatres, performers would go to great lengths to whet the public's appetite for their particular talents with some sort of bill matter, a descriptive line on the bill posted outside the theatre. It might read something like: 'Arthur Grimshaw: A Smile, a Song and an Exploding Haddock!' and people whose particular taste was for an evening of musical comedy climaxing with the senseless destruction of a fish would know this was the show for them.

There was a conjurer in those days called Kardoma, whose speciality was to produce an impossible quantity of flags from his Tardis of a trouser pocket until they were strewn all over the stage. His bill matter was: 'Fills the Stage With Flags'. Maybe, I was thinking, Vicky could steal the line from him. For the time being, word of mouth, you should pardon the expression, seems to be doing the job.

For artistes who insist on remaining clothed, however, Benidorm is no picnic, especially for comedians. Audiences can be brutal. I went to two shows a night for four nights and concluded that if you cannot produce items of interest from your private parts, you'd better be able to tell obscene or racist gags peppered with four-letter words. You wouldn't do it if you didn't need the money, which I am told is not very much, but it is Euros in the pocket, no questions asked, and does come with some basic free accommodation and plentiful supplies of cheap food and alcohol.

Benidorm undoubtedly appeals to some turns, because of the regular work, the sunshine and cheap booze or, more likely, because it keeps them out of the clutches of the taxman, who is the Benidorm entertainer's equivalent of the bogeyman. Every time I get my notebook out to interview an artiste, I find myself regarded with the kind of suspicion normally reserved for a small wriggling creature with an excess of legs that you have just found in your mashed potato. 'You're not from the Inland Revenue, are you?' asks Mike St. John, jokingly, when he catches me outside Steptoes, making notes and taking a few snaps.

Mike, who does the early shift at Steptoes, is a club singer of the type comedian Vic Reeves used to lampoon in his TV show. He is from Blackpool and years ago would have found plenty of work back home in working men's clubs, cabaret clubs or summer shows. But frankly, there is no demand these days for what he does. Even working men's clubs prefer young boy and girl duos or karaoke nights, so Mike has shipped out to Benidorm, where the nostalgia season never ends.

From about half past nine till half ten each evening he joins in with backing tapes on a fairly mawkish selection of hoary old sixties and seventies 'classics' – Gary Puckett's 'Young Girl', Dr Hook's 'A Little Bit More', the Drifters' 'Like Sister and Brother' – while elderly couples gently tap their feet and the younger crowd use him as background to get tanked up at the bar.

Mike is about sixty, short and paunchy, with long silver hair tied back in a pony tail. His shoes are black patent leather and he wears tight trousers, with a razor-sharp crease, and a white shirt, open to reveal a gold medallion, which he wears without irony. He could be a minor Mafia functionary, the type of guy who gets rubbed out in the second reel.

He does a little bit of unremarkable patter between songs, which goes down well with the oldies, who are Benidorm's bread and butter for most of the year until school holiday time. Mike is also the first guy I have heard for several years introduce a song by saying, 'It goes a-something like this ...'

'Let's go back to the sixties now,' says Mike. 'I remember this one when it first came out. I had jet-black hair and zits, and I was eight stone, dripping wet.' And you believe him. In fact, you can imagine him in his leather jacket looking mean, fronting some Blackpool rock 'n' roll group. There are chuckles of recognition from the flowered dress brigade as they clutch their halves of lager and lime, and Mike launches into some cheesy old tune, which does not sound radically different from the one before. He looks bored when he is performing. And so he might, singing the same old songs night after night. He does a desultory little shuffle from one side of the performance area to the other as he sings and you wonder whether it might not be kinder to take some of these songs off the life support machine and allow them a dignified death.

You hear the old tunes wherever you go in Benidorm. Mike's act was the first I went to see after arriving in the resort on a Friday night. As I walked down from the Palm Beach Hotel towards Steptoes I heard old songs spilling out from every bar I passed and never particularly ones I wanted to hear again:

'Especially for You' by Kylie and Jason, Cyndi Lauper's hit, 'Girls Just Want to Have Fun', 'September' by Earth, Wind and Fire, 'Teenager in Love' by Dion. At breakfast in the hotel they were playing 'We're All Alone' by Rita Coolidge. The music never stops. Eating or drinking in silence is not an option in Benidorm. It is like being trapped inside a radio permanently tuned to a golden oldies station.

It is terribly difficult, I am finding, to write about Benidorm without sounding like an insufferable snob. Everything you have heard about the resort is true. It is hot, dry, noisy and crowded. It recycles its water. Around 1.2 million British tourists come here every year, packing the skyscraper hotels and ticky-tacky apartment blocks that crowd Benidorm's streets. You are never more than a minute away from egg, bacon, sausage, beans and a fried slice.

The pubs are awash with British bitter and there are fish and chip shops here, lots of them. The proud boast of one is 'English fish fingers', for those worried their little ones might have to go two weeks without their fix of artificial additives, breadcrumbs and fish-style filling. See, I told you it was difficult.

The Queen Mary is my local. There are mini-cheddars and scampi fries behind the bar and the entertainment includes Alun Echo, a Welsh-Irish vocalist, singing the songs of Buddy Holly and Johnny Cash. Lest everything seems a little too foreign to you, though, the pubs invariably inform you of the provenance of mine host and hostess: the White Horse, the Tartan Bar, the Yorkshire Pudding, run by Pat and Tom from Manchester, Maggie and Jim from Arbroath and Alan and Jean from Castleford respectively.

I walk into one pub for a livener at 11.30 one morning. The place is deserted apart from me and two young Liverpudlian women behind the bar talking. It smells of Ajax, and the huge TV screen with which I share the bar is playing at full volume some Euro music channel with which I am not familiar. The music videos are interrupted by an advert for diarrhoea tablets voiced by the former punk princess Toyah Willcox. 'Hey, that's whatsername,' says one of the girls. 'Toyah,' says the other. 'Oooh, she's done well.' In Benidorm, could anything be more important than diarrhoea tablets?

Then again, Benidorm does not pretend to be anything it is not. The mayor is actually quite bullish about his town's reputation for cheap and cheerful holidays. 'Anyone who insults the five million people who come here every year is insulting the ordinary people of Europe,' he says. Quite so. Show business personalities and politicians who claim to be in touch with the common folk should be made to spend their holidays in Benidorm. 'Tuscany, my arse,' as Jim Royle might say to the Prime Minister.

Ricky Tomlinson, by the way, leaves Steptoes long before the Sticky Vicky segment of the show. I need to make that clear to avert any 'TV Ricky in Sexy Strip Show Shock' headlines. He is here for the same reason as me: to see Crissy Rock, whom he knows as a fellow member of the formidable Scouse comedy mafia, and who, like himself, is a veteran of the films of the great British socialist film-maker Ken Loach.

In 1994 Loach cast Crissy, who was then a barmaid doing a bit of stand-up comedy, as the lead in his film *Ladybird, Ladybird*, in which she played Maggie, a feckless mother of four fighting social workers for the custody of her children. It was a sensational debut. Roger Ebert, one of America's most respected film critics, wrote of it:

> Crissy Rock, who has never acted before, gives the strongest performance in any film of the past 12 months. Seeing the movie for the first time at the Telluride film festival, I walked out of the theatre and saw Rock standing there, and wanted to comfort her, she had embodied Maggie's suffering so completely. The Oscar nominations will be incomplete if they do not take this performance into account.

There was no Oscar, though, and less than a decade later I am sitting at a table with Crissy outside Steptoes, where she is to do the midnight show, 'the graveyard shift' as she calls it. She is not happy about going on so late in the evening. It is early in the season – late May – and the crowd in Steptoes consists mostly of oldies, who like to go to bed early to make sure they don't miss the buffet breakfast in the morning. So the club will be thinning out once it is Crissy's turn to go on. What is more, there have already been three comedians on, so there is a chance that what audience remains will be all laughed out. Crissy, who is in Benidorm for a fortnight, has already had a week of this and she seems ready to jack it in and go home. It is not just the bad time-slot she's been given but also the need to do some pretty cheap and vulgar material in order to survive.

Chaps who have had too much to drink and are possibly over-stimulated by too much junk food will shout, 'Get yer tits out,' and Crissy will shout back, 'They wouldn't fit in that fucking mouth,' and quickly get back to her act before the heckling takes hold. 'It's soul-destroying,' she tells me. 'It's like you're playing some card game with the audience. Show me what you've got and I'll see you. Ninety-five per cent of the time I go for the throat and get them to back off but you get fed up with it sometimes, the constant battle.'

I worry that I am depressing her, asking her to get too introspective before a gig. She's not going to go on and it will be all my fault. But Crissy is no quitter. She even carried on at Butlins after some guy decked her. Right in the middle of her act, he came up and whacked her, knocking her to the ground. Probably would have stuck the boot in as well, if security hadn't grabbed him and threatened him with another week. Imagine that, hitting a comedian just because you don't like the act. I would never do that, I tell Crissy, even if it was Hale and Pace. Crissy considers the outrage and says, 'Ah, fuck 'em,' and adds, 'Excuse my French.' That's Crissy all over. One minute as rough as an old pair of docker's boots, the next surprisingly proper, almost childlike.

Roger Ebert summed her up best in his review of *Ladybird, Ladybird*, although he may have been confusing her with her character, Maggie:

If you hang around bars where a lot of steady drinking goes on, you will have met someone like Crissy. She is short, blonde, pudgy, in her 30s, with a nice face tending to fat. She's a 'character'. On karaoke night, she grabs the mike and brings down the house. She's good company, tells jokes, gets bawdy, holds her own. She likes to laugh, but there is sadness inside, and after too many drinks she may start to sob. She's in the bar looking for comfort, reassurance, a sense of belonging, and so she's a pushover for guys who buy her a drink and seem to care.

Actually, on second thoughts, the doyen of American film critics was almost certainly writing about Maggie rather than Crissy, who is in her forties and doesn't drink. But the rest fits fine and Ebert's confusion unwittingly offers a clue as to why Ken Loach chose this unknown for the part.

The film led to a whirlwind of acclaim for Crissy; not just Ebert's review but a best actress award from the London Film Critics' Circle (Hugh Grant, best actor), the Berlin Film Festival award (Tom Hanks, best actor) and prizes in Hamburg, Dresden, Chicago, as well as invitations to film festivals all over the world. But no glittering film career, although Crissy acts regularly in the theatre and is offered small parts on TV, work about which she is endearingly non-precious, treating it rather like the stand-up, as 'just another gig'. It is not altogether surprising that her head has failed to be turned by the blandishments of the international film world. You are not likely to be terribly impressed by the artifices of film when you have had as much contact with real life as Crissy has.

The headlines are as follows: brought up in grinding poverty in Parliament Street in inner-city Liverpool with a confusion of siblings and relatives; managed to pass through the school system without learning to read or write; married at sixteen to a husband who administered regular beatings; at twenty-four diagnosed with cancer of the womb and had a hysterectomy; also in her twenties, married second husband, Ian, an alcoholic; at thirty-one fell victim to skin cancer, later given the all-clear after treatment.

And that in a fairly inadequate nutshell is Christine Thompson. Also, to an extent, it is Crissy Rock, as she incorporates episodes from her life in her act. She does a song called 'Then He Punched Me' to the tune of the Crystals' hit 'Then He Kissed Me', which is quite edgy and dark but which in Benidorm is greeted as knockabout comedy, as it were. There are lots of gags about male uselessness, both in and out of the sack, greeted with hoots of laughter by a corner table of chubby girls I take to be a hen party. It is not exactly radical feminism but at least Crissy does no racist gags.

Elsewhere, it is as if the eighties, nineties and the new millennium had never happened. At the start of virtually every act the comedian will ask people in the audience where they are from and the answers come back: 'Salford', 'Bradford', 'Rotherham', a litany of solid Old Labour towns that used to be at the heartland of the white working classes, when Britain was white and working. The comedians seem to pander – and the only way to survive in Benidorm is to pander – to the audience's desire to return to the old certainties when they, and not big business or the Pakis, ruled their streets.

In the seventies there was a TV programme that used to include this kind of material – minus the four-letter words, of course – called *The Comedians*. When it crops up on nostalgia channels, one is struck by how hopelessly old-fashioned it appears. In Benidorm, though, not only is similar material *de rigueur* but some of the original performers are actually out there, doing it. One of them, George Roper, has been in Benidorm for 20 years. He has been ill of late and sometimes appears on stage in a wheelchair. Johnny Hackett, another old-time comic and long-time resident of Benidorm, is in even worse shape, leading to this exchange between two of the town's performers: 'Johnny Hackett died.' 'Well, he's died before. He'll get over it.' 'No, he died, as in "they're burying him on Tuesday".'

Liverpool singer Tony Gustafson, who reported this exchange to me, swears it is true. I was going to offer the observation that old performers never die, they just go to Benidorm, but obviously that is not quite the case; although as Johnny Hackett's picture was still up outside the Town club and he was billed to perform several days after his unfortunate demise, who knows?

As I said, Crissy manages to survive – just – without the racist gags. 'I was brought up by a black surrogate mother,' she says, 'so I would never do that.' I do not ask for details. Crissy is so open about her life that you hesitate to probe, for fear of uncovering another layer of tragedy. I do not wish to be hard-hearted but I am on the verge of saying, 'For God's sake, Crissy, no more cancer. I'm on my holidays.'

Crissy learnt to read at twenty-two, encouraged by her second husband – and the current incumbent – Ian. 'I always wanted to know how to do jelly,' she tells me. 'I thought you put it in the oven. I learnt to read so I could follow the instructions and make it properly.'

Her act, which I have seen twice now – once at a working men's club in Bradford – is unremarkable, although it includes a great version of 'You're My World' (or 'You're My Whereld', as she calls it, in the thickest Scouse accent I have ever haired) where she fails to keep up with the backing track, and manages a viperish swipe at both Cilla Black and cruise ship singer Jayne MacDonald.

Crissy never set out to be a stand-up comic. She fell into it when she was still working as a barmaid and was forced to deputize at the last minute for a turn who had failed to show up. Instant success and a need for ready cash propelled her into more gigs, but I am not sure it is the right medium for her. Perhaps a one-woman show, based on life in her beloved Liverpool, performed in front of an attentive audience, would display her talents to better advantage.

Tonight in Benidorm the spot before Crissy is occupied by Danny Downing, also a Scouser, and he appears much more comfortable in it. He is commendably light on the racist material, although heavy on Britain's most popular four-letter word, which from his mouth sounds more natural than it does from Crissy's.

There are two types of performer in Benidorm: those like Crissy, booked out by their agent for a three- or four-week run in a pub or club, who take the money and run; and guys like Danny, who have settled here, work like stink all summer and then go back to Britain for a few weeks around Christmas time.

Danny, a cheerful forty-seven-year-old with blond hair and big picture-frame glasses, bears a superficial physical resemblance to TV comic Vic Reeves and his style is certainly closer to Vic's than to some of the old-time comics. Coincidentally, shortly after returning from Benidorm I was in London's Comedy Store and frankly I find the gap between comedians like Danny and the supposedly 'modern' comics in

London's West End is now pretty negligible. There is more masturbation material at the Comedy Store but that is about it.

Danny does some good, if rather cruel, stuff about the old folk who flock to Benidorm out of season. On performing to a roomful of pensioners, he says, 'I told a joke and the audience pissed themselves ... but nobody laughed.' He does some Quasimodo stuff – 'What's that lump in your pocket?' 'It's a picture of my dad.' – and a lot of stuff about drunken driving. It was the drink-drive issue, Danny is frank enough to admit, that was behind his move to Spain six years ago. In Britain he was constantly being stopped – 'My licence has been back to Swansea more fuckin' times than Neil Kinnock' – but now he has a little bungalow near Benidorm market, walking distance from the bar, and can get pretty well tanked up every night. He likes to hang around till very late, drinking with the other turns, joshing with the bar staff, before rolling home to sleep till the early afternoon. Then he will go out for a spot of fishing and next day he will repeat the cycle. This is what he means when he says, 'I like the lifestyle over here.'

My view is that Danny should be more ambitious. He is a good comic, winning over a difficult audience. As well as the oldies, there are people in the bar with young children, and if you can command a crowd against a backdrop of electronic games machines and over-stimulated little darlings running wild, you have a rare gift.

An earlier turn, Billy Fontayne, who bills himself 'Mr Blackpool', struggled horribly, constantly shushing the audience, and at one point brandishing his microphone at some children and saying, 'See how much fuckin' noise you make with this up yer fuckin' arse,' adding, 'and that's the last time I'm being fuckin' nice about it.' When he wasn't saying 'Shut the fuck up' he was moaning about the riff-raff in the crowd. 'Thomson's fuckin' Square Deal,' as he put it. Underneath it all, Crissy tells me, he's a lovely chap. I will take her word for it. Danny, though, is a class above. He should be on TV.

While Danny fishes, Crissy returns to Liverpool, and more theatre. She is starring in a play at the city's Royal Court called *Night Collar* (Liverpool slang for night work) and I go along to see her in action. The play is written by two local lads with experience of working in the taxicab business, Jimmy Power and Tony Furlong. It is essentially a monologue by a driver – played by Scouse comic Mickey Finn – working the night shift on Christmas Eve. The set is a black cab on stage into which various passengers step, interrupting Mickey's soliloquy. Crissy plays two parts: a woman returning from hospital, where she has been told she is dying of cancer, and a lippy prostitute.

The play is full-on Scouse, glorying in everything that ensures you will never mistake Liverpool for Guildford: poverty, casual criminality, ditto sex. At one point, Mickey makes a call on his mobile, a comically unwieldy device. 'You can't be too fussy about knock-off,' he says conspiratorially to the audience (big laugh), 'I got it next door' (even bigger laugh). This is a reference to the Penny Farthing, the pub next door to the Royal Court, which Crissy has already told me has 'the cheapest ale in Liverpool', is full of every thief and scoundrel in the city, and is a legendary marketplace for stolen goods. She advises me not to go in there with my camera around my neck. When I make to leave it behind in her dressing room, she says she is only joking. They wouldn't really rip it off my neck. 'But don't put it down anywhere.'

I have mixed feelings about Liverpool. When I first started out in radio back in 1976 I was offered a job in Liverpool but took up an alternative offer from a station in Sheffield instead. The two cities could not be more different: Sheffield, rather puritan, industrious, dominated by solid working-class values, home of the priggish David Blunkett; Liverpool, by contrast, a flashy fly-by-night city, home of the vacuous, bejewelled Derek Hatton.

So I never went to Liverpool to live, but have visited frequently to work, and it has always struck me as a warm, uninhibited, vibrant city, where a night out is invariably a joyous, uplifting experience, as long as you don't mind getting back to your car to find your stereo's gone. Whoa, damaging stereotype. Normally, I shouldn't indulge but several of the Scouse comedians I saw in Benidorm – is stand-up comedy now Liverpool's chief export? – drew freely on their city's reputation as the light-fingered capital of Britain, so I am just following accepted practice.

Two comedians on the same bill, less than 90 minutes apart, told an identical joke, about four Scousers who turn up at the pearly gates craving admission to heaven. When God asks St Peter to bring them to him, St Peter, turning round to fetch them, says, 'They've gone.' 'I wonder why they have done that,' says God, to which St Peter replies, 'No, I mean the gates have gone.'

'Round our way,' says another comedian, 'they think Robin Day is a bank holiday.' And so it goes on. New York comics used to take a similar line about their city's perceived reputation for violent crime. What is it all in aid of? Attention-seeking, maybe. 'Hey, look at me, from the roughest, toughest town in Britain and still I can joke. Aren't I lovable?'

Understandably, the rest of the nation sometimes gets a little irritated with Liverpool, looking at us with its big googly eyes, pleading to be treated like a recalcitrant but charming child. Instead of writing plays and making jokes about how crap you are, we feel like saying, why don't you do something about it?

Another annoying thing – and I promise you, this is my last whinge about Liverpool – is the continuing obsession with the Beatles. I yield to no one in my admiration for the popular singing quartet, who were undeniably fab (as can easily be proven with the aid of a home computer), but it is 32 years since they last joined voices in harmony. Why, then, when I am driving into Liverpool on a balmy Tuesday evening in June listening to Radio Merseyside's events guide, are two of the three recommended gigs Beatles-related? There is a concert featuring the Backbeat Beatles, a soundalike band, with the Royal Philharmonic Orchestra, and there is an exhibition of Paul McCartney's paintings. Enough Beatles already.

As I approach Liverpool, a passing bird makes a hefty deposit on my car. Best case scenario, I thought, it has only hit my windscreen, and I will be able to clear it with the screenwash. I did not quite achieve that. Instead, I managed to smear the excretion all over the windscreen, reproducing exactly the effect of driving through vanilla custard; which led to my missing my turning. When this happens in Liverpool, you find yourself very quickly in some rather mean streets. You can see the city's magnificent Victorian buildings tantalizingly out of reach through the rear-view mirror but the road you are driving along – I think it was Scotland Road in my case – is full of shops cowering behind metal grilles.

Having executed a U-turn somewhere in Everton, I am soon circling the Royal Court looking for somewhere to land, marvelling at the scale of some of Liverpool's buildings – St George's Hall, the council building, an old railway goods depot that has been turned into a conservation centre – as I drive past them for the third or fourth time. Eventually, I park in Cheapside, an alleyway next to the city's main cells, and note that the windscreen is the least of it. The car looks like it has spent the past six months parked next to the bird house at Chester Zoo with the word 'conveniences' stencilled on the roof, but at least the outrage should deter anyone with designs on my radio cassette player.

I make for the Royal Court, a typically art deco thirties theatre, rather like one of those nice old Odeon cinemas, and, as tends to happen in Liverpool, within minutes I have chums. The authors of the play are hanging around the foyer as I explain my mission to the guy in the office. They insist I am given a ticket for one of the best seats in the house, usher me up to Crissy's dressing room and then take me next door for a pint. In several years of theatregoing in the West End this has never happened to me.

The mix of criminals and theatricals in the Penny Farthing is probably unique outside of a biography of the Kray twins. Alongside the cast of the play, who are taking advantage of the £1.40 a pint looseners, and the local ne'er-do-wells, are Jimmy McGovern, creator of several TV hits, including *Cracker*, and Colin McEwan, founder of Liverpool Film Studios and one of the guiding lights behind long-running TV soap opera *Brookside*. That is the thing about Liverpool. You could drink in Leeds every night for the rest of your life and never meet a writer or stand-up comic. Twenty minutes in Liverpool and I am in a pub full of them.

The theatre is packed and the play is greeted with rapturous joy. Here is a typical joke, in the original Scouse, on which it depends. Mickey to Crissy, sitting in the back of the cab: 'Ay, dere's been a big fire at one o' dem supermarkets in town. Crissy: 'As dere?' Mickey: 'No, Tesco!'

An Elvis impersonator gets into the taxi and Mickey asks him if he will sing his favourite Elvis number, 'Blossom

Arsehole'. That's 'Blossom Arsehole', as in 'Blossom arsehole, what's wrong with me? I'm all shook up ...'

It is not, you will have gathered, a sophisticated evening. People heckle. In the interval, one of the young chaps sitting near me is telling his friends how his girlfriend has caught him looking at other girls. 'At least she knows I'm not gay now,' he says. 'She knows I'll always be the postman, never the letterbox.' This is a truly Liverpool night out.

In the pub afterwards Jimmy McGovern has rather a lot to drink and tells Crissy the play is 'an outrage'. He says it does not make sense dramatically for Crissy's cancer victim not to return later in the play. This leads to a full and frank discussion among writers and cast members, in which the consensus appears to be that the big hotshot TV writer can go and fuck himself. Speaking of which, throughout the evening I have been introduced to a bewildering array of people as 'Martin Kelner from the *Guardian*' but after a few drinks, Colin McEwan, for reasons which escape me now, doubts my credentials. 'If you're a reporter, I'm the fucking Pope,' he says, the correct answer to which is, 'Well, fuck you, your Holiness,' but as I am not a Scouser this only occurs to me on the drive home.

If the measure of a good evening is how much you laugh, I had a great time. I have yet to go to Liverpool and not laugh an awful lot – apart from when I had to queue up all day for a new passport. Sure, Bill Bryson is right when he says it is a city with 'more of a past than a future', but if it is no longer sending great ships out into the world, at least it still exports laughs, in the shape of people like Crissy and Danny and Ricky, not least to Benidorm, which with its cheerful vulgarity often feels like Liverpool on holiday.

But what next for Crissy? By the time you read this there is a chance she could be almost famous. A couple of independent film-makers were in the audience for *Night Collar*, talking about 'doing a project' with her, and certainly the story of a woman who could not read a word until she was twenty-two, and now learns pages of lines for a play, is worth doing, I should have said.

Fame is certainly a spur for Crissy but even more so is the need to escape. 'Whether it is stand-up or theatre, I love it,' she tells me, as we sit outside Steptoes. 'I couldn't be without it. When I come to work I leave Christine Thompson behind. For one hour a day I can be Crissy Rock, and unlike Christine, Crissy Rock has no problems.'

For performers of all sorts, from radio presenters to gravy jugglers, escape is a pretty powerful motivation. I am convinced, though, that Benidorm is not the right place for Crissy to escape to. It is no place for a nice girl to be. She should leave it to the Paki-bashers, the tax-dodgers and Sticky Vicky with her flags.

4

MR ENTERTAINMENT

As it happens, Crissy and I share an agent, Roger Davis. Most of what I laughingly call my career is self-managed but I do have an agent to handle my after-dinner speaking engagements, which is a bit of a joke really because I am not exactly beating off with a shitty stick people demanding my post-prandial *aperçus*.

Roger's efforts to pitchfork me onto that lucrative after-dinner circuit have mostly been in vain. He has actually got me one gig in the past five years, which may be one more than what I am pleased to call 'my routine' warrants. This, by the way, is not me trying to be cute, saying, 'Ooh, look at me, aren't I useless, but charming with it?' I am actually, provably, useless. If anyone ever devised a mathematical formula for measuring after-dinner speakers, I should be down there below freezing.

I always used to start off by saying, 'Don't expect anything too radical from me, I'm from Radio 2, where we are not exactly hip ...' (A beat.) 'More sort of hip replacement.' But then Radio 2 sharpened up its act, slung out the Mantovani and the shrimp boats, and bang went my nice self-deprecating opening. (The shrimp boats reference, by the way, is to a record that, in Radio 2's old light music days, always seemed to be scheduled in my programme, and was called, if memory serves, 'Shrimp Boats Is A-comin'. It was utterly inappropriate for Radio 2's middle-aged, middle-England audience, conjuring up a vision of little old ladies in Tunbridge Wells fruitlessly scanning the horizon for dem ole shrimp boats a-comin'.) Anyway, despite my material being as dangerously past its sell-by date as the shrimps, I still do after-dinner speeches when asked, simply because it seems like ridiculously easy money.

I once wrote a magazine feature about the growing

popularity of sportsmen's dinners, which involved my following a well-known former football manager around the country as he picked up lots of fat brown envelopes stuffed with £20 notes in exchange for tired old footy stories. A solid week of hearing the joke about the uncompromising Scottish defender who was so hard he had his gravestone inscribed with the legend 'Who're you looking at?' led this observer, who was being given a substantially slimmer envelope by Associated Newspapers for his finely crafted words, to think, 'Hey, wait a minute …'

Roger has kind of given up on me but sometimes misguided folk who have read my newspaper column or heard me on the radio book me directly under the misapprehension that I will provide an evening of rip-roaring entertainment. Which is how I ended up at the Huddersfield Society of Chartered Accountants' annual dinner recently, floundering somewhat. I ascribe my downfall at this sort of function to two factors: firstly, I am invariably put to dine at the top table, where it is odds on there will be someone with far more experience than me in public speaking, and this has a destabilizing effect; and secondly, once I am actually on my feet, there will be a line – however well the thing seems to be going – that I consider to be a sure-fire winner that will fall on inexplicably stony ground. When that happens, it is as if you have placed your foot unthinkingly on a stair that is suddenly no longer there, leaving your limb flailing helplessly.

The sight of a couple of hundred accountants and their spouses done up to the nines in full evening dress is something I find intimidating. They look so very expectant and I know that what I have to deliver is a rather slight, undernourished thing that I can feel shrinking as I rise to my feet. And why do they always position a large lady in an extravagantly low-cut dress directly in front of me? You try getting your timing just right while you are concentrating on not looking at a woman's breasts. Or maybe it is just my material that needs updating, possibly by the inclusion of some snappy eighties one-liners. Whatever it is, it looks like I'm never going to be Peter Ustinov, which I can live with; and it is a burden which may be lightened by spending some time with people who will never be Barbra Streisand or Bob Hope or Barry Manilow.

Roger Davis has a lot of these people on his books. He is, after all, West Yorkshire's Mr Entertainment, according to an article I once read in the *Halifax Courier*. In the past my dealings with Roger – the gig, that is – have been over the phone. When I propose a visit, his son, Mark, who runs the business with him, sends me an A4 sheet of closely typed directions, full of winding roads, old barns and country pubs and finishing along a gravel track through a graveyard. It may be the most difficult place in Britain to find. Were Roger a secret agent rather than a showbiz agent, he might have found himself the perfect hideaway. He runs his business from his home, which strictly speaking is in Halifax. But it is not in the centre of Halifax, rather in a village called Luddenden Foot. But not in the centre of Luddenden Foot. Instead it is halfway up a Pennine hillside, just off the A629 Halifax to Burnley road.

Interestingly enough, my literary agent is in Newman Street, W1, at the heart of the West End of London, giving me representation in both of our two nations. Mind you, I once interviewed the comedian and actor Freddie 'Parrot Face' Davies, who had agents in Yorkshire, London, Sydney and Los Angeles. 'I'm out of work all over the world,' he boasted.

Roger seems to be doing well enough out of his stable of old-style comedians, club turns, and through booking people like me – most of them rather busier than me – for corporate functions or after-dinner speaking. His house is like the house of a football manager or the sort of comedian he handles, when you see them all spruced up for *Through the Keyhole*, with polished imitation wood floors, an interesting staircase and lots of knick-knacks. In the driveway is a posh car, a Lexus, with the registration ROG 9, also some sort of a four-wheel drive vehicle, and his son's Porsche.

The office where the two Davises work alongside two women assistants is at the top of the house, illuminated by the light coming from what I can confidently name as Velux windows, being a veteran of a loft conversion myself. Yellowing cuttings from long defunct showbiz papers jostle for space with computers. The phone rings fairly frequently, although, by Roger's own admission, not as frequently as it used to.

Were he not so clearly prosperous, Roger would cut rather a

sad figure, the emperor of an empire that no longer exists. He manages 14 comedians, none of whom is of the type you see regularly on television these days. The best known is a chap called Johnnie Casson, who has in fact appeared on Des O'Connor's TV show a few times and still manages to fill medium-sized theatres in Blackpool, as well as appearing at corporate functions and sportsmen's dinners.

As I remember, in the *Halifax Courier* feature, Roger is pictured holding a poster for a Casson gig at the Grand Opera House in York, reading 'Ladies and Giblets, Leisure Management in association with Roger Davis presents the classic comedy of Johnnie Casson.' The poster includes a quote from Shirley Maclaine: 'I love this man, he is so funny.'

Even Casson, however, who used to do 300 shows a year, now has quiet times. He used to be the drummer in a pop group called the Cresters, who once toured with the Beatles in Scotland. He has kept souvenirs of the tour, signed concert bills and so on, which are his pension, and which he carries around the country with him in an old suitcase. (Insecurity is endemic among entertainers. Show me a performer on ten grand a night and I'll show you someone with a stash of cash somewhere for when it all goes horribly wrong.)

One look at Roger and you know he was in a beat group too. He is getting on for sixty now but his hair is younger than he is, swept forward, with only a hint of grey, and he wears a neatly trimmed beard. He smokes a pipe, giving him the air of Derek Smalls, the bass guitarist in Spinal Tap. The details of Roger's pop career could have come from Spinal Tap as well. He started in 1959 in a group called the Chessmen, playing rock 'n' roll at village dances in Yorkshire, made a single – for Elite Records of Shipley – and then went to Germany, where the group played for GIs and in clubs around Frankfurt.

Back in Britain, the group disbanded and Roger 'went into the motor trade', as he puts it. (I am fairly sure it is only people of Roger's generation who talk about 'the motor trade', taking their cue from the Beatles' song 'She's Leaving Home', in which the heroine, as I recall, skips off to meet a man 'in the motor trade'.) In 1970 Roger formed another band, Simplicity, 'a four-piece with a girl, a kind of New Seekers act'. Their zenith came when they performed the theme tune for *The Sky's the Limit*, a quiz show of the era starring the late Hughie Green. An even later incarnation was Claret, who performed covers of hit songs on cruise ships.

At the same time as failing to become a pop star, Roger worked with showbiz agents booking acts into the casinos and cabaret clubs that flourished in Britain in the seventies – the so-called chicken-in-the-basket circuit – before striking out on his own in the mid-eighties. He is undecided about what killed his business, or at least forced him to diversify. He hates karaoke with a passion, feeling it has killed live music. The tribute acts, which continue to proliferate, he describes as 'glorified karaoke'. TV is his other *bête noire*, or at least producers whose talent-spotting fails to take them beyond the London comedy clubs. 'It is impossible for my type of comedian to get work on the TV these days,' says Roger, lamenting the lame game show and chat show formats some of the more fashionable comics come up with.

He is right when he says some of the working men's club and cabaret-style acts could give the newer performers a lesson in professionalism but the truth is they are craftsmen in a craft for which there is no longer any great call, at least not in Britain. They might as well be hand weavers or guys who set type in hot metal. And there I am, amongst them, on Mr Entertainment's roster of (highly) available artistes, and with my own entry on his website, www.comedians.co.uk. According to this, my chief asset – and, believe me, it took some considerable thought to come up with anything – is that I have spent 25 years in broadcasting and journalism, in the course of which I have accumulated a wealth of amusing anecdotes. That is the theory, anyway. Unfortunately, as most of my stories involve disc jockeys either being drunk on air or being caught *in flagrante* in a studio, putting the mixing desk to non-standard use, they are probably of limited interest to Huddersfield accountants.

Incidentally, in my younger days I used to find that if you were involved in that sort of activity in the studio there were all sorts of hidden hazards. The turntables tended to have remote starts in those days, so it was quite easy in the heat of passion to nudge the wrong button and find your new friend's backside rotating at 45 revolutions per minute (which rather spoils you for anything in the future). These days, of course, it is all digital (please feel free to insert your own smutty joke here, I'm trying to cut down).

One radio story that almost qualifies as a bona fide amusing anecdote concerns a colleague of mine who went to work for a radio station down south, where he conducted a radio swap shop on his afternoon show. Housewives (we still had them in those days), mainly, would phone the show and try to exchange baby buggies that were no longer of use to them for Dimplex heaters. This chap kept the telephone numbers of the women he liked the sound of, and then rang them back after the show. But he was not offering to relieve them of their unwanted items. Deary me, no, it was relief of another sort he had in mind, usually successfully achieved during the course of his uniquely obscene telephone calls.

I find the idea of a broadcaster stalking his listeners a rather neat turning of the tables, but the problem is that there is no real punchline to the story, unless you count an eighteen-month suspended sentence and an invitation to leave the radio industry.

Another favourite radio story, again of limited use in an after-dinner context, concerns Roger Moffat, a golden-voiced and very funny broadcaster, and also an enthusiastic and quite spectacular drunk, whom I was privileged to count as a friend and colleague in the seventies. One of his gigs was to act as stooge to two puppet piglets called Pinky and Perky in a Sunday afternoon children's TV programme. Roger, as I recall, played the manager of a radio station, staffed by the two piggies, who sang a Chipmunks-style song and did all sorts of silly and naughty things. Hilarious consequences, I expect, ensued. Also, I believe, a beat group mimed to their latest hit.

One Saturday morning, having recorded a couple of these programmes in the BBC studios in Manchester, Roger decided to call in at the BBC Club in Piccadilly, where he enjoyed a long and leisurely midday meal, not at all affected by the fact that no food was available in the BBC Club at lunchtime on a Saturday. Emerging somewhat unsteadily onto Market Street, Manchester's main shopping thoroughfare, at around four in the afternoon, Roger was recognized by two little boys, about six and seven years old, out shopping with the family. 'Ooh look, it's Pinky and Perky's dad,' they shouted. 'Where's Pinky and Perky?' Roger, who was pretty well incapable of speech by this time, and certainly in no position to meet his public, sort of flailed his arm a little, which was meant to shoo the children away. But they continued to follow him down Market Street, shouting all the while, 'Where's Pinky and Perky?' One of them, I think, started grabbing at his jacket, while the other one kept repeating the question, 'Where's Pinky and Perky?' to which Roger eventually snarled the reply, 'I've fucking eaten them.' Cue tears, angry father, desultory fisticuffs and a by no means unique meeting between golden-voiced broadcaster and Manchester pavement. Again, not one, I think, for the Huddersfield accountants.

The problem with spending 25 years in my trade is that you never actually do anything. You meet some famous people, go to some interesting places, but you never really achieve anything. At least I haven't.

Invariably, when I am at a function, one of my co-speakers will say something like, 'So, as we went out to open the batting for England in that fateful second test, I said to Geoff Boycott ...' or 'So there it was in front of me, in all its savage beauty, the Kalahari Desert ...' What am I supposed to counter this with? 'So there I was at Murrayfield, pissed in the bar, and 900 words to produce by 5.30 for the first edition ...' To make things worse, there will sometimes be somebody who can entertain the diners with some mind-reading or a bit of close-up magic, which I take as a cruel taunt, underlining the paucity of my talents.

I only became aware quite how useless I was when I landed a big television gig some time in the late eighties, co-presenting a programme for Yorkshire Television called *Living It Up*. The idea of this programme was that elderly folk, instead of spending their retirement in carpet slippers watching *Question of Sport* on TV, might want instead to fulfil their lifelong dreams of going skydiving or doing a dance routine in a stage show.

Although the show was ostensibly a local documentary project, a hotshot light entertainment producer was brought in to make it sexy enough for a network repeat. He was a chap called Phil Bishop, fresh from the Saturday night hit *Game for a Laugh*, whose values he imported wholesale. This meant that we – myself and my co-presenter, the late John Diamond – were required to plunge ourselves comically into whatever activity the old person in our film had chosen to do.

While John could pretty well handle anything thrown at him – banjo playing, dancing, riding a unicycle – I was unable to rise to even the pathetic minimum level required to make it look semi-convincing on screen. They spent a whole day trying to teach me a simple kick-step sequence for a basic dance routine, by the end of which I looked like I was doing some sort of tasteless send-up of Douglas Bader. This is why, when I thumb through the pages of *Showcall*, which has become my regular bedtime reading, I am particularly impressed by those artistes who can do things. It beats me that entertainers will spend all their leisure time and risk personal injury to acquire a range of abstruse skills when they could probably earn twice as much as an under-manager in their local supermarket.

Take Tony De La Fou, 'an act of quality and comedy for all ages'. His entry lists skills including juggling (five balls), unicycling (giraffe and standard), fire-eating, fire-juggling, diabolo, balloon-modelling, pocket-magic and clowning. Just as I was intrigued at the career path that had taken Sticky Vicky into the business of producing interesting and occasionally dangerous items from her lower orifice, so I wondered about the way Tony had chosen to earn his weekly envelope, particularly the fire-eating. There must have been one moment, one defining moment – a dull afternoon, possibly, when there was nothing much on the TV – when he first decided it would be a good idea to put a flaming torch in his mouth. And that is almost exactly how it happened, he tells me when we meet in a pub near Waterloo station.

Tony was performing nearly every day and every night and could not have been happier to cooperate. His *Showcall* entry says he is 'suitable for corporate work, promotional and themed occasions, staged or street shows, festivals, fairs and community entertainment,' and there seems to be an awful lot of that kind of thing about.

'Let me see,' says Tony, consulting his diary. 'Friday night at

Odiham RAF base, just off the M3, entertaining in the officers' mess, their summer ball, back home for 2 a.m., then up at 8 a.m. for a circus skills workshop in the Milwall football club car park, part of Southwark Council's action day. Finish about 4 p.m. and then in the evening, off to the Honourable Artillery Club for an Arabian themed entertainment, very popular for corporate nights.'

The next day it was street entertainment in Bromley during the day and an Indian couple's very posh wedding in Ruislip in the evening. He does children's parties as well, which is an interesting development given that Tony arrived at his unusual career choice via the anarcho-punk route. Yes, the man who founded a magazine called *Ripped and Torn* and another called *Kill Your Pet Puppy* is now available for children's parties.

Tony started the *Ripped and Torn* fanzine in 1976 but all I could find in the way of archive on the internet was an interview with a band called Raped, which mentions other bands of the era with similarly provocative names, like the Moors Murderers and Belsen Was a Gas. It also quotes a sweet little lyric from a demo by a band called Foreplay Playground, which goes as follows (and do feel free to join in at home): 'Jenny's got her nose in a library book/She's so into masturbation she's forgotten how to fuck.'

So it must be a bit of a change for Tony doing children's parties, although from my recollection of some of those to which I have escorted my children, a Moors Murderers gig could be ideal preparation. Tony, I should imagine, goes down really well with the kids. He is one of those chaps you just can't help warming to, one of the nicest anarcho-punks I have ever met, in fact. I bet they call him Uncle Tony. He actually calls himself Mr Laffo for his children's party gigs, which do not pay much, but he does them because, as he says in true show business style, 'The work is there.' He demonstrates his children's party material for me by whipping out a couple of balloons and, in double quick time, making them into a lovely flower. I don't know about the children, but I am entertained.

Tony says he could teach me to do the balloon shapes at one of his workshops. Don't count on it, I say. When Yorkshire Television tried to teach me to unicycle, I broke a trestle table and 40 quid's worth of crockery in their rehearsal room. I did actually teach myself some years ago to juggle three balls but to take the leap into proper juggling I need to work on my weaker hand, says Tony. I need to spend hour after hour, day after day, practising until I get it right. 'I can't be arsed,' I say. 'That could be your problem,' concludes Tony.

I will regret moving on from this chapter because Tony has become my new friend. When I met him, Tony and his girlfriend, Michelle, were due to have their first child, so I kept in touch with him for developments on that front while charting his progress as he cut a swathe through southeast England, eating fire and entertaining children.

Conversations would go something like: 'Tony, can you talk?' 'Well, I'm on stilts in northeast Kent at the moment.' Later I would ring him at home and ask how the stilt-walking had gone. 'It was a bit breezy,' he said. 'Is that a problem?' I ask. 'Yes, you have to wear the big trousers, and the breeze, well, you know ...'

There was a time when it would have been a sign of arrested development for a forty-four-year-old man to spend his time worrying about the wind whistling through his big trousers. It might even have been seen as a vaguely absurd concern to have when you are on the point of bringing a new human being into the world and buying a flat in Leytonstone. But hey, who am I to talk? I spend my time watching football matches on TV and making up sarcastic jokes about John Motson, and I have four little ones who call me Daddy, and look to me for their Coco Pops and fashionable sportswear.

Maybe this is why there is such a bond between us (that's Tony and me, rather than my children and me). We are part of the generation born between 1945 and 1965, which grew up with the Beatles and punk and have discovered you don't have to put on grown-up trousers to make a living.

Tony, bless him, does not even ask me to go to the flat in Leytonstone to interview him. I am in London to guest on the *Hawksbee and Jacobs Show* on Talksport and it turns out that Tony is a big fan of the programme. He agrees to meet at Waterloo, near the studios, if I will introduce him to the unsung geniuses of afternoon radio. We do better than that and actually get him on the show, where he explains how to eat fire and comes close to libelling the chairman of a non-league football club.

The important thing is I have not had to travel to Leytonstone. I have a Northerner's aversion to travelling to unfamiliar areas of London and apart from the West End, and a few areas of north and west London, most of it is unfamiliar to me. It never used to bother me in the early seventies, when I would happily drive around in an old Mini ferrying four mates and a couple of bottles of undrinkable wine on a quest for some bloke's party in East Dulwich or Turnham Green or Wandsworth, at the same time wondering why the *London A–Z* is not categorized as a work of fiction. But these days, driving in London is just another of those things I cannot bear. I hate travelling anywhere by tube as well. London is such a fascinating city that I begrudge time spent underneath it so if I have the time I walk to where I need to be. Even an ostensibly undistinguished, traffic-choked area like Holloway, I find, is worth a leisurely stroll if you don't mind ingesting a year's supply of carbon monoxide in an afternoon.

I used to share a flat in Drayton Park, roughly halfway between Highbury Corner and the Holloway Odeon, while my brother's place was further up the road towards Archway, so at some time or other I have tramped every yard of Holloway Road, drinking in its entrancing delights. (Sorry, for a moment there I thought I was writing a travel piece for the *Sunday Express*.) All right, no entrancing delights, but I never failed to be impressed by the idiosyncratic range of shops missed by motorists rushing down the A1 to the City, and the poor overworked saps forced down onto the Piccadilly Line. I like the fact that there is a shop selling bondage gear and transvestite supplies just down the road from an old-fashioned baker's. Where else can you buy a nipple clamp and a Cornish pasty on the same trip?

For my first meeting with Tony I walk from King's Cross station to Waterloo. King's Cross/St Pancras is, I think, a highly underrated area, and I have to say that over the years my sympathies have always been with those high court judges and MPs who have been caught trying to enjoy its architecture by driving around it very slowly.

The station was built in 1851 on the site of a former hospital for contagious diseases, several of whose displaced inmates appear still to be hanging around in the nearby slot machine arcades or have found work behind the counter of one of the many kebab and fried chicken places. Cross over the road into Argyle Street, though, and it is a different world. There used to be a programme on the radio that claimed to stop 'the mighty roar of London's traffic' and that is the effect you get the moment you leave Euston Road and head towards Bloomsbury, past those terraces of dubious little hotels. (It is years since I stayed in one of those price-buster establishments but I suspect they still supply you with the toenail under the washstand and the single pubic hair on the nylon pillowcase, which I have always thought of as the budget alternative to the little chocolate mint.)

Through Bloomsbury, Holborn, Covent Garden, and over Waterloo Bridge – the best view of the Thames in London – on a mild and sunny Tuesday afternoon, and that gag Dr Johnson used to do about the man who is tired of London being tired of life is striking me as a real winner; although if you live in Peckham or Catford you might be inclined to take a different view. When I arrive at the Hogshead pub in Stamford Street, which is an awful pub but a convenient meeting place, Tony De La Fou, né Drayton, is taking calls on his mobile.

I had not realized that people with the ability to juggle flaming torches were in such demand but Tony is on the books of several agents, and unless he has set up all the calls to impress me, he is a definite candidate for the Hardest Working Man in Show Business. A lot of the requests fall into the category of 'meet and greet, mix and mingle', which was a new one on me, and a term I have now taken to using for social engagements. ('Just a little mix and mingle,' I will say if I am meeting chums down the pub.) These are often corporate gigs, where large companies apparently believe that they can either increase productivity or get away with sacking a few people if they treat their workforce to a slap-up meal with some bloke breathing fire in the background. Other engagements are for local authorities, where Tony will juggle and unicycle all afternoon in shopping centres and distract local ratepayers from the fact that their bins haven't been emptied and there is nowhere to park their car.

We get our diaries out to sort out a further meeting when I can watch him eating fire, and his puts mine to shame. Mine tends to have six blank pages, followed by something like 'Haircut, 2.15', whereas in Tony's there is something different every day: 'Thursday – Dartford shopping centre, dressed as jester, handing out leaflets for computer course, 5 p.m., Cricklewood, Beacon Bingo Hall seventh anniversary, do some fire.'

Then there are the children's parties. 'The problem there is, once you knock on that door, you're on. "The clown's here," they'll shout, and you've got to be full on, right from the offski, till you get in the car and drive round the corner. It's hard work and not much money but, you know, what with buying the flat and having a baby, and so on … I read one of those books, *How to Make a Million*, and it said, "Don't be too proud to pick money up off the floor." Well, children's parties are maybe £2,000 a year just lying around on the floor.'

Not that he seems at all unhappy with his lot. Avuncular is definitely the word for Tony. His hair is steely grey and thinning slightly. In his anarcho-punk days, he tells me, it was blond: 'But then I was in Thailand for a while, went swimming every day, and it washed all the colour out of it.' His grey hair makes him look like a cross between a slightly chubby Sting and the film star Steve Martin. He does not look much like a fire-eater in his civvies but when he performs he sometimes goes bare-chested and wears a pseudo-Arabian bolero type of thing.

The next time I see Tony he is doing a little bit of 'meet and greet' but without the 'mix and mingle'. Leeds Grammar School, a very wealthy private school with a vast new campus to the north of the city, is celebrating its 450th anniversary, with a dinner dance, a big black tie do with a tasteful little jazz quartet playing in the foyer, speeches from local worthies and later a pop group and a disco.

Tony has been booked as 'background' and as people arrive, between 6.30 and 8.30 p.m., he will be at the entrance, eating fire and juggling his flaming torches. He is being paid quite a few hundred pounds for this one but he has to find a female fire-eater to perform alongside him and he has to drive up from London.

He normally does his boy/girl gigs with a fire-eater called the Duchess – which, apropos of nothing in particular, is how Jimmy Savile always refers to his late mother – but she is unavailable (that's the fire-eater, not the late Mrs Savile). There seems to be a network of female fire-eaters, though, mostly from a vaguely anarcho-hippy background, and Tony zooms up in his Toyota Corolla carrying Sorcha Ra, a rather striking-looking Irish lady with pre-Raphaelite tresses and a neat dancer's body. Unlike Tony, who merely slips on a black shirt with a flame effects design, Sorcha makes an effort with the costume and make-up with a little sequinned top and a jewel for her forehead.

Not only is this a gig that pays well, but there is free food as well, a facsimile of the grand meal the guests will get, served in the school canteen. Tony is anxious he and Sorcha are fed before the gig because afterwards everything will taste of paraffin, and if you are going to do that, you might as well eat at the Little Chef.

Over tea, Sorcha tells us about an engagement in Majorca – performing for the 18–30 club – from which she has recently returned with burns on her arm after somebody sold her the wrong sort of fuel for use in her body-burning routine. A lively discussion on types of paraffin, to which I am able to contribute little, ensues. I gather there are hundreds of sites on the internet offering specialist materials from America to fire-eaters and the like.

Tony has suffered burns lots of times, he tells me, particularly when he was first learning to fire-eat. After the *Ripped and Torn* fanzine, which he started in Glasgow in 1976, he moved to London and became heavily involved in the punk scene, living in squats and selling his political magazine, *Kill Your Pet Puppy,* at gigs. By 1984, though, the New Romantics had more or less taken over the music scene and Tony segued neatly from punk into New Age travelling, going to the Stonehenge Festival, taking acid and hanging out with a bunch of like-minded people, arsing about, as some might call it.

'At the time I was living in a house with about 12 people, the Black Sheep Housing Cooperative,' he says, 'and I started learning circus skills just for something to do, really. The idea was to go out with bands, you know, musical circus stuff, to get out of London and live Gypsy style. Not to go out and do corporate gigs.'

Sorcha smiles knowingly. She travelled round Europe for a while, living in a camper van in a sort of performing/arsing about interface that she thought might last forever, and now here she is as well, providing colourful background for dinner-jacketed fat cats who can afford to have their children privately educated.

The weather is not ideal for what they do. There is an uncertain breeze, and if you are not careful, when you breathe fire the wind can blow the flames back at you and you end up getting singed. 'I used to have a much bigger quiff,' says Tony. Also, it is a light summer's evening and their show is obviously much more spectacular performed in the dark. They throw themselves into it with commendable enthusiasm, though, doing the fire-eating, juggling the flaming torches ('Three flaming torches, one flaming idiot' is Tony's line) and trying to engage the guests, who arrive in their finery in twos and threes. It is a fairly thankless task, however, as people just seem a little taken aback to be greeted by fire-eaters. Tony and Sorcha are quite literally background, booked, one suspects, because the budget was there for them.

'It is all experience,' says Sorcha. 'Every gig is. I mean, some of them are just bread and butter gigs but you get a glimpse into a lot of different lives, and I enjoy that. I think of myself as a dancer more than a circus artiste, so what I should like to do is perform a piece choreographed to music but that is not going to happen five days a week so I do these other gigs.'

Sorcha seems very centred, either that or very spaced out. She is calm and the pitch of her voice rarely varies, even when she is talking about being burnt in Majorca by the wrong kind of paraffin. She smiles a lot, a pretty smile, and her approach to her fire-eating, stilt-walking and so on is almost transcendental.

'It takes perseverance to acquire these skills,' she says. 'It can be ever so frustrating, trying for hours on end, for days even, to master something, going over it again and again, but when you can do it, body-burning or fire-eating, whatever it is, it gives you the knowledge that everything is attainable.'

Tony is a little more down to earth, if you like. When he talked to me about his fire-eating, he talked in terms of physics.

'It is all a question of having a lot of saliva in your mouth and then putting the torch in at the cut-off point below the flame. The flame will then burn the oxygen in your mouth and go out.' I think I have got that right, but to be on the safe side, I shouldn't try it at home.

The problem, once you have acquired all the skills, is where to go from there. There is a sort of macho juggling scene, which the surprising number of specialist magazines for jugglers – *Jugglers' World, Cascade, Catch* and many more – covers fully, with stories about chaps juggling chainsaws and unfeasible numbers of bowling balls.

'That kind of thing's all about gym work,' says Tony. 'I can't see the point. I can do four flaming torches but I usually stick to three, and I can juggle five balls if I want, but I don't believe it's about how many you can do. Some jugglers want to do four, then five, six, seven. There's a guy in Las Vegas who can do twelve rings and seven torches. But that kind of thing is tedious. I like to concentrate on the entertainment, work on the patter and so on.'

Which would be fine were there some sort of variety stage for Tony to appear on, maybe an alternative cabaret circuit. I am not saying it is something I would go to but it would keep jugglers out of shopping centres and would make a change from bright young comics whose idea of entertainment is a slick 20 minutes of masturbation jokes.

For the moment, though, Tony must nuzzle up to the capitalist teat, which is probably the last thing he thought he would be doing when he did a degree at the University of East London from 1991 to 1994, delivering a thesis entitled *Street Entertainment, Part of the Secret History of Revolt*, with subheadings like 'The Monstrous Brood', and 'Inspired Lunacy – Itinerant Performance and Timeless Themes of Spiritual Significance'.

How to square all that with a gig in a bingo hall is a conundrum I shall leave to Tony. 'I do what comes my way,' he says. 'About five or six years ago I did give some thought to the future but then the gigs started coming in and as long as that keeps happening it sort of stops me looking for a proper job.'

I have no idea how long you can go on juggling and eating fire. Can you still do it at fifty-four? Or sixty-four? It is the sort of dilemma pretty well every entertainer has to face at some time or other. I thought about it myself, when I was still disc-jockeying at forty, but then I looked at John Peel, still doing it in his fifties, and Jimmy Young, who was still presenting a regular show at one hundred and four or whatever it was.

To some extent, everybody in this book – and I include myself in this – keeps on performing as a means of avoiding looking for a proper job, even into their fifties and sixties. And retirement, of course, is an option that is clearly just too ridiculous to even contemplate. We would rather think about death.

While I was mulling over these issues, the phone rang and it was Tony, telling me that little James Jack Drayton had just arrived in the world, and mother and child were doing well. He and Michelle had wanted a hippy water birth but Michelle had a ligament strain, so that was impractical and they were stuck instead with a traditional dry land delivery. But, my goodness, he could not have been more chuffed to be a father for the first time.

Would he, I wondered, at this momentous time, be taking a step back to reassess his life? 'Well, er, maybe, but not tonight. I'm booked for a Caribbean theme night in Slough.'

5

GOLDENOLDIELAND

When Brian Wilson of the Beach Boys wrote his famous lyric about East Coast girls being hip, and went on to express his admiration for those styles they wear, I think we can safely assume he was not thinking of Scarborough, on England's east coast.

That is not to accuse Scarborough of a lack of comely and personable girls but, as I look around the predominantly female audience at what I have been assured is the absolute top night out for Scarborough's women, 'hip', it must be said, is not the first word that comes to mind. At the table nearest to me, for instance, are four women, ranging in age, at a gentlemanly guess, from thirty-five to somewhere north of fifty-five, office colleagues, possibly, all of whom wear a similar uniform of blouses and tight blue denim jeans. They are not slim women. A lot of denim is being asked to spread itself over quite a wide area. Zip fasteners are having to work a good deal harder than Whitcomb Judson probably envisaged when he patented his Clasp Locker Device in 1895. It would not surprise me to hear their metal tangs screaming out for mercy, were I able to hear anything above the sound of Seaside Danny Wilde.

Seaside Danny Wilde. The name alone sold me on the absolute necessity of going to see this performer long before I knew anything about his act. There is a Leeds University lecturer I know, Steve, who organizes a minibus several times a year and goes over with a bunch of his colleagues to enjoy an evening's drinking, rounded off with a visit to pay tipsy homage to Danny. Steve tells me similar pilgrimages take place from Sheffield University. It is also a popular outing for coachloads of nurses from northern hospitals. Danny may be close to being Scarborough's number one visitor attraction.

Here is a story about Danny, frequently told: when the

British film *Little Voice* was being filmed in Scarborough, the cast learned of Danny's near legendary status and one of the stars, Michael Caine, said he would like to meet him. 'If he wants to meet me, he'll have to come down to the pub, I'm not going to see him,' Danny is reported as saying. Not in a belligerent way. He is just a little shy, doesn't like to hobnob. It is a story Danny neither confirms nor denies but Caine apparently did show up at Scarborough's Lord Nelson pub and told Danny he had enjoyed the show. Brenda Blethyn came, too, and bought one of Danny's CDs. Ewan McGregor got up on stage and sang with him.

So what is it about Seaside Danny Wilde? The name helps, certainly. As the Lancaster pub, his latest residency, fills up, his female fans start chanting it to the tune of the Gap Band's 'Oops Upside Your Head': 'Seaside Danny Wilde, I said Seaside Danny Wilde.' They are mostly – although not all – of a generation that will remember sitting on the floor at discos in the late seventies pretending to row a boat to this tune.

The first thing to make clear is that Danny's reputation owes little or nothing to any musical ability, or at least not to any of his own. Like the singers I had seen in Benidorm, he sings along to backing tracks of other people's songs. His voice is a pleasant light baritone, nothing more. He strums a guitar, too, but that seems to be mostly for effect. His repertoire is unremarkable, comprising chiefly songs made famous by late-period Elvis, such as 'Let It Be Me', 'Suspicious Minds', and so on, some Roy Orbison numbers, 'Dance the Night Away', as heard on the Renault advert on TV, a rock 'n' roll medley of 'Let's Dance', 'Chantilly Lace', 'Heartbeat', as heard on the popular Sunday night TV series and, oh look, do I have to spell it out for you?

Here we are once more in the country where the British music business has more or less taken up residence: Goldenoldieland.

I turn up at the pub on a Thursday night, at 8.45 when Danny is billed to begin, and he is already on the little stage at the end of the Lancaster's long bar. The pub is plastered with posters advertising 'The Danny Wilde Experience', dubbing him 'King of the Seafront', and 'The Ayatollah of Rock 'n' Rollers', so I was expecting some sort of a build up, but it appears the

Great Man just wanders onto the stage, plugs in his tapes, and starts working his way through Elvis's back catalogue.

It seems a quiet night. The seats are mostly taken by elderly couples nursing their drinks – pints of bitter for the men and halves of lager and lime for the ladies. There are a few groups of women, like the one described, and some lads at the bar not taking much notice of the Legend. So far, it is not my idea of a knockout evening. I think I may have been led to expect too much. The way Steve, my university friend, had described it to me, I was expecting some wild old geezer in a cowboy hat ripping the place apart but Seaside Danny Wilde does not seem markedly different from those bored-looking blokes trotting out oldies-by-numbers in every other bar in Benidorm. He's wearing the same uniform for a start – the bright white shirt with a ruffed front, undone nearly to the waist, black slacks with a razor-sharp crease, and very shiny, black patent-leather shoes. When I take a picture of him he even uses the same line as the guys in Spain: 'You're not from the DSS, are you?' I was beginning to wish I was. At least it would give some purpose to listening to another mediocre version of 'Let It Be Me'.

Danny is a good-looking chap in his late fifties, maybe even sixty, but making a conscious effort to look fifteen years younger, and actually pulling it off. He is slim, which makes a big difference, and has what your granny would call 'nice hair'. There is certainly plenty of it, without a trace of grey, and if it is dyed, someone is doing a heck of a job. You somehow know his hairstyle has remained unchanged since around 1975, when he walked into the barber's and showed him a picture of one of the Bee Gees.

My companion for this evening at the Lancaster is local chiropodist Charles White. I would not normally choose a chiropodist as an expert witness at such a gig but, unusually for a small-town foot doctor, Charles is the official biographer of rock 'n' roll stars Little Richard and Jerry Lee Lewis and an acknowledged expert on the subject, with writing credits including the *New Yorker*. You may even have seen one of his books, possibly *Killer! The Baddest Rock Memoir Ever* by Jerry Lee Lewis and Charles White.

I will run that by you one more time. To Charles White

MChS, who with his chiropodist wife, Annie, runs a little parlour up the stairs from an optician's, where for nearly 40 years he has tended the troubled feet of well-bred ladies who run seaside tearooms, to this happily married middle-aged Scarborough man, fell the task of chronicling the years of sex and drugs and rock 'n' roll, and then more sex, of two of that lifestyle's most enthusiastic devotees.

I first met Charles, or Chas as he prefers to be called, or Doctor Rock, which he prefers even more, 12 years ago, when I wrote a piece for the *Independent* about how he got to write Little Richard's biography. (To cut a long – 1,300 words – story short, he's an enthusiast; he met someone who knew someone who knew Little Richard, ended up visiting this friend of a friend in Los Angeles and spent the time virtually camping on Little Richard's lawn, eventually beating off competition from two hotshot American authors when Little Richard announced, 'God has sent Doctor Rock to tell my story'.)

The book, which Doctor Rock wrote together with one of his old drinking buddies, Barry Hampshire, retired features editor of the Scarborough *Evening News*, was a hit. Later, in one of those rare instances of a multi-million dollar Hollywood project being entrusted to a chiropodist and a local newspaperman from an English seaside town, they were commissioned to write a screenplay. Then they wrote Jerry Lee Lewis's story, and got screwed somewhat on the money, although when you are collaborating with a man who carries a gun everywhere, was accused of the murder of his fifth wife, and is said to set fire to pianos, what do you expect?

Put this point to Doctor Rock and he does not so much roar with laughter as explode into it. Never have I met anyone who laughs as readily or as infectiously. He is neither a ha-ha-ha man, nor a hee-hee-hee man, but a hoo-hoo-hoo man. He whoops with laughter, reaching in record time the point where he appears to be afflicted with whooping cough, catching his breath helplessly, and beginning to wheeze. The mildest witticism will bring this on. You would hesitate to take him to see one of the films of Leslie Nielsen, say, for fear he might have a seizure.

The Doctor Rock thing, by the way, goes back to 1978 when the local technical college was running courses in rock 'n' roll and enlisted the local chiropodist, with his well-advertised passion for the music, as guest lecturer. That kind of thing was fairly novel in those days and the *Daily Mail* ran a story about him, dubbing him Doctor Rock, a tag not only embraced by Chas but incorporated into his letterheads, which must have caused confusion for a while amongst some of his more straitlaced patients.

Doctor Rock and I wander along the beach for some lunch. At this point, working for a great public service organization like the BBC, I feel I should just issue one warning. Do not, under any circumstances, however hungry you may be, even should you be 'faint from lack of nourishment', as old Granny Grove used to say, ever, ever buy any of that shellfish they sell in little polystyrene trays from those stalls down by the seafront. This applies in all British seaside resorts but especially in Scarborough's South Bay. All right, you expect to pay over the odds, but standing there on the edge of the sea, you have a right to expect equally that at least the seafood might be fresh. Yet the six mussels for which I paid £1.50 tasted as if they had been frozen around the time of Gracie Fields's first hit. Not only were they the most tasteless mussels I have ever eaten, they were the most tasteless objects that have ever entered my mouth, and that includes the plastic end of the biro I stick in my mouth whenever I sit down to write. They were not so much mussels as mussel-shaped pieces of rubber, or Rowntree's fruit gums from which all the flavour had been sucked, painted to look like mussels. If you are in the market for something possibly toxic, do yourself a favour and eat a kebab.

Scarborough's casual disregard, disdain almost, of the gifts of the sea is a big thing with Doctor Rock. For the past 20 years he has been a member of the Sons of Neptune, a group of local nutcases who make it their business to swim in the North Sea off Scarborough all year round. I am not sure much of this swimming actually goes on, but the thought is there, and so the Sons were horrified to discover that Yorkshire Water, backed by Scarborough Council, had built outfall pipes to dump raw sewage into the sea.

For 15 years Doctor Rock and his mates ran a fierce, occasionally hilarious, campaign against Yorkshire Water and its hapless handmaiden, Scarborough Borough Council. Doctor

Rock himself stood up at Yorkshire Water's annual meeting and said, 'Every member of this board should be behind bars.' As part of the protest, the Sons of Neptune sailed up the Thames in a floating toilet they called a Thatcherloo, under the command of local war hero Captain Sidney Smith, then in his eighties, holder of the Burma Star, the VC, and various other medals.

Doctor Rock tells me that Captain Sidney, when under attack by German bombers in the Second World War, stood on the deck, looked up at the planes and kept on firing up at them till the moment he saw the bomb hatches open. Only then did he dive for cover.

Unfortunately, the Thatcherloo's voyage took place when the royal yacht *Brittania* was in town and at the height of a terrorist alert, so Doctor Rock, the war hero and the rest were slung into cells at Wapping police station. When reprimanded for the stunt by the superintendent in charge, Doctor Rock replied, 'You can tell Inspector Scott in Scarborough. I'm playing squash with him tonight.' 'Are you Irish?' said the police chief. 'You're lucky we didn't shoot you.' 'Hoo-hoo-hoo,' countered the chiropodist. 'I'd be the first Irishman to be shot trying to save England from its pathogenic sewerage.'

Doctor Rock talks like this all the time and from him it sounds just right. 'I don't drink at lunchtime,' he says, when I suggest a beer, 'but in the evening I might caress the shores of inebriation ... hoo-hoo-hoo.' His stories are peopled with extraordinary characters, like 'Swift-half' Jenkinson, who acquired his soubriquet when he told his wife he was slipping out to the Shepherd's Arms up on the moors for a swift half and failed to arrive back home until the next day.

The truly remarkable thing is that this funny old chiropodist and his colourful cohorts actually won their battle against the might of Yorkshire Water. The water company has abandoned its dumping plans and is building a £120 million sewage treatment plant, a decision its executives marked by going for a dip in the sea with the Sons of Neptune.

Patrick Argent, a lecturer in graphic design and another of Doctor Rock's chums, whom I meet in the Doctor's waiting room, shows me a letter he has sent to the Scarborough *Evening News*, saluting the Sons' victory. 'The whole unfortunate saga of the council's wholly irresponsible attitude to Scarborough's sewage problem seems, in retrospect, incredible,' he writes. 'A child's logic would have told any reasonably intelligent person that condoning the polluting of a resort's bathing waters with raw sewage was a monumentally stupid position to adopt.' He compares the council's blind-eye stance over sewage with that of the mayor in the film *Jaws*. He is equally contemptuous of their replacement of fine old Victorian buildings in the town with brutal modern architecture, a viewpoint you do not have to be an arty-farty, pinko, liberal art college lecturer to understand.

Elsewhere, Scarborough is gradually falling to bits. A perfect metaphor for the town is the story of the Holbeck Hall Hotel, a stately Victorian pile, which looked out from the cliffs over the resort's magnificent coastline, and which in 1993, quite literally, and rather spectacularly, slipped into the sea, providing front page pictures around the world.

Less spectacularly, buildings seem to be gently crumbling around the town. Scarborough has a suspiciously high number of sites 'ripe for redevelopment'. The Futurist Theatre on the south shore, which used to attract moderately well-known TV turns in the summer, is one. The wallpaper is peeling off, and when it rains, buckets are put out to catch the leaks. It is, says Patrick, 'a great place for whiffing urine samples'. It is not even fit for the Krankies.

The next morning, when the sun shines, Scarborough seems in much better fettle. What has survived in Scarborough, its grand hotels and villas on the cliffs, is still impressive. As Doctor Rock says, 'The only thing holding this town together is what the Victorians did and the beautiful scenery. We're lucky the Big Man Upstairs spent an extra half-day on us, otherwise we'd be in trouble ... hoo-hoo-hoo.'

Even so, look more closely and your doubts return. The Grand Hotel advertises 'Soap and towels' and 'Hand wash basin' among the attractions of some of its rooms. What, soap *and* towels? Such luxury not to have to wipe your hands on the candlewick bedspread. 'Nearby Shared Bathroom Toilet Facilities' is another great sales pitch. How nearby? It's that old dilemma we international travellers had almost forgotten; is it close enough to stop you having a leak in the washbasin at 2 a.m.?

The Grand appears to have recreated the British seaside hotel of the past as a treat for its customers, who are now almost exclusively old people. At regular intervals throughout the day, coaches pull up outside, disgorging into the Grand's impressive entrance hall a sea of tight white perms and beige loafers. These folk should feel more than comfortable with the dinner menu that is being posted up around the hotel.

There is stuff on there I have not seen on a restaurant menu for 30 years. The starter is a choice between 'Freshly Made Cream of Vegetable Soup served with Bread Roll and Butter', 'Carmen Miranda Fruit Cocktail served in Sparkling Wine' (Carmen Miranda!), and 'Chilled Fruit Juice.' Just a thought. Does anyone serve soup without some sort of bread these days (what, soap, towels *and* a bread roll?), and who doesn't chill fruit juice? Call me a dangerous radical if you like, but I think we're all getting quite used to refrigeration in Britain now.

The main course harks back to an era when the art of fine living was indicated by slinging in the odd French word here and there. So, you are asked to choose between 'Chicken Breast cooked in a Classic Chasseur Sauce' and 'Roast Ham served with Warm Pineapple Compote'. Chef's vegetables of the day are roast potatoes, creamed potatoes, garden peas and diced buttered swede (or buttered Swede, which is how it is actually written).

In small print at the foot of the menu, we find the punchline: 'A wine waiter will visit your table should you require a drink from the bar.' Should you require? Should you require? If I am eating warm pineapple compote and diced buttered swede, 'require' doesn't quite cover it. That wine waiter had better be on permanent stand-by.

I used to go to Scarborough quite a lot when my children were little and were happy playing on the swings or walking round Peasholm Park. We would stay around the North Bay, the quieter end of the resort, and swim in the open-air pool, which was called Watersplash World for a while and then Atlantis, but basically never stopped being the municipal baths. When I drive round to have a look at the pool for old time's sake, it seems, like everywhere else in Scarborough, desperate for a lick of paint. These days, more exciting rival attractions always seem to beckon our offspring, so family outings to

Scarborough are rare. Patrick is not surprised: 'Our museums still have everything in glass cases. There's none of that hands-on stuff that kids are used to these days. They're stuffy, like museums used to be. Walk into the natural history museum here, and you expect to be handed a ration book.'

As mentioned, I was chaperoned to Danny's gig by Doctor Rock, something he did with reluctance. He had seen Danny once before when he accompanied a TV producer friend of ours who was considering making a film about the phenomenon, and had not been impressed. 'Sub-moronic brain damage' was, I believe, the expression used. So, after about three-quarters of an hour, Doctor Rock deserts me to go to the Indigo Alley, a pub over the other side of town, where his friend and co-writer, Barry Hampshire, is playing sax in a pick-up band. At which point Danny starts to raise his game a little. Almost imperceptibly, the Lancaster has filled up. The Danny Wilde Experience seems to be not the whole experience. People will go to another pub or two first, then to see Danny, before hitting the town for a spot of clubbing, fights and kebabs optional.

Danny has been a fixture at either the Lancaster or the Lord Nelson, which are less than a casual vomit apart on Scarborough's South Bay, for more than 20 years, four nights a week in winter, five in summer, and this I am guessing is one of the secrets of his success. Somehow or other, his gig has become a tradition, something you go to. It is like Christmas. Everybody knows it is a nonsense yet we go through it every year and all agree what a fantastic time we are having. With Danny, also, the fun has become exaggerated in the telling.

It is said women throw their knickers at Danny. I never saw it but, if true, it would explain at least part of his appeal. The prospect of women in such a state of abandonment that they are dispensing with their undergarments is not to be underestimated as an attraction for visiting males. To his credit, Danny is as mystified by his success as I am. He has sort of settled for being world famous in Scarborough after harbouring hopes at one stage of being a rock 'n' roll star.

Born in Rochdale, in the fifties he was in a skiffle band called the Vikings, with whom he played in the evenings, while working with his father, a painter and decorator, during the day.

Later, he joined a band called the Ramblers, covering rock 'n' roll hits of the day, from whom he split to go solo, calling himself 'Karve – the best-dressed folk singer', with a repertoire, heaven help us, that included the songs of Bob Dylan and Donovan.

Danny Wilde was born – he is as coy about his birth name as he is about his age – with the boom in northern cabaret clubs in the seventies. He became something of an Elvis copyist, which was much rarer then than it is now, and which made him an instant hit in Scarborough when he first performed there in 1979.

I don't know whether this makes sense but Scarborough is just the sort of place where I should expect Elvis to be popular. Having travelled extensively around Britain, and having played several thousand requests over the years on Radio 2, I think there is a definite regional pattern to musical preferences. England's east coast, I have observed, has a distinct leaning towards old rock 'n' roll, especially Elvis, and maudlin country 'n' western music, with a small but significant vote for the sentimental Irish tunes of Daniel O'Donnell. The same applies to Cumbria and rural Scotland. In urban areas like Manchester, Birmingham and Newcastle there is a dwindling but still healthy enthusiasm for heavy metal music, alongside what I believe is called indy music, crypto-punk rock that involves its followers dressing entirely in black and piercing unlikely areas of the face. In places like Hampstead, Wilmslow and Guildford, meanwhile, interest is more likely to centre on organic chickens and second homes in France.

So Danny has undeniably found his spiritual home in Scarborough, where he has refined his act over the years. Whatever your reservations about Danny, he is a consummate professional. The care he takes over his backing tapes is crucial. The sound is crisp and very loud, loud enough to discourage conversation and, more importantly, drunken heckling. He reminds me of Sticky Vicky in a way, in that he knows his audience, understands what it wants and tends not to chance anything new or original. Why should he? That would be the equivalent of Vicky suddenly starting to pull things from her back bottom, and would just confuse the audience.

I stay with Danny long enough to gain a grudging admiration for him. The pub is full now, and loving it. He has an applause track on his tape machine, which he is using to crank up the excitement. I leave before the big finish, which is Elvis's 'American Trilogy'. I have seen enough to imagine how that goes.

Many years ago, when I was a disc jockey, I used to go out and do guest spots in discos, at Sheffield Polytechnic, or at big insurance firms' Christmas parties. I would finish by playing an old EMI single of Vera Lynn singing 'Land of Hope and Glory', inviting the crowd to sway along to it. I used to get a few people up on stage and hold up a football scarf while I led them in community swaying. On a good night, when people had drunk well, it would be a great finish. People would cheer as the song reached its climax and thank me for a fantastic night, although all I had done was put the record on. 'American Trilogy', I expect, is much the same sort of idea.

People do want to have a good time, I find, and are enormously grateful if you can facilitate that. I remember once doing a disco for the Young Farmers organization in a huge cowshed on the Chatsworth House estate in Derbyshire and running some sort of contest on stage. I used the old Monty Python line, 'I can't decide who has won so I'll just award the prize to the girl with the biggest tits', and to my surprise these girls took off their tops. I had not realized that just because you were on stage holding a microphone, girls would show you their naked breasts. It was an epiphanous moment.

As I leave Seaside Danny Wilde and head across town to join Doctor Rock at the Indigo Alley, I pass another pub featuring a chap like Danny, singing along to backing tapes. The contrast could not be more stark. The place is empty save for a couple of businessmen who are ignoring the turn and do not look to have knicker-throwing on their mind. Danny clearly has something.

It is a steep climb up from the Lancaster, then a walk past St Mary's churchyard and the grave of Anne Brontë who died here in 1849, at the age of twenty-eight, of consumption and a false belief in the magical properties of the sea air. I continue along a road called Paradise. 'That's what this place is to me,' Doctor Rock had said to me earlier in the day. 'I have had a wonderful life here. I have loved every minute of it. Every minute.' Despite everything, that is: the sewage, the crumbling buildings, Danny Wilde, the petty bourgeois dunderheads on the town council.

When I arrive at the Indigo Alley, Doctor Rock, aged sixty,

is dancing with much the same extravagant flourish as he talks. Hard to believe but on him it looks fine. Actually, everybody is dancing. It is the one place in town, apart from the Lancaster, that is jumping. Only this is real fun, not an artist's impression of fun. It is a band called AMOS, standing for All Manner Of Stuff, with which Doctor Rock's friend Barry Hampshire guests on a few numbers on sax and vocals. They are thirty-and forty-something musicians, who have played in bands for years, and know what to do with an old Fats Domino number. Good-time R&B is what you would probably call it. Barry has his own band, Hamp's Tramps, who do similar material.

Barry sings a song called 'Whisky Heaven' extolling the virtues of a place where 'it rains Jack Daniels all the time' and recommending 'getting high with the angels'. You do not like to judge from appearances but my strong suspicion is that getting high is not exactly an alien concept for much of the crowd. By the time Barry gets into a kicking version of 'Woolly Bully' the little dance floor is heaving and those unable to find space there are jumping up and down on the banquettes.

This is alternative Scarborough. Real ale is served here, and Barry and Doctor Rock are drinking pints of something called Hooligan. I go easy on the Hooligan front but still have a marvellous time. I could not be more pleased to have abandoned Seaside Danny Wilde, who has turned out to be less interesting than his name. Barry Hampshire, on the other hand, is someone with whom you want to spend time. He is sixty-six years old, tanned, shiny-faced, fit as a flea and one of those chaps who appears entirely, radiantly happy with his lot.

In 30 years on the Scarborough *Evening News* rarely a week went by, as is the way on small-town daily newspapers, without a colleague leaving to go on to bigger and better things but Barry always stayed. He had joined the paper at fifteen as a print apprentice, being given his chance in journalism after ten years of inky fingers, eventually becoming features editor, where he remained until 1981. 'I never hankered to leave. I love Scarborough,' he says. 'Others left but going away never held any attraction for me. I was playing in bands in hotels and nightclubs and actually earning good money at the time.'

Barry started playing the sax in 1957 when he was twenty-

Top Benidorm – jewel of the Mediterranean.

Above Scouse reunion in Spain – Danny Downing and Chrissy Rock.

Right Mike St. John.

Above left Flame, remember my name – Tony De La Fou.

Above Sorcha Ra.

Left Mark Fletcher – Blackburn's No. 1 Freddie Mercury tribute.

Opposite top Abba Girls: 230,000 miles on the clock.

Opposite bottom Golden oldie – Seaside Danny Wilde.

Left Sun, sea and sax – Barry Hampshire.

Below We do like to be beside the seaside – Barry Hampshire and Chris (Dr Rock) White.

Opposite Cruisin' – Island Escape cruise director Bruce Maher.

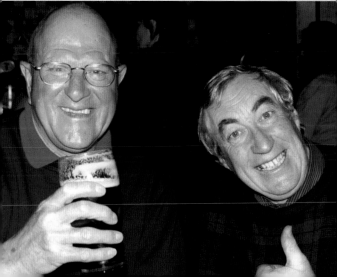

Opposite top Wot, no medallion? The author takes advantage of Island Cruises' generous hospitality.

Opposite bottom Eyes and teeth: Claire Phillips (l) and Danielle Murphy (r).

Above Boogie nights aboard the Island Escape.

Overleaf top left Barry Young – the Stardust's genial host.

Overleaf top right and bottom Meeting and Greeting: Edmond Wells as John Cleese (top r) and Chris Bylett with Charlie (b).

one, after hearing the records of Little Richard and Fats Domino on the radio and asking a colleague what the glorious sound was in the instrumental break. Duly informed, he then went out and bought a tenor sax and taught himself to play. 'Entirely self-taught, with all the faults,' he tells me. In the late sixties and early seventies he played big band music with the Jeff Laycock Band who made two or three appearances on television, and had a residency at Scarborough's Candlelight Club (the temptation to call it Scarborough's 'fabulous' Candlelight Club is almost too strong).

He married in his early twenties, had two children, but later embarked on a passionate affair with Jeannie Hobson, a local artist. Together they bought a handsome two-hundred-year-old guest house, the Flower in Hand, nicknamed the Gland in Hand by local wags because of its ancient history as a brothel catering for the seafaring community.

The Flower in Hand overlooks the harbour and is itself overlooked by Barry's marital home, thus enabling his two women to keep an eye on each other, a story I was told by Doctor Rock, this being a town where everybody knows everybody else's business. I got the impression that women like Barry a lot, and the feeling is mutual. A guest from the Flower in Hand, a lady in her late thirties, is dancing to his music in the Indigo Alley and is quite gushing in her assessment of her host.

Barry has grandchildren and when I ask him if he is a good granddad he answers without hesitation and quite cheerfully, 'No, not at all.' 'Is that because you have not really grown into the role of a sixty-six-year-old?' 'Absolutely, that's it.'

He is running the Flower in Hand on his own now. Jeannie, who had something of a reputation as a local femme fatale, is living in Glossop with a writer from the *Guardian* who used to come to Scarborough to review Alan Ayckbourn's plays. (There is a deep irony in this, which those of you who have enjoyed the playwright's impish take on the relationship merry-go-round will recognize immediately.) I am told – not by Barry – that Barry currently has 'two or three girlfriends'.

His big love is Scarborough, though, and like everyone who cherishes the place, he has his theories about why it is in less than sturdy health:

The demise of Scarborough can be summed up in two words: Ken Goodall. Scarborough was bombarded by German battleships in 1914, the first shots really of the First World War. They knocked a hole through the lighthouse and smashed up the Grand Hotel, which had been built by the Victorians. Nineteen people died and there were propaganda posters at the time: 'Remember Scarborough – The Death of the Innocents.'

Well, everybody panicked and started selling their homes and hotels and moving out of town. A local estate agent, J Lucas Goodall, picked up most of the property for next to nothing and when he died it passed to his son, Ken, who wouldn't give you the steam off his piss.

He refused to make any improvements. When Jeannie some years ago tried to rent a studio off him, a room in a run-down block he owned, he asked for £100 a week when she could only afford 50. He said, 'I'd rather let it rot than rent it out for £50 a week,' and that's what he did.

He's dead now but Scarborough is still paying for years of neglect.

I wish I could have stayed in Barry's hotel but its three rooms were taken so I go to another Georgian guest house, the Stewart Hotel, right opposite the Grand, whose slightly bizarre decor – the entrance hall has a ridiculous tartan carpet and a man-in-armour standing guard over the reception desk – I was going to make merry with, until Doctor Rock told me he did the proprietress's feet and she was 'a lovely lady' struggling to run the place on her own after the tragic early death of her husband.

That is the trouble with using Doctor Rock as your guide. He knows everybody and will usually divert you from whatever angle you are pursuing with an irrelevant but entertaining story about some Scarborough character: 'Tom Laughton kept the Pavilion. His third wife was a strange one, used to smoke cigars.' From which he will segue seamlessly into a story about Bram Stoker's great-niece, whose feet he saw to, and who told him not to mention 'that dreadful book' because her great-uncle wrote many better, lesser-known works. 'As it happens, he didn't write

Dracula at Whitby as is often thought,' he tells me, 'but at Ravenscar where we play golf.'

Every time he embarks on one of these tales, Barry or Patrick or whoever we are with at the time will shush him and endeavour to bring him back to the point. They seem to have an enviable life, these middle-aged professional chaps in Scarborough; not working too hard, playing a little golf, dancing, playing a little sax, writing a little, and they are undoubtedly good company.

Refugees from real life love seaside towns, where the amusement arcades and crazy-golf courses create an air of frivolity, which is distinctly appealing to such fugitives. The whiff of corruption and dodgy dealing is stronger by the sea, too – sometimes strong enough to mask the smell of chips and rotting seaweed – thanks to the regular summer influx of cash in pockets.

Scarborough, on all counts, scores higher than most. And all of its weirdness and naughtiness is played out in the magnificent setting of one of the most spectacular stretches of coastline in Britain and amongst the faded grandeur of a town whose golden age was maybe 150 years ago, the constant cawing of the seagulls providing an eerie soundtrack. (Actress Maureen Lipman, apparently, staying with Alan Ayckbourn, asked: 'How do you live in this place, with all these fucking seagulls?')

But I have decided this is a story about denim, the fabric that keeps us all forever young. I am fairly sure my father never wore a denim garment in his life. Certainly, when he was fifty and I was fifteen, had he come down to breakfast in a pair of denim jeans, I should have been shocked. But these days, we all wear it. The audiences for Danny Wilde and Barry Hampshire – oceans apart in class and attitude – are united in their jeans. Denim keeps us young, or maybe we just think it keeps us young, prolonging notions of an active and interesting sex life; and in essence sex is what all this cheap music is all about.

'I'm just a hunka hunka hunka burning love,' sings Seaside Danny Wilde, and no one is laughing. Like Michael St. John in Benidorm, he sings 'Young Girl': 'Young girl, get out of my mind/My Love for you is way out of line.' Now when Gary Puckett sang the song in the sixties, he was about twenty-five, and his love for a teenage girl probably *was* slightly out of line, but Danny is old enough to be the girl's grandfather, and still nobody is laughing, or threatening to enter his name on the sex offenders' register.

Are we all in denial? Refusing to grow old? Is that what being at the seaside, with its memories of fresh air and fun, is all about? Would Danny Wilde be as popular in Stevenage? I think not. The only poem I have ever committed to memory is 'The Love Song of J. Alfred Prufrock' by T S Eliot, and it comes back to me when I am walking back at midnight from the Indigo Alley to my hotel.

The stuff about 'half-deserted streets' and 'restless nights in one-night cheap hotels' seems particularly appropriate (It's £35 in the Stewart, including a rather fine breakfast). Not wishing to tangle with the estate of the late great poet, who may well have a battery of razor-sharp copyright lawyers protecting him from beyond the grave, I do not intend to quote from the poem in any detail, but I notice that in my heavily annotated copy of *Selected Poems*, issue of Stand Grammar School for Boys, I have underlined words like 'insidious' and 'tedious', and the gag about Prufrock measuring out his life in coffee spoons.

I expect Mr Garnett, our English teacher, pointed up these bits as indicative of Prufrock's state of mind; full of weltschmerz, ennui, and all that European stuff. A mid-life crisis, we would call it these days, and the young Eliot showed extraordinary imagination in describing it so well. I, of course, am rather better placed to know what such a crisis feels like. All that stuff about what trousers to wear, worrying about eating a peach, and the visibility of the bald spot. It could be me, or if not, Frank Bough.

Good to know that Eliot and I agree on the importance of trousers. I wear blue denim for my walk upon the beach before leaving, and looking back at Scarborough from the seafront, in the sunshine, it really is the most impressive sight. From that distance, the crumbling behind the Victorian facade remains a guilty secret.

It is tempting to see Scarborough as a sad metaphor for all the forty-, fifty- and sixty-somethings giving it one last fling with Barry's good-time band, or with Seaside Danny Wilde, but

I prefer to take the view of Kate White, a contributor to *Greenguide* (the 'hippy' guide to Scarborough) who – albeit on the subject of circle dancing – writes, 'The rhythmic music and repetitive movements can have the therapeutic effect of connecting us with the Eternal.'

We will all, of course, be connected with the Eternal eventually – some of us sooner than others – and the runaway success of Seaside Danny Wilde would seem to suggest that growing old gracefully is no longer considered a desirable way to prepare for meeting our maker.

If we are all going to rage against the dying of the light, then Danny's message would seem to be: let's put our blue jeans on and do it to some decent old rock 'n' roll.

6

IT'S A KIND OF MAGIC

'Come and sit on my hot seat of love.'

It is a sweet thought, isn't it, although the line I am afraid is not one of my own. It is one of Freddie Mercury's, from his song 'Good Old-Fashioned Lover Boy'. I think it says everything Shakespeare was trying to say in all those sonnets but in a much more direct way. And please don't think of my filching of the line as plagiarism, nor any failure of imagination on my part. Think of it more as a tribute.

There is no theft any more, no copying. Everything is a tribute. No taking off, as my dad used to call it. 'He's just taking off Dean Martin,' my dad would complain when some vocalist he disapproved of showed up on a Saturday night variety show. These days, that would not be a criticism, that would be his act.

When I log on to the *Showcall* website to plan my schedule, it seems that everybody is taking off somebody else; and if I want to see any live entertainment, it will have to be a bunch of pretenders (there is, in fact, a band pretending to be the Pretenders, calling themselves the Pretend Pretenders).

I remember a comedy sketch from years ago on TV featuring John Cleese, in which a chap goes into a bookshop seeking a copy of *Bleak House* by Charles Dickens. As the assistant goes to fetch it, he calls after him, 'That's Charles Dikkens with two 'k's, the famous Dutch author.' The sketch gradually gets more manic as every classic work and author the customer asks after is spelt just slightly differently from the standard. For some reason, this sketch comes to mind as I look down the list of tribute acts performing over the next week or two. Here, for instance, is Jamm (that's Jam with two 'm's), here Alison Moyhet, and here that well-known band that brought the rock 'n' roll craze to Britain. I refer, of course, to Phil Haley and the

Comments. Your most important asset, it seems to me, when you go into the tribute business, before even you get hold of the backing tapes which will make you sound vaguely like the act you are imitating, is a smart-arse name.

You can approach this in one of three ways. You may want to choose a name similar to that of the act being copied, like State of Quo (these are all genuine, by the way), UU2, Twin Lizzy, Daz 'n' Chave and so on, in the hope of hoodwinking the customers. ('Mm, I see the Korrs are on tonight at the Lower Ackworth and District Working Men's Club and Institute. Do you think they are the famous Grammy-award-winning Irish songstresses who have sold millions of albums worldwide?' 'Oh yes, dear, almost certainly. It's £2 to get in.')

Another strategy is to come up with something clever, based on one of the records or distinguishing features of the act being copied. Stayin' Alive, for instance, is a Bee Gees tribute, Buffalo Souljah, God help us, are Bob Marley copyists, while Abba Dream, well, take a wild guess what they do.

A third and increasingly popular tribute band wheeze is the scatter-gun approach, whereby you sling in a lot of vaguely related imitations under a catch-all name; Glamarama, for instance, cover a whole range of glam rock bands, while Marvin Ruffin or Baby Love will seek to persuade you you are watching the entire stable of Tamla Motown acts.

In quoting these names, though, I do not even scratch the surface of the tribute business. For instance, my by no means exhaustive research turned up more than 30 professional acts alone going round Britain pretending to be Abba, with names like Abba Solutely, Abba Forever, Fabbamania. There are probably many more. What is more disturbing is that there is a band called Step by Step, paying unnecessary tribute to Steps, another tribute band wittily named S Club Heaven and at least two singers who earn their living pretending to be Celine Dion. Not only do you no longer need to be dead to qualify for a tribute, you do not even have to have been in show business for much more than ten minutes.

The act I have chosen to follow for the next two nights is called, simply, Freddie, and I assume he is paying his own personal and highly felt tribute to the late lead singer of the pop group Queen rather than to some other Freddie – the cricketer Freddie Trueman, perhaps, or the philosopher A J 'Freddie' Ayer (now, that is an act I *would* like to see).

It is a highly competitive field that thirty-one-year-old Mark Fletcher from Blackburn has chosen to join. The half of the country that is not impersonating Elvis, it seems, is having a go at Freddie Mercury. A survey in the *Stage*, acknowledging tribute acts as the biggest growth area in show business, sought to discover which were the most copied artistes, and Queen were beaten only by Elvis. Elvis impersonation, by the way, is apparently one of the fastest growing industries in the world (I am a particular fan of El Vez, the Mexican Elvis). According to a statistic I read somewhere, if Elvis impersonation were to continue growing exponentially at the same rate as it has year-on-year since his death in 1977, by the year 2040 or something everybody in the world would be imitating Elvis. Not Mark Fletcher, though. He has invested too much in the Freddie gear.

Mark does four costume changes and, for a married former landscape gardener with a wife called Kath and two children back home in Blackburn and an unblemished record of staunch heterosexuality, he makes a very creditable stab at Mercury's brand of camp insolence. Also he has a moustache. Mark claims the moustache pre-dates his Queen imitating, which is probably quite a brave move in Blackburn. He says he became aware of Queen's music through his parents' record collection but I get the impression it is the easy money and semi-fame which appeals to him rather than any genuine desire to pay tribute. He is a professional, though, even trying to mimic Freddie Mercury's strange boy-from-nowhere mid-Atlantic way of speaking in the patter between songs. The Blackburn burr gives it an extra layer of exoticism of which the late singer would undoubtedly have approved. The irony, of course, is that someone like Freddie Mercury, who would not have been seen dead in a working men's club, is now suffering that exact fate.

Mark's singing voice sounds close enough to Freddie Mercury's for me, but then I am not a fan. His manager, Mike Allen, who has accompanied his star to the gig, explains to me that the act is meant to be more of a homage than a direct imitation and it would be wrong to measure his boy up against the records. 'I was in the bogs in one of these clubs once and some bloke says to me, "He's all right but he doesn't sound *exactly* like Freddie Mercury." "You're right," I said. "If he sounded exactly like Freddie Mercury he wouldn't be working here for two hundred fucking quid."'

Mike becomes more blunt as the evening wears on – which is a pretty fair description of what the evening does. A bright young chap called Sean, who does design work for Mike and sorts out his computer problems, has driven the boss over from Lancashire to the club near Halifax, so Mike is free to take advantage of the place's very reasonably priced alcohol.

Freddie, reckons Mike, is the perfect act for clubland because you can't not watch it. I see what he means. Mark is loud, and he appears through clouds of dry ice: 'This is a tribute to Freddie Mercury, the greatest rock legend the world has ever seen,' booms out an overblown introduction from the speakers, and then some guff about how 'we feel overwhelming grief'. It was recorded, says Mike, by a local disc jockey, Derek Webster. 'He charged us a tenner.'

The act also has a brand new pyrotechnic effect, a sort of mini-explosion to herald Mark's arrival, but he forgets to ignite it. 'That's why they're acts,' complains Mike. 'They wouldn't be acts if they weren't lazy bastards. They just want to sit around all day watching TV and then turn up at night hoping somebody else has got everything sorted.'

But at least Mark and Mike and the boys are giving it a go. All right, it is only a tribute act, but there are those four costume changes – covered by musical bridges – a new backdrop produced by Green Brothers of Manchester, the professional sound and lighting, and a genuine attempt to get customers onto the dance floor. All in all, Mark is rather good, probably too good for the Siddal Cricket and Athletic Club.

Siddal is another of those end-of-the-line places, with the twist that it is at the top of a very steep hill. You leave the M62 motorway, go down into a valley, then turn right up a vertiginous road to a grey housing estate on the road to nowhere. Well, strictly speaking on the road to Halifax, but you know what I mean. It is the kind of place where you know the most popular Friday night activity for local young people is going to be hanging around outside the off-licence; and sure enough, as I slow down to look for the club, I come across a group of youngsters, one of whom mysteriously throws a cap down in the middle of the road in front of my car. I carefully drive around it, but when I stop to ask one of the kids the way to the club, he asks if, in return for his directions, I will drive over the cap. This is obviously part of a game they are playing with the unwitting connivance of passing motorists: a throwing-things-in-the-road-and-guessing-whether-drivers-will-drive-over-them-or-not kind of game. And they say kids are incapable of making their own entertainment.

Whatever it is they are doing, it looks like more fun than the Siddal Cricket and Athletic Club, which lowers my spirits the moment I catch sight of it. In fact, it might have been designed for that very purpose. It is an ugly, squat, prefabricated building the colour of cold gruel, and about as inviting. Every effort has been spared to make the place look welcoming to visitors. Worse, inside they will be playing bingo.

Bingo is without a doubt the most important thing that goes on in a working men's club. I visited four in a fortnight – the Crigglestone Working Men's Club, the Lofthouse Gate Club, this one in Siddal (all in Yorkshire) and the Higher Broughton Conservative Club in Manchester – and was left in no doubt that whatever else you treat lightly, you respect the bingo games.

The players even have special pens, about four inches long and rather stumpy, with which to mark off their numbers. You just bash the pen down as each number on your card is called and it blobs it out. I am told these pens are called dabbers and they help the smart bingo player avoid those embarrassing errors which might occur using conventional ballpoint technology.

I did not take part in a bingo game myself, as I did not altogether understand what was going on. There seemed to be a prize for completing a full line of numbers, and then another for completing a full card, but I could never be sure which game was being played, and did not want to risk the ignominy of ruining a game with an erroneous shout. I am sure bingo is quite simple but it does have the feel of an alien religious ceremony, with all that shout and response stuff as the card checker calls out the numbers, the caller responds, and ultimately the honoured one is anointed, or at least given the £25 prize. I thought it best not to get involved.

Some years ago I worked at a commercial radio station in Leeds, where the boss, in a misguided attempt to ingratiate the station with the local community, decided we ought to get into the working men's clubs. He struck some sort of deal whereby our newsreaders would guest as bingo-callers for a night and call out all the numbers in the local clubs. This would have been fine, had he not neglected to inform his staff that all that clickety-click, two fat ducks stuff of popular legend was about as welcome in a working men's club as Jackie Mason at an al-Qaida benefit gig. Stony faces all around as our cheerful commercial radio types tried to put a smile on the face of the proletariat with some poptastic ad libs. The undoubted faux pas of a very uncomfortable night came from one Mark Easton, now a very important figure in the world of television journalism, who donned full monty evening wear and read the numbers out in the plummiest voice he could manage, which made him sound uncannily like Princess Michael of Kent.

There was always the danger, of course, that, with so many games of bingo being played in so many different clubs, the number 69 would crop up sooner or later. I suppose it was just unfortunate that Mark – who had not endeared himself to the crowd by appearing to be a rich, posh southerner, and possibly a homosexual one at that – was the radio personality who got to call it. For the record, the correct way to call the number is 'Six and nine, sixty-nine' and not 'Here we are, ladies and gentlemen, always popular, and a personal favourite of mine, soixante-neuf.' It is also probably as well not to wink at one of the committee members as you are saying it.

The only surprise was that a promising television career was not nipped in the bud by a public lynching, although Mark will never again be able to set foot in the East Leeds Social Club, which must really rankle as he sits in smart Chelsea restaurants dining with the big names from the world of media and politics.

The scope for personal expression in the area of bingo-calling is extremely limited. In Siddal, for instance, the portly sixtyish lady who does the calling allows herself just a little latitude, saying, 'On it's own, the number's five' and 'One and two, the number's 12' instead of the more conventional 'On it's own, number five' and 'One and two, number 12'. See, a little bit of individuality, the extra beat in the sentence just cranking up the tension slightly. But not too much. Soixante-neuf would not go down well (do feel free to add your own joke if you wish) in Siddal.

When I was at Lofthouse Gate near Wakefield, a comparatively small club which I merely went to one Saturday night because it is near where I live, I bought a round of drinks, for which I was charged a pitifully small amount (bottle of Pils, £1.06, which makes the BBC's claim of being the best bargain in Britain look a little sick). Feeling obliged, as a non-member, to top up my order with another purchase, I bought myself and my wife some elaborate variations on the potato crisp theme. Problem was, a bingo game was in progress, and every time I started to open the crisps, I could feel a dozen pairs of accusing eyes burning into me. It could be that while everybody is quite happy to chatter away in libraries or in the cinema now, a bingo session in a working men's club is the last place in Britain where silence is obligatory.

The caller there obviously felt confident enough in his material to deviate just slightly from the script. Whenever the number 11 came up, he said, 'Those legs 11' and a chap sitting at a nearby table wolf-whistled. It seemed to be something they had worked out between them. Knowing the clubs' love of unnecessary bureaucracy, bingo-whistler is probably an executive position, and unofficial ad-lib whistling would undoubtedly be viewed as severely as any other interruption of the ritual.

Everything you have ever heard, read and seen about working men's clubs is true. Peter Kay's TV show *Phoenix Nights*, in which he plays overbearing club boss, Brian Potter, is exaggerated only very slightly for comic effect.

Mark Fletcher gets quite morose talking about the clubs. 'If I have to sit through one more game of bloody bingo, I'll scream,' he tells me, as we sit glumly at a table in the club in Siddal waiting for his first spot of the evening. He has to go on at nine for forty-five minutes and then wait until 10.30 or so, when he will return with another forty-five-minute set. They usually insist on two forty-five-minute spots in working men's clubs, which Mark can do, although he much prefers to do a single one-hour set so he can begin his act with a crescendo and work his way up to a climax. Also it means he doesn't have to sit around through another six games of bingo.

Mike Allen is something of a character and used to be a performer himself. He is a cheerful bloke, on the paunchy side, with hair swept back: an upbeat Lancastrian and ever so helpful. He used to be a 'singer/entertainer' and, more recently, a hypnotism act called the Mike Jason Hypnotic Experience. For a couple of years he lived in Tenerife, which is where he met his wife, Carol, who went on holiday in search of some winter sunshine, fell in love with the crooner and stayed. If youwere making a bittersweet British movie set in the north of England you would have no hesitation in casting Mike, probably as a former singer, now managing a Freddie Mercury tribute act.

Mike has brought along a little presentation pack about Freddie's act, including a poster, declaring it to be 'The ULTIMATE Tribute to Freddie Mercury' and detailing some of the act's past triumphs. There is a picture of the artiste alongside 'lead singer Dave Bartram of Showaddywaddy' at the Rhine Army Summer Show, an Anglo-German military festival held in the NAAFI live entertainment marquee. Artistes who appeared alongside Freddie, we are told, included 'Billy J Lewis and the Drifters, Racy, the Searchers, Slade, and Fish of Marillion fame.'

Other high spots in Mark's career as Freddie Mercury include an appearance alongside Kris Akabussi at a corporate event for the Going Places holiday company at Butlin's Skegness, a gig for the NSPCC in Wilmslow attended by 'Rovers Return barmaid Shelley Unwin (Sally Lindsey) and on-screen boyfriend, Peter Barlow (Chris Gascoyne)' and a cabaret performance at the Custom Car Show, Doncaster, with 'the girls from the Adult Channel'.

In Siddal tonight, though, Mark will have to rub along without the Corrie characters or the Adult Channel girls. Frankly – and I do not make a sexist point here – there is nobody in the club for whom you could imagine the removal of clothes to be a commercial proposition. It is a quiet night and the meagre crowd consists mainly of quite elderly people.

Apparently – and this emerges during conversation the following night in Manchester – there was what Mark describes as 'a nice little blonde' in the club, although I never spotted her. 'I signed her arse,' he remembers. 'She had a nice little thong on and everything.'

The set-up does not change much from club to club. There will be a concert room, with trestle tables and upright dining chairs, usually upholstered in red crushed velvet, with a stage at one end and a long bar at the other. The lighting, apart from when the act is on, is usually rather harsh, possibly to enable bingo cards to be read more easily. Depending on the size of the club, there will be two or three other rooms to accommodate a large TV, gambling machines, a full-size snooker table and a dartboard. You would not say the atmosphere is made for entertainment. You get the impression that acts see the clubs almost as a rite of passage, an ordeal they must suffer before plunging their maw into the corporate honeypot.

Mark has been paying tribute to the late king/queen of pomp rock for six years now. Before going solo and hitting the clubs with his tapes he was in a pub band called Galileo, which began as a rock band playing a few Queen numbers and then morphed into a full-on tribute band. 'But what he doesn't say,' chips in Mike, 'is that he never made a penny till I took him on.' Around our table with Mark and Mike are Andy and Dane, two young shaven-headed types from Blackburn College, who understand computers and mini-discs; they travel everywhere with Mark, looking after his sound and lighting. Another young mate has come with them just for the hell of it, and to cheer and dance and generally shoulder the thankless task of creating an atmosphere. The fact that Mark travels with his own sound and lighting boys singles him out as a cut above most club acts. Clearly, a little care and attention has been lavished on him, unlike other performers I saw who spent the interval between songs with their back to the audience while they fiddled with tapes and volume controls.

Mike is quite proud of Mark, calling him 'one of the busiest tribute acts in the world', which I am not in a position either to confirm or deny. He tells me his boy is booked solid until the end of the year. 'In December he has seven days off but is working the other twenty-four,' he says, adding, 'We have had enquiries from Zambia.'

However, this is no place in the sun, this is a working men's club in the north of England, and given the way performers are generally treated in working men's clubs, it's a wonder they bother. The audiences can't exactly be described as forgiving. Where an act gives the audience an excuse for not watching, that act will quickly perish.

I witnessed such a death at Crigglestone Working Men's Club, near Wakefield. Paddy Green, a nervous comedian of a type that used to be called zany, who came highly recommended to me by my agent, Roger Davis, lost the audience from the start with some joke about Yasser Arafat, which involved him (Paddy, not Arafat) crouching under a table. It died in the air and Paddy never recovered.

It can be intensely uncomfortable watching those acts which depend on the performer appearing to be not entirely at ease or in control – people like the heavily perspiring Lee Evans or a heavily Guinnessed Johnny Vegas. When they pull it off, it is wonderful but when, like Paddy, they pretend to be awkward and uneasy, and they really are, it is like a nasty road accident. You want to avert your eyes but are unable to. With no dry ice or well-known hit tunes to ride to his rescue, Paddy was on his own. All that stuff about the loneliness of the stand-up comic had never seemed truer. The sound failed him – he was using the club's PA – but still he carried on for nearly a full hour, leaping rather self-consciously around the stage. He told a joke about someone drowning in a cake mix after being dragged under by a strong currant, which signalled to me that he might have misread the crowd. They showed him no mercy – not heckling or anything, but their indifference spoke volumes, and later in the evening I spotted him slinking out of a side door.

Roger assures me that Paddy often goes down a storm, although an edgy act like his – another joke concerns a chap being dragged out of his house and lynched by the Ku Klux Klan, after asking a genie if he could be 'hung like a black man' – is always a risk in working men's clubs. You can see why acts take the safe option of coming along with some noisy tapes and running through a selection of Abba hits.

'To be honest, it's the one-armed bandits, the bingo and the gambling games that keep the clubs going,' says Roger. 'Concert secretaries have always treated acts badly, trying to screw them down on fees, and wielding what they thought was their immense power over them, and I suppose that is what is still going on, even though the influence of the clubs is far less than it was.' Working men's clubs declined dramatically in the nineties, he tells me, although in recent years the downward trend has, in the word favoured by newspaper circulation managers, 'plateaued', and the movement is still quite strong in South Yorkshire, the Midlands and in the Manchester area.

Sheffield, particularly, still boasts some big clubs, although probably only about half as many as there were in the fifties and sixties, when in one area alone – Manor Top – there were three huge clubs, all 800-seaters, within one mile. The pavement between them was worn away as people played bingo in one club and then scuttled along to play in the next.

Roger tells me some horror stories about closed societies of concert secretaries – they still exist in the Burnley and Huddersfield areas, apparently – holding kangaroo courts before which acts could be hauled if they 'had committed an offence'. By that he doesn't mean the Ku Klux Klan joke or a dodgy version of 'Tomorrow' but turning up late or displeasing the concert secretary in some other unspecified way. An act can be blacklisted as a result of one of these hearings.

Each area has its own concert secretaries' meeting every month, followed by a showcase, not unlike those you may have seen in the TV show *Phoenix Nights*. Acts audition before this unforgiving audience and hope to pick up bookings as a result. A common approach, says Roger, is for a group of concert secs to get together and say to an act, 'We'll all book you if you drop your fee.'

Mike Allen confirms this: 'At the Burnley concert secretaries' meeting you get about 20 of them, sitting there with their notebooks and pens, looking important. Their opening line to any act is nearly always the same, "We're only a small club, we haven't got much money." Sometimes they'll find an act who is new to the business and offer £100 for a night, then say, "Are you free New Year's Eve?" What's the act going to say, he's never worked before? That way, they've got themselves an act for New Year's Eve and it has only cost them a hundred quid.'

Mike also lists a bewildering array of gambling games, most of which are variations on a similar theme, but which interest the customers enough to keep the clubs alive: games like 'pick black', where you reach into a bag of snooker balls and gamble on picking out the black one; or 'open the box', a similar gamble but involving the purchase of a key; and 'joker', similar again but with cards stuck on a board. Most of the clubs operate the games on an accumulator principle, with the prize rising each week if nobody wins. 'It can get up to £1,000,' says Mike, 'and then the club will be packed.'

Let me make it clear that, despite all the above, I am broadly in favour of working men's clubs. They stand for two causes in which I believe passionately: the leisure and entertainment of the working classes and the sale of cheap booze.

Having felt the sharp point of the capitalist boot up my backside on a number of occasions, I am a staunch supporter of labour against management. I have always resisted any temptation to join the managerial classes. My experience of management, admittedly mostly within the media industry, is that it is chock-full of people whose skills start and end with the ability to wear a suit convincingly. The idea of an institution where you can plot their downfall, while drinking bottles of Pils at £1.06, has my vote.

It's a pity, though, that working men's clubs have travelled so far from Henry Solly's prospectus when he founded the Club and Institute Union in 1862, which spoke of 'rational recreation', of a place where working men 'can meet for conversation, business, and mental improvement', of places of 'wholesome and constructive amusement'. No word of Pils at £1.06 a throw from Henry, who was strictly teetotal, but I am sure it was in the back of his mind somewhere.

If there is any wholesome and constructive amusement going on in 2002 at the Higher Broughton Conservative Club, there is a powerful countermovement there designed to keep you away from it. When I arrive to see Freddie, there is a chap standing in the car park guarding the door, which has a combination lock. 'I've come to see Freddie,' I say. 'Is he here?' 'There's four of 'em,' he tuts, seemingly outraged at the thought of a solo performer arriving with a back-up team of three whole people. 'Well, can I go in and see him?' He punches a few numbers resentfully and says, 'It's £1.50.'

You get the impression that, like socialism itself, the working men's clubs have been suffocated by too much officialdom. When I ask Roger Davis to deconstruct for me the hierarchy of the working men's club, he says, 'There's a president, and up to about 14 people who want to crawl up his arse.' Typically, there will be a secretary and treasurer, and then a number of committee men, between eight and fourteen, who divide all the rest of the jobs up between them – concert secretary, calling the bingo numbers, standing in the car park to discourage potentially sarcastic authors from entering, and so on.

On penetrating the Higher Broughton Conservative Club's ring of steel, I find Mark Fletcher and his vast team sequestered in a small sepulchral side room whose only concession to wholesome and constructive amusement is a prehistoric and rather ragged dartboard. The room is empty save for Mark, Andy and Dane, and a third shaven-headed mate called Steve. The bingo, snooker, and economy-priced drinking is going on elsewhere.

Spending a second night watching a Freddie Mercury tribute act is, I have to say, not my idea of rational recreation. Mark puts on a good show but I was around for Queen's first incarnation and even then I never shared the popular enthusiasm for their brand of showy rock music. It was 'Bohemian Rhapsody' that did it for me. I mean, 'Thunder and lightning, very very frightening'? Do me a favour. Having presented many of those radio shows where you spin the listeners' favourite platters, I have had to play 'Bohemian Rhapsody' several times, which has had the effect of hardening my heart against Mr Mercury. Don't like to speak ill of the dead and all that, but there it is.

The club's clientele is mostly old, white, working class types; the women are in the concert room, the chaps playing snooker or watching football on TV. You would cast any of them in *Coronation Street*, or at least in the *Coronation Street* of the Ena Sharples/Len Fairclough era.

Mark doesn't reckon they are his type of people. 'We've been moaned at since we got here,' he tells me. 'People were covering their ears during the sound check.' The concert secretary, a decent chap called Colin, comes over and asks Mark if he is going to be loud. 'Yes, of course we're loud,' he replies. 'It's rock music. That's what rock music is all about.' 'Oh, well. Just keep it to a nice level, will you?' says Colin affably, and leaves the room.

'Colin's all right,' says Mark, 'but we haven't had much of a welcome from some of the others. It means a lot to me how I'm tret [treated] when I first walk through the door. If I'm tret bad, it affects me for the rest of the night.' He and the crew console themselves with reminiscences of more glittering gigs. The NAAFI gig in Germany was a good one, getting to play with Showaddywaddy, and hundreds of pissed-up squaddies screaming for more. Even better are the gigs where there are girls. There was a tour of holiday camps, where there were girls, and it was good to be the star, or with the star; and a caravan park in Carlisle, when one of them found a thong in his pocket the following morning. At a nightclub in Buxton, awash with young women, they were given free drink as well. 'They had some lager with icebergs in it that costs £3 a pint,' says Steve, who has come with the team for the sole purpose of dancing, 'and I had 12 pints of it. Brilliant.'

Steve is something of a hero. 'Wait till you see Steve,' the lads kept saying to me, and sure enough, once Mark swung into action, Steve, a great big shaven-headed bear of a chap with a Gypsy-style gold ring through one ear, whipped the crowd into a frenzy. If you had told me beforehand that anyone could throw himself so wholeheartedly into a Queen tribute gig at a working men's club, I would not have believed you. First he flung himself extravagantly around the little dance floor to the bemusement of the audience, then he started grabbing middle-aged ladies with tight white perms and wrinkled cleavages from their tables to dance with him, writhing suggestively in front of them and making them giggle.

In between Mark's two segments Steve returns to the darts room with three rather sad sandwiches, all of which are for his own consumption – 'I said, "Anything you've got as long as there's no egg in it."' Remarkably, the boys had spotted another 'nice little blonde' that had escaped my attention. 'She didn't stop,' said Steve. 'I knew she wouldn't. She had a birthday card in her hand. They just come in for a couple of cheap drinks then bugger off.'

Aside from the girls and the free drinks, though, does Mark see anything else coming from his Freddie act? 'Well, I'd like to do some more of my own stuff,' he says. 'I've written a song with my brother who's got a website, 'Unsigned FM', and we've put it on there. We're thinking of getting some session musicians together as well and going out as a band, doing bigger venues. I'd like to do more corporate stuff as well, less of the clubs.' It's a long haul, though. When I ring Mike to check a few facts I ask if Freddie is still busy. 'Oh, always, he's doing a club in Carnforth tonight, Newport Pagnell tomorrow.'

If my conversations are anything to go by, the mileage clocked up in the name of entertainment on Britain's crowded roads is little short of phenomenal. If just a few of us were prepared to sacrifice our right to watch Abba tribute acts or dodgy comedians, billions could probably be taken out of the road-building programme overnight.

The act I am to see the following day, for instance, Abbagirls, have been in Bridlington, are on their way to Woolacombe in Devon, and are stopping off at Bury in Lancashire to perform at a wedding. They do all this travelling in a Ford Transit van decorated with the blue and yellow Swedish flag on the front and sides and the legend 'Abba Girls'. Colin Cross, who shares the driving with the girls, and whose other duties include being married to one of them, Kim Graham, and taking care of the sound and lighting, tells me the van has 230,000 miles on the clock and averages 50,000 a year.

The evening before I'm due to meet the girls, I stay overnight at the Travel Inn just a few miles north up Bury New Road, near where much of my childhood was spent.

When I was growing up, the thought of a sixty-room hotel in our undistinguished suburb of Manchester would have been laughable. We had Tower Buildings, a big Co-op department store where we used to go once a year to buy bits of school uniform to go with the blazer my dad had made me, a cosy little cinema called the Plaza that housed an interesting selection of insect life, and Prestwich Clough, a relatively untamed area of parkland. But nothing really to tempt anybody to go as far as actually stopping in the place. Unless they had relatives in Prestwich Hospital.

The hospital was what made Prestwich famous all over Manchester. It was, I believe, the largest mental hospital anywhere in Europe, with its own electricity and gas supplies, its own farm and fire station. It was a classic Victorian mental institution – opened in 1851 – full of people who probably should not have been there. Still, when I was at school, Prestwich Hospital was a source of endless fun. 'I'm from Prestwich,' you'd say to some kid. 'Oh, they've let you out of the loony bin for the day, have they?' would come the inevitable hilarious quip. The irony is that tonight, for the first time, I *am* actually in the loony bin, or at least where it used to be.

The huge tract of land that started life as the Lancashire County Asylum in 1851 is now junction 17 of the M60 motorway, and since all human life appears to be conducted on motorway turn-offs these days, there is an enormous Tesco store, selling pimento-stuffed olives and four different sorts of tortilla chips where once electric shock treatment used to be administered to truculent and independent-minded patients; there is also a branch of the TGI Friday's American restaurant chain, and the Travel Inn. The mental hospital itself is now a scaled-down community something-or-other, and a good thing, too.

The Travel Inn, by the way, is not an inn. My dictionary defines an inn as 'a public house or small hotel providing food and accommodation' and in my book three custard cream biscuits do not constitute food. I intend to take this up with Whitbread Group PLC as soon as I get home. You can order breakfast but you have to go next door and take your chances at TGI Friday's, which is not a smart move when you can wander into the supermarket and get a bottle of freshly squeezed orange juice and a fairly recently baked bagel.

My room at the Travel Inn is sparse. There is no phone, there are not even any of those little sachets of shampoo. It is clean, but in a sterile kind of way, as if someone has been round with a super turbo-charged vacuum cleaner sucking up dirt and dead spiders but at the same time sucking all the life out of it, hoovering up everything that makes it seem like a room. The bed is a good size, big enough for me and two air hostesses, which, frankly, would be the only way to make your stay there mildly interesting. There is not even anything in the room you could use in a suicide bid, which is probably a wise precaution. When you find yourself in a Travel Inn on a motorway slip road just outside Manchester on a Saturday night, the Big Sleep must begin to look an attractive option.

I eat the three biscuits instead – finding myself unaccountably lacking in the air hostess department – and flip round five terrestrial TV channels and three radio stations, which is no fun when you have hundreds you can flip round at home. That used to be one of the joys of hotels, the extra channels. The thrill of watching a Scandinavian tractor-pull on Eurosport or finding out in which fine hotels CNN was available. You could be staying in some shit-hole somewhere, watching the footage of the Raffles Hotel on CNN, and persuade yourself you were part of some high-living community of international travellers.

I drift off to sleep, of course, with the TV on. As Jerry Seinfeld says, the last part of the human body to require sleep is the finger with which you operate the TV remote control.

The next day is a ridiculously pleasant late summer Sunday, mingling memories and desire, as I think T S Eliot might have said. The sky is cloudless, there is scarcely a breath of wind, and I decide to repeat a journey I have made hundreds of times, south along Bury New Road, the four miles into Manchester city centre. First, though, I visit 3 Lichfield Drive, the house I lived in from the age of three until I left for university at eighteen, the house I suppose where all the damage was done. It is a brick-built three-bedroomed semi, mock Tudor, more mock than Tudor, with a postage stamp garden at the back on which the sun never shone and a little patch at the front that my dad paved over for his Vauxhall Velox.

The house has barely changed. I stand across the road and I take pictures, getting that odd feeling in the pit of my stomach, which I suppose is nostalgia (from the Greek: *nostos* – 'homecoming' and *algos* – 'pain').

We often forget the *algos* when we talk about nostalgia. Abbagirls would probably be described as a nostalgia act but there is no *algos* in listening to some catchy pop tunes that frankly have never disappeared from the airwaves anyway; not the kind of *algos* I am feeling, remembering the smell of my mum's cooking, remembering the times I had to act as intermediary for my parents because they were not talking to each other. My dad would sit cursing in the dining room, counting out my mum's housekeeping money in pound notes and thrusting it into my hand to take to her in the kitchen or in the front room; I was an eight-year-old Dr Kissinger.

The *algos* does not entirely disappear as I head for town along Bury New Road. The names of the clubs I used to visit come flooding back: Top of the Town, the Jungfrau, Brown's, Mr Smith's. I went out mostly to escape the atmosphere at home, although even when there was a ceasefire there was invariably something like *The Lulu Show* on TV, so home and hearth held little attraction.

Sometimes I would just buy a meat and potato pie from the stall near Salford bus station, wander around town a bit and get the bus home again, just to be out. Mostly, though, I used to go out 'pulling' with a friend; a serious misnomer, as we rarely met any girls, and the only pulling that went on was usually after the evening had finished, alone, in the privacy of our respective bedrooms.

I was twenty-one before I had a proper girlfriend and I am sure those awkward sexless years, along with all the soul music I absorbed, fuelled my dreams of show business, and partly accounts for what I am doing now: preparing to spend an evening with Abbagirls.

I remember I haven't eaten anything, and going to see an Abba tribute act on an empty stomach is not recommended, so I hunt round for someone to sell me a meat and potato pie for old time's sake. A fool's errand. What you can get now is a Thai chicken wrap in spinach tortilla, with Thai green mayonnaise, in the Hogshead pub, which is OK, an artist's impression of foreign food.

It is just as I bite into my wrap that I get a call from Colin Cross, genial *éminence grise* behind Abbagirls, who supplies me with regular updates on the progress of their journey from Bridlington to the Village Hotel, Bury, where they are to perform at a wedding. The hotel is another one on a motorway roundabout, about eight miles out of Manchester city centre.

In the same way as the Travel Inn is not really an inn, the Village, it will hardly startle you to learn, is not really a village. More of a tribute to a village. There are a few of these hotels around Manchester. They are the exact antithesis of the Travel Inns, selling themselves on the quality and variety of their restaurants and bars, and the facilities in their health clubs, none of which I feel qualified to pronounce on, having merely shared a coffee with Colin and his Abbagirls in the reception area.

Abba, you will recall, were a Swedish group, comprising two boring bearded chappies who made up the tunes, and two attractive girls, one blonde, one a redhead, who sang them. In the seventies we thought their music was the epitome of ephemera: transient, easily disposable pop. I hardly ever played it on the radio – except for 'Dancing Queen', because that was such a good radio record – preferring to play really important music from Saxon or the Salford Jets. Who would have thought that 20-odd years later it would be Abba's music – minus the two boring beards who wrote it, of course – rather than Saxon's that would be considered the perfect crowning touch to John and Lorraine's special day, and worth every penny of £800?

I am beginning to get the message with these tribute acts. Once you have the name, and the backing tapes, your big selling point is the costume changes, and whereas Freddie could point to four, Abbagirls boast seven. Of course, there are two of them, so they can do a kind of flip-flop thing, one handling the vocals while the other disappears into a side room and slips into a little mini-kimono, then rushes back and makes way for the other to scurry off. Freddie has to cover his own costume changes with tapes of guitar solos or Montserrat Caballe's bit in 'Barcelona'.

Colin tells me about Abbagirls' quick-change routines over coffee and I must say it does occur to me that, with most of the audience being tired and emotional after a day of wedding celebrations, and not necessarily Abba purists, they might try and get away with five or six. But, blow me, I counted them all out and I counted them all in. They completed the full complement. Kim Graham as Frida and her partner, Sarah MacDonnell, the third Agnetha in the six years of Abbagirls, were in and out like Errol Flynn on his wedding night, as I believe they used to say during the war.

During my time on the road, I must say one quality above all others has impressed me about the tribute artistes, and that is the professionalism of the acts. Faced with the grimmest working men's club, the sparsest comedy venue in a pub's top room, the most blasé crowd at some stomach-churning corporate function, not one act I saw reacted the way you or I might – with the words, 'Why bother?' The minute I meet Colin, I know Abbagirls will be no exception. Colin is a tecky, as we showbiz types like to say, a technical whiz, the type your heart longs to see when you are out on a gig, a real steady Eddie. Most of his life has been spent in rock 'n' roll.

On leaving school Colin took an apprenticeship in television engineering, ended up in a hi-fi shop bamboozling fools like me with talk of sub-woofers, and eventually joined the famous Edwin Shirley Truckers, handling the sound for the biggest names in music. He has adjusted mikes and pumped up the volume for Michael Jackson, the Stones, and the Who, among others, and hesitates for barely a second when I ask him what it was like working with such legendary talents. 'Pain in the arse,' he says. 'You can work for an hour on the drummer's sound. "Ooh, my snare's not quite right" so you adjust it. "Yeah, that's better, but it still needs nudging a tad" so you put it back to where you started, and they say, "Yeah, that's it. I told you."'

It is difficult to imagine Colin getting too rattled, even by rock music's egos. He is a short, stocky chap, with grey hair swept back, and grey stubble. He is tanned, and smiles a lot, which gives him a sort of shiny showbiz look. Since meeting Kim, and getting off the rock treadmill ten years ago or so, he seems to have found some inner peace. Actually, he probably always had it, absorbing it from his technical background, from knowing how things work, a sort of *Zen and the Art of Motorcycle Maintenance* thing.

Kim was a dance band singer, did cabaret on cruise ships, and before she and Colin came up with the idea of the Abba act, somewhat bizarrely used to tour as an Olivia Newton-John tribute, for which you might think there would be a limited popular appetite. Kim does actually bear a more than superficial physical resemblance to Olivia Newton John, which I suppose gave the act a certain novelty value.

Sarah joined Abbagirls just over a year ago, after answering an ad in the *Stage*. Her background is in musical theatre, pantomimes and so on. She has sung and danced on cruise ships, worked in a kind of meet and greet capacity at the Dome, and danced for one of the doyens of the song and dance world, Peter Gordeno. 'I was doing summer season when I saw the ad,' she says, 'and I wanted to try something different, so I auditioned.'

I expect the chance of regular work was something of a lure as well. Even a successful act like Abbagirls, booked solid until Christmas, seem haunted by the possibility that the gravy train will hit the buffers at any moment and so they refuse little. The wedding in Bury, I suggest, is a little way off their route from Bridlington, where they have been performing on Saturday, to Woolacombe, where they are due to be on Monday, but their answer is simple: 'It's a Sunday night and we're working.'

Although they are slightly up the food chain from Freddie, they will very occasionally still do working men's clubs. They have the two forty-five-minute spots if required but think of themselves more as a cabaret act – 'Not so much cabaret, as Abbaret,' in the words of their press handout.

Actually, Abbagirls were nearly on television. Colin tells me – here comes the hard luck story – that they were performing at a function when they were approached by a chap who asked if they could work with a band rather than tapes, and Colin declined, saying they didn't have the sheet music. 'Turns out the chap was a producer doing a show for the BBC. We would have been on BBC1. Somebody else did it eventually and we had to take action to stop them calling themselves Abbagirls. In the end they called it Fabbagirls. But who knows what might have come from the TV exposure.'

I suppose they could have charged more but they could not be much busier. They do a regular gay night at the Two Brewers, a cabaret club in south London, near their home, and this has resulted in a two-week tour of Philadelphia and New York, playing gay venues. With virtually the same act, they can play family holiday centres in north Devon, party nights at football clubs, and corporate functions. Thank heavens for post-modern irony.

I am not sure what to make of tribute acts. Before spending time with Freddie and Abbagirls my view was that they were as pernicious a feature of modern life as children's menus. (Who decided our kids were not fit to eat proper food and had to be fed fingers and nuggets? And what part of the chicken is the bloody nugget, anyway?) Or hot-air driers (wet trousers anyone?) and Rosie Millard (personal, don't ask). But in some cases – certainly in the ones I saw – the performance had been polished to an extent and, without hitting any musical heights, a fairly decent act has ensued. Admittedly, it wasn't strictly speaking *their* act, but given that neither Queen nor Abba is likely to turn up in the immediate future at the Siddal Cricket and Athletics Club or for a wedding in Bury, a reasonable facsimile was provided.

If you share my view that going out is intrinsically preferable to staying in, offering as it does the chance for some sort of social interaction, and that a desire to relive the old days to some extent is understandable – and I write as someone who took pictures of his old house, for goodness' sake – then we should not be too harsh on these copycats.

Whether we like it or not – and my personal preference is still to be entertained by something I have never seen before, which becomes increasingly unlikely the older you get – the tribute business is no passing phase. What has changed the entertainment landscape, I think, is the fact that people of forty, fifty, and sixty even, are going out much more than they ever did. Thirty years ago, if you were bringing up a family, you were inclined to take Bob Dylan's advice and not stand in the doorway or block up the hall. Your place was at home. Going out was for the kids. These days, I suppose, older people have the money to go out. Also, with the increase in marriage break-ups, there must be more people of advanced age out there on the pull and I expect they want some recognizable tunes to do their pulling to.

Some of you may be familiar with L P Hartley's novel *The Go-Between*, the opening lines of which I quote, merely as a tribute, of course. They go: 'The past is a foreign country: they do things differently there.' Well, not any more they don't.

7

AT SEA

There are times in everyone's life when they wish they'd stayed at home. Perversely, for me, one of those occasions was when I was on what on the face of it seemed my most plum of assignments: interviewing young and attractive lady dancers on a cruise ship, touring some of Europe's choicest real estate.

First thing: I am not a good sailor. I may be guilty of perpetuating a racial stereotype but I don't think Jews are natural sailors. Round the world yachtsmen tend to be called Francis Chichester rather than Chaim Finklestein. Obviously, over the years, Jews have had to go to sea from time to time. There was the business with the pharaohs, when I think some of our boys may have found themselves below decks rowing like stink and getting a sound thrashing for their pains. Then there were the ships carrying migrants from Europe to the New World around the turn of the twentieth century. Full of Jews.

In Charlie Chaplin's film *The Immigrant*, for instance, you see Charlie comically sliding from side to side as the ship is tossed about on the high seas. What you don't see are the three Jews throwing up down below. Need more evidence of Jews and the sea not getting on? Shelley Winters in *The Poseidon Adventure*. And then there was me, on the four-star cruise ship *Island Escape*, sailing southwest – or are you supposed to say sou'west? Who knows? – out of Toulon towards the Balearic Islands, with the weather stormy and the ship being tossed about like, well, rather like a ship in choppy water.

That is the thing about the weather. It pays scant regard to the brochures, which unsurprisingly fail to mention, in amongst the panegyrics about five-star international cuisine, well-stocked bars and comfortable, well-appointed cabins, that you will actually be on a moving bloody ship and there may come a time when you will be lying in your well-appointed cabin, with your stomach being flung from port to starboard, begging for merciful release.

My view is that the sea is not terribly keen on sharing its charms with boatloads of the comfortably off and likes to let us know from time to time that if it really wanted to it could make life very difficult for us. Clearly in some cases – and I am thinking of the popular motion picture *Titanic* here – it goes too far. On the *Island Escape* it restricted itself to flinging a few dinner plates around in the style of Sissy Spacek in the film *Carrie* and making anyone unwise enough to try and move around the ship lurch unsteadily like a Newcastle kebab queue at 2.30 in the morning.

When the sea was at its most vindictive I was in the Island Restaurant eating dry cream crackers by the dozen on the recommendation of our waiter, Mohammed, who seemed something of a sea dog and assured us this would soak up the liquid in the stomach and create a kind of ballast. Mohammed's advice seemed to be working when a particularly fierce wave caused a tray to cut loose from the servery. As the hot chicken à la something or other sizzled at my feet, and I manoeuvred my tongue to dislodge a mush of cream cracker from the roof of my mouth, sitting quietly in my conservatory at home suddenly seemed a very attractive alternative.

To be honest, I had begun to doubt the wisdom of my mission before even boarding the ship. It is inevitable, I suppose, when you are writing a book about something as transitory and illusory as fame that the ground will shift beneath you as you write. The story of Tony Blackburn, for instance, with whom I spent some time around Christmas 2001, seemed a strong one; formerly nationally celebrated disc jockey clings on to vestiges of fame by parodying himself for modern audiences with a sense of irony. Then he is chosen to appear on the so-called reality TV show, *I'm a Celebrity … Get Me Out of Here*, wins the damn thing and suddenly becomes the most famous man in Britain again.

I knew all along he was going to win. I told everyone he was an absolute certainty, while neglecting, of course, to put any money on it. One gesture, when I was with him in his room in the Malmaison Hotel in Newcastle, convinced me he had the qualities needed to win a popularity contest of this type. A complimentary bottle of red wine had been left on the table for him and he immediately opened it and poured me a glass. Not much, I know, but believe me, most 'personalities' would not have bothered. The poor sap with the notebook would have been left to fend for himself.

Tony is, basically, just a nice guy. The worst you can say of him is that he can be a little boring at times. But for TV to pick a bunch of 'celebrities' and then find that one of them turns out to be a half-decent human being, well, no wonder it made headline news. So I was already wondering whether my Tony Blackburn story was still valid when I discovered that the very cruise ship I was about to board in order to tell the story of its floating entertainers was to be the subject of a ten-part docusoap on ITV.

What was it Oscar Wilde said on the subject? To be scuppered once by reality TV is a misfortune, to be scuppered twice is a real pain in the arse. There I was, then, at the foot of the gangplank ready to board, wondering if my trip was really necessary or if I could have stayed at home and watched the whole thing on the telly.

The *Island Escape* is a 40,000-ton former car ferry. First Choice, a British package holiday firm, and Royal Caribbean Cruises, got together, spent around £7 million on a refit, and formed a company called Island Cruises, with just this one ship, capable of taking 1,500 passengers a time on one- or two-week trips around the Mediterranean. The first voyage was on 26 March 2002.

The intention of the new company was to make cruising more attractive to a wider audience. When marketing people talk about 'a wider audience', of course, what they really mean is a younger audience but that is difficult to say without appearing to slight your existing clientele. The problem is, when you have a product that is enjoyed predominantly by older people, a proportion of your customers will disappear each year through, what shall we say, natural wastage. Oh, fuck it, people die. We're all going to die. You're going to die. I am going to die. And the old geezer lying on the sun-lounger snoozing gently as his wrinkled skin turns a deeper shade of mahogany is certainly going to die, possibly before he can book next year's cruise.

The prospect of your customers being poached not by competitors but by the Grim Reaper is by no means unique to cruise ships. The *Daily Telegraph*, for instance, noticed some years ago that it had a disproportionate number of elderly readers and realized that after death people's desire to buy the paper tended to taper off. It tried, with some success, to bring in younger readers by printing lots of pictures of Liz Hurley and filling its arts pages with reviews of noisy pop bands its readers had never heard of.

Where the BBC has radio services that appeal mostly to an older constituency it tries to bring in what it calls 'a replenisher audience', which is a delicate way of admitting that some of your listeners will shortly be going on a journey where a transistor radio may be surplus to requirements. Radio 2 has been notably successful in attracting so-called 'replenishers' through the simple expedient of a slightly sharper playlist – minus anything too likely to frighten the horses – and some livelier disc jockeys.

It is more difficult for traditional old consumer products – I don't know, Marmite, HP Sauce, that kind of thing – but you always know when the research has shown their products appeal more to people in bathchairs than pushchairs. That is when their advertising starts to include colourful cartoon characters and voice-overs from formerly edgy stand-up comics eager to clamp their formerly foul mouth around the corporate todger.

Island Cruises' big idea is 'casual cruising', which turns out not to be what George Michael gets up to when he's in Los Angeles but a 'friendly, innovative' style of cruising, 'with all the features expected from a traditional cruise, but presented in a more informal way'. The other key word in Island Cruises' publicity is 'relaxed', the main thrust of all this being that they do not expect you to dress for dinner, which came as a bit of a blow to those of us who had gone to the trouble of packing two suits, a selection of smart shirts and the cufflinks we had been waiting since Christmas to wear. I was also carrying a suitcase full of smart pre-teen girlie wear for my twelve-year-old daughter, Martha, a late addition to my party after Island

Cruises had not only given me one of their best cabins free of charge but also invited me to bring along a guest, in the hope no doubt that I would counteract some rather bad publicity about to emerge from the reality TV show, *Cruise Ship,* on ITV.

The show's endlessly questing cameras and microphones had apparently sought out pipes leaking sewage into corridors, tiles falling from walls, disgruntled guests, restaurant managers harassing crew members and other outrages to entertain Sunday evening TV viewers.

As one of Britain's most corruptible journalists, I am happy to confirm that none of this was going on when I was on board; and in case Island Cruises need some help with their casual cruising pitch, let me add that they are the freshest, funkiest, wickedest, kick-ass cruises on the planet, man, and yo need to get yo ass down on that ship, 4 sure. Will that do?

Whether the casual cruising thing is going to work or not is difficult for me to say as our trip was in October, after school and college holidays were over. At the height of the summer, apparently, there were quite a few families with young children on the ship but as I ascended the gangplank in Majorca, the sea of tight white perms before me told its own story. Actually, we had already got an idea of the cut of our fellow cruisers' jib in the queue at Manchester airport, when some chap of about seventy whose clothes were a bizarre mix of cowboy gear and mid-period John Lennon – a suede jacket with tassels on and a black leather flat cap – embarked on the most surreal conversation. 'Cruellest thing you can do to a Chinaman,' he said to Martha, 'is cut his pigtail off. Chinamen, you see, always used to wear pigtails, and little pillbox hats. You hear a scream in the cinema, and the lights go up, and someone's sat down behind a Chinaman and cut his pigtail off,' at which he smiled knowingly and presented his passport for inspection. I can only presume his Chinaman riff was sparked off by Martha's ponytail.

The next time we saw the chap was on the ship. He was wearing a Bob Marley 'Lion from Zion' T-shirt decorated with a ganja leaf motif, combat trousers and highly polished black brogues. That is the kind of gear I am going to wear when I am seventy and I can hardly wait. His wife, interestingly, looked perfectly conventional in a nice black cardy and skirt.

About the flight I do not intend to go into great detail, especially as my intention is to give Island Cruises the kind of top-notch publicity their gracious hospitality merits, and thus advertise my availability for further bribery and corruption, but I really must say the food on their aeroplane over to Palma was an insult. I know now why they take your weaponry off you at the airport, because if they did not, the temptation to seek out the joker responsible for the 'smoked turkey and cheese melt' and give him a good stabbing would be overpowering. I don't know what got in amongst me more, the abomination itself or the announcement that we were to be served complimentary tea or coffee alongside 'something from the Air 2000 Deli'.

What is really, truly frightening is that some smart-arse marketing type has come up with the concept of the Air 2000 Deli. He or she probably spent three years in higher education, falling in and out of love with fellow students, wearing stupid trousers, crowding the bar at the Fenton in Leeds so that honest toilers like me have to join the crush or go thirsty. After which there was maybe a postgraduate diploma in 'leisure management' or one of those subjects. And what is the end product? The Air 2000 Deli.

What do they think? That we are stupid or something? I saw the plane. There was no deli on there, and in any case there is not a deli in the world that would serve the two slices of hot smoked cardboard inside a polystyrene ciabatta that was slung our way – not if it had ambitions to stay in business. A suggestion to the airline: either stop pretending to serve a free 'meal' or take all the money you put into the in-flight magazine and put it into the catering instead – unless, that is, you have solid evidence that there are people who actually want to read features with titles like *Salad Days With Jamie Oliver*. As if all this were not enough of a downer, when I slip the headphones on to listen to the in-flight audio, I hear all sorts of former colleagues coining it – the bastards – doing voice-overs for the airlines.

As the purpose of the cruise was to watch the shows and talk to the entertainers, Martha had packed a number of different outfits for evening wear; and as most twelve-year-old girls' idea of dressing up for the evening is to look as much like a Puerto Rican hooker as possible, I had been given strict instructions not to allow her to wear anything 'too tarty'. This is an awesome responsibility for a chap. 'Does this go together?' she would ask, appearing before me in a swirl of tight-fitting primary colours. 'Sure,' I said, making a mental note not to include her in any photos her mother was likely to see.

Given that I had no particular desire to be on a cruise ship, I must say our cabin was fantastic; it was one of only five on the ship with a balcony, with a free bottle of wine and bowl of fruit thrown in, all courtesy of Island Cruises, who I am sure will not mind my saying once more what a marvellous company they are. I should also thank RDF Media, makers of the ITV show *Cruise Ship*, without whose unforgiving cameras I am sure the hospitality to me and my fellow reptiles from Her Majesty's press would not have been nearly so lavish. We were there to let the world know that, despite the picture emerging on TV, the *Island Escape* was not necessarily the cruise ship from hell.

But what was the ship doing on TV in the first place? Why is everyone in such thrall to television? I remember a *Simpsons* episode once where the children, for some reason, all flung their arms around the set and hugged it. For me that sums up our attitude to TV: it feeds us rubbish, it persuades our kids they need junk food and piles of meretricious gewgaws, and yet we love it, worship it. (I do not include myself in this. Like most middle-class people, I only watch it for the news and wildlife documentaries.)

The Simpson kids, mind you, you can understand. They are, after all, cartoon characters, but the former managing director of Island Cruises should have known better. There he was, with a new company, a newly converted car ferry, a multi-national staff of staggering inexperience, a boatload of probably the most demanding travellers in the world ('How can you tell when you've got a planeload of Poms on the tarmac?' 'When you switch the engines off, you can still hear the whining.') and a letter on his desk from a TV company asking if they can come on the ship for ten weeks and film the whole bloody thing. 'Sure,' he says. 'Come right on in. Do a number on us. Oh, and the assistant director would like to massage my grandmother and you want me to eat my shoes? Well, if you think it will make a better programme.' Does nobody ever think of turning television down? Just say no, is my advice.

The TV people had been and gone by the time we turned up and the two captains of the *Island Escape* were busy picking up the pieces. Captain Stuart Horne and Captain John McNeill work one month on and one month off, and although I am sure they are both adept at driving the ship, they have a stake in the company, so seem to spend at least as much time trying to keep their customers happy as drawing lines on charts and doing all the seafaring stuff. I suppose as there are no icebergs in the Mediterranean, they can leave the steering to their juniors.

When Martha and I arrive on board it is handover day for the captains, so both of them entertain us and fellow hacks to lunch. Captain Horne, a handsome chap on the cusp of having to admit he is going bald, is the more comfortable with his PR role, making a big fuss over tasting the wine, giving it the full nose performance and so on, and appearing quite relaxed about the TV programme. To show how relaxed he is, he wears crisp blue denim jeans with his smart navy blazer, an outfit my neighbour at the luncheon table, a funny, boisterous diary writer for the *Daily Express*, tells me to view with deep suspicion.

Captain Horne, who is already achieving a little fame through the TV show, looks a little like the former Liberal leader David Steel, whereas Captain McNeill's resemblance to David Bowie is striking. It is the first thing that hits you about him. He is the older of the two skippers, fifty-three as opposed to forty-three, and seems less comfortable with all the glad-handing. His announcements over the ship's public address, on which he appears at regular intervals to explain sailing matters, are more reminiscent of a speak-your-weight machine, or John Major before he suddenly became interesting, than the androgynous hit-maker he resembles.

We missed our first port of call, which was to have been Malta, he announced, because of strong easterly winds slowing us down. At least, I think that was the reason. The skipper, bless him, gave so much unnecessary meteorological detail in his address I may have dropped off halfway through. Kate, my *Daily Express* friend, suggested his address might have been more effective had he simply broken off after the first sentence or two and announced – in the style of his *doppelgänger* – that there might have to be some 'ch–ch–ch–ch–ch–changes'.

If Captain McNeill seems vaguely embarrassed by all the mixing and mingling he is called upon to do – not just wining and dining the press, which is bad enough, but doing a fairly embarassing boogie at 'seventies night' – the entertainers on the ship throw themselves into it with the kind of youthful, bright-eyed gusto that makes Mary Poppins seem like old man Steptoe.

The entertainment is bought in from a Cyprus-based company called Viva Entertainments, who advertised for performers in the *Stage* (of course) and started rehearsing their shows in the January before the *Island Escape* set sail. I thought they were all marvellous, but then I am probably biased, having interviewed some of the singers and dancers and fallen in love with them a little. There is something infectious about youthful optimism, especially when you are on a ship full of people around your own age or older who have lost their hopes and dreams, along with several of their teeth. I mean, I am not saying I am one of these chaps in his fifties about to start creeping round twenty-eight-year-old weather girls, but the young performers' refusal to accept they were headed anywhere other than the top of the entertainment tree, and their rather sweet, uncomplaining willingness to be shamelessly exploited, well, the older you get, the more willing you are to accept that Vladimir Nabokov had a point in *Lolita*.

The age thing is actually quite an important issue aboard the *Island Escape*. As previously indicated, Island Cruises are keen to widen the appeal of cruising, so Viva Entertainments were charged with coming up with a package to appeal not just to their present customers – predominantly middle-aged, middle-brow, working-class folk who had pulled themselves up by their bootstraps, self-employed painters and decorators who, after making sure their grandchildren were looked after, wanted a few drinks and a bit of a laugh, and maybe to see Naples before they die – but also to their potential new customers.

Island Cruises, bless them, believe that alongside the so-called grey pound there is the pound just speckled with grey – maybe we should call it the slightly balding pound that doesn't always feel too good first thing in the morning – couples in their late forties, say, or early fifties, whose children have grown up and left home, and who now find themselves with money and time on their hands. This generation, the argument goes, that grew up with the Beatles and cannabis and round tea bags, might demand something a little more radical than the traditional cruiser.

To ensure the balance is achieved, a cruise director is employed. This is a position that has interested me ever since I discovered that it was the job that Hank, the marvellous character played by Jeffrey Tambor in the *Larry Sanders Show*, used to do before becoming Larry's sidekick.

Before meeting any of the delightful young entertainers, I had to speak to this real-life Hank, and he did not disappoint. Not that he is pompous and mean-spirited like Hank. Outside of the darkest of dark sitcoms, who could be? But, like Hank, he takes his vaguely ridiculous job absolutely seriously. Physically, Bruce Mather is not unlike his TV counterpart, but this round-faced teddy bear of a man is relentlessly cheerful, friendly and helpful; a little like a taller, chubbier version of Tony Blackburn. He lives to please.

Where Hank is rampantly heterosexual, Bruce gives the impression of being less so. In fact, when you try and deconstruct his maddeningly fluid accent – a mix and match thing that tells of a life in polyglot theatre companies – the prevailing tone is camp. You certainly would not guess from his voice that he is Canadian. He was born in Toronto 43 years ago and, as he puts it, 'I have been in show business all my life.' He started out as a swimmer and lifeguard – which stretches the definition of show business somewhat, unless he did a full Busby Berkeley routine when he dived in to save someone, which I should not put past him – but always saw his future in theatre:

> I studied to be an actor, but actors weren't working, so I took up dance. Dancers worked, I found, while actors were waiting tables. Because I was a swimmer, the dancing came easy. I knew how to fine-tune the body. I did all the musicals in Toronto: *Cabaret*, *Best Little Whorehouse in Texas*, anything you care to mention.

Bruce's life, he tells me, has taken 'a very bizarre path'. But –
and he looks me straight in the eye, and tells me in all
seriousness – 'everything I have done has been leading up to
this.' If it was anybody other than Bruce talking, I should have
laughed, since the 'this' to which his whole life had been leading
up was 'The Solaris Trio play Salsa in the Bounty Lounge',
'Groovy Nights deck party with DJ Johnny G' and the 'Ocean
Theatre Players in "All You Need Is Love"', their interpretation
of those classic Beatles songs. But Bruce is utterly sincere about
it, and refreshingly, in a business where most of the people he
works with are on the make to some extent, and see cruise ship
entertaining as a stepping stone to something else, he views it as
an end in itself. He does not see the entertaining of a retired
newsagent from Rotherham and his wife as beneath him, and
for that you have to love him a little.

Bruce's home when he is not at sea is Barcelona:

> I've lived there for the past 15 years. I moved there for
> work originally but then when I found that in my block
> there were five different shops where you could buy a red
> rubber nose, I thought, I'm home. I am a party animal. I
> have always had a talent for throwing a party and that is
> why this job is made for me.

He has quite a spacious office at the top of the ship, up the
sharp end (the prow, as I believe they like to call it), with his
own fridge and a decent-sized cabin off it, with plenty of room
for his costumes. These include a rather impressive gold lamé
evening dress, which he will wear for the Groovy Nights deck
party, when Captain McNeill, carrying out the kind of duty they
somehow neglected to prepare him for at navigation school, will
prove what a wag he is by pushing him into the pool. Bruce is
perfectly happy with this:

> I have been with Viva Entertainments for three and a half
> years. I like the way they do things. A lot of cruise ships
> do the traditional tits and feathers shows but that's not
> for me. I danced at the Lido in Paris for a year, where we
> did those kind of shows on the grand scale, and either

you do them like that or you don't do them at all.

To be honest, we could never store enough feathers and jewels to do that kind of show properly. I'm sorry, dear, but 12 sad-ass ostrich feathers just doesn't cut it.

So the girls and boys who answered the advert in the *Stage* and passed the audition do a Beatles pastiche instead, leaping around in sub-Mary Quant gear and proving how very difficult even the Beatles' simplest songs are to recreate, and making their audience – well, me, at least – wish it was 1964 again and they were hearing the songs for the first time on the LP their mum and dad had bought them for Christmas. Or they do their seventies show, and a Parisian-style thing, including some racier numbers from *Moulin Rouge*.

Every night Martha and I and our two new friends, Kate from the *Daily Express* and Jane from the *Sunday Express*, settle down to watch the singing and dancing in the Ocean Theatre, a 500-seat cabaret bar done out in blue crushed velvet, reminiscent of seventies chicken-in-the-basket palaces like the Batley Variety Club. The seats, comfortable swivel chairs with wide arms, just made for lounging in, drive Bruce mad. 'You want your audience upright and alert, ready to pay attention,' he says, 'not slumped in their chairs, about to nod off.' It is a surprise to find Bruce such a puritan when it comes to seating arrangements but it is possibly a legacy of his upbringing:

I was brought up in a very very strict religious house, Baptist and then some. Till I was fifteen I was allowed no TV, no cinema and no music apart from hymns. But it meant I had to use my imagination. I don't think kids these days are encouraged to use their imagination enough.

I agree, of course. It seems odd to be sitting down lamenting the state of kids today with a camp Canadian cruise director who owns his own gold lamé evening dress, but he has a point and he is not the first entertainer to complain to me about modern audiences. Colin Cross, the chap behind Abbagirls, reckoned that young people were so used to watching TV that they did not quite grasp the concept of sitting quietly in public watching live performers. The implication was that the only way to keep them quiet was by playing backing tapes of Abba songs they already knew, at ear-shattering volume. If he thought he could make a living with anything more original, he said, he would give it a go.

Similar seems true of comedy. I have been watching a fair bit of comedy of late, as the time approaches for me to do my own stand-up gig, and I have noticed that a certain directness pays. You may get away with subtle irony in a six-part TV sitcom but try it in an open spot at the Comedy Store and they will have you. In a stand-up contest recently on ITV there were several rather astute observational comics, and a couple of clever character comedians, but the winner was the comedian who told this joke: 'I went to the opticians and he said, "You're going to have to stop wanking." "Why?" I asked. "Is it making me short-sighted?" "No," he said. "It's annoying the other patients."' I might use that in my own act.

Unlike me, though, Bruce would not for one moment consider he was appealing to any kind of lowest common denominator with his seventies shows and all that *Moulin Rougerie*. He is proud of his young performers. 'Those kids are awesome,' he tells me, wide-eyed. 'I cannot believe they are actually here and not in the West End.' And he directs my attention towards the Ocean Theatre version of the TV show *Stars in Their Eyes*, in which Gareth, a twenty-three-year-old singer of whom Bruce is particularly proud, 'comes on as Meatloaf, and sings the royal fuck out of "Bat out of Hell".'

Bruce's deputy is Lesley Carol, a twenty-eight-year-old from Ilkley in Yorkshire, who would like to be a television presenter. And why should she not be? She is blonde, attractive, has that classless, vaguely upmarket northern accent that TV quite likes, can work with complete meatheads and, thanks to the *Island Escape*, knows how to keep smiling when everything around her is falling to bits. Perfect for telly.

Lesley has spent six years on cruise ships, before which she worked in holiday camps for four years: Pontins, Prestatyn, Haven on the Isle of Wight, Caistor, Great Yarmouth, Devon Cliffs, the very names redolent of British seaside afternoons spent in a fug of bacon and burger smells, looking for breaks in the cloud while watching rivulets of rain stream down café windows. She was a Bluecoat entertainer, which she went into straight from dancing school, dancing in little rock 'n' roll shows for the holidaying working classes, and you can see why she has risen up the cruise ship ladder. Positivity is her strong suit. She actually says to me, 'I'm a people person.'

'We're mother and father to the boys and girls,' says Bruce, and Lesley agrees. 'Most of the girls are aged nineteen to twenty-four,' she says, 'so I know what they are going through because I have been there myself. My door is always open for any of the girls to discuss problems.' 'You have to grow up pretty fast on a ship,' says Bruce, 'and those performers work pretty hard. You want to look after them. They are so, so, talented.'

Well, up to a point. I am no expert but I spot a tendency to confuse volume with talent. The young chap who screams the Meatloaf number, and a girl called Rebecca who goes full pelt at Edith Piaf's 'Non, je ne regrette rien', are generally thought of as the top turns in the Ocean Theatre but I find it difficult not to share to a degree my agent Roger Davis's lament that this is glorified karaoke.

They are nice kids, though. I just hope all that enthusiasm and energy is not being channelled in pursuit of a chimera. It is unlikely any of them will become famous or even particularly well known. Chances are, most of them will not even work regularly. The job ads in the *Stage* tell their own story: 'Hostesses required for busy nightclub in Central London', 'Do you have a great American accent?' (if so, you could work booking out cars for USA Rent A Car), 'Costa Coffee are looking for enthusiastic and motivated team members'. And if they do achieve some measure of success in their twenties and early thirties – especially the girls – what then? I may be an old cynic, but my travels in light entertainment have taught me that once the light has gone from your eyes and expensive cosmetics have become the permanent stand-in for the once youthful glow, it becomes desperately difficult to remain out there craving the love of an audience. Such concerns, though, seem far from the minds of dancers Danielle Murphy and Claire Phillips when I talk to them one afternoon in the empty Ocean

Theatre before their rehearsals, after Martha and I had returned from our lame-brained half-day coach tour of Naples.

The dancers had spent their time in port more sensibly than us – a phone card, a call home and a coffee in a quiet place free from the pressure of smiling at passengers. I know it is part of the training but the smiling must get to be really irksome after a while. Claire, who at twenty-six is a little older than most of the singers and dancers on board, certainly seems all smiled out as she slumps wearily into a seat next to me in the empty theatre. This is understandable, as she is the only entertainer left who has been working since the ship's troubled early days eight months previously. She was there when sanitation problems forced 1,500 passengers off the ship and onto flights home or into hotels in Majorca. Her practised smile and performing skills were enlisted to try and mollify holidaymakers who had suddenly found the cruise of a lifetime had become a week in Magaluf. This is not easy work. You try smiling with the righteous indignation of Middle England bearing down on you in a Majorcan hotel lobby at three in the morning:

> People kept asking me all sorts of questions about refunds and getting them on flights home and so on. They were getting very angry and we were just left to our own devices to sort it out. We were given no information or anything. I just wanted to say, 'Look, I'm a dancer, there is nothing I can do to help you' but you just had to be pleasant and do your best to pacify people.

The temptation to say, 'I can't get you a new hotel but I can do you Liza Minnelli's show-stopper from *Cabaret*' must have been almost irresistible.

Among the problems faced by the entertainers in those early days was a plague of flies in their living quarters, which meant that several of them suffered from diarrhoea. 'How do you dance, with diarrhoea?' I asked Claire. 'It isn't easy,' she replied. The additional pressure of a TV camera up her nose must have been just what she needed.

Then again, Jayne MacDonald, a singer of limited talent but boundless enthusiasm, had become a star of sorts after appearing on a previous TV show about a cruise ship. So you could see the intrusion as an opportunity. One of the girls on the *Island Escape* did: Penny Taylor, a twenty-seven-year-old (no longer on board by the time I joined the ship), was either chosen by the TV people as a particularly good subject or she pushed herself forward at every opportunity, depending on your point of view. She was blonde, homely and trying to lose weight – one of TV's current obsessions – which I suppose made her more of a natural TV subject than her colleagues, but her playing up to the cameras did not win any popularity contests in the crew bar, as Claire confirms:

> There were clashes. Penny fell out with the girl she was sharing a cabin with, so she had to move out. We saw Penny as a bit of a diva, quite frankly, and you can't be doing with egos on board ship. There are too many other things to contend with. You have to stick together.

Claire is in a searingly honest mood. So far, every conversation I have had with crew and entertainers aboard the *Island Escape* has been all smiles. As well as journalists, there are travel agents on board the ship, from Brazil, where it will spend the winter, so a major charm offensive is clearly under way. But Claire is in the kind of mood to let rip. It happens to a journalist very occasionally. You sit down with your notebook or tape recorder and opposite you is someone determined to tell it like it is. Rare moments, but a joy. Invariably, the interviewee will move up close to see what you are writing and will make sure you are getting the most damaging invective down correctly. 'Yes, that's "complete bastard", spelt b–a–s–t–' and so on. Occasionally, they will say, '… and you can quote me on that.' As if you wouldn't. That, anyway, is the kind of mood Claire is in:

> You are living so closely with the others you have to consciously make an effort not to get annoyed with little things. I did this at first but there have been so many problems on the boat, with the flies, the toilets and so on, that now I cope by just sort of cutting myself off. I have withdrawn now, really, and am just waiting to go home.

Let me tell you about the toilets. They are, apparently, eco-friendly, as Captain McNeill, in his frequent broadcasts on Radio McNeill, never misses an opportunity to tell us. What this means in effect is that less water is used to flush them than might be the norm in their land-based cousins. The waste pipes, I believe, are narrower than those we are used to at home. All very politically correct, but when you base part of your appeal on the availability of 24-hour buffet dining, and when that buffet might well include a delicious lentil and chickpea salad ... Look, how much detail do you want me to go into? Our toilet got blocked three times in the week I was on board and according to Claire the toilets in the entertainers' quarters remain blocked five days out of seven. 'It is three days before anybody comes and unblocks them, because the passengers take priority,' she explains. 'We have only just got fans backstage and we have been asking for them for months.'

She took up some of her grievances at a crisis meeting on the ship attended by Viva's director of operations, a Russian lady called Ludmilla Koplykova – a gold medal Olympic gymnast, according to Bruce. ('I won't tell you which year but she has still got some bod on her, that girl.') 'I told Ludmilla about the flies and everything,' says Claire, 'but she started screaming at me and threatened that my complaints might stop me getting other work. But I don't care what they say about me, because when you audition, they judge you on what they see before them. '

Claire says she would work on cruise ships again – a sought-after gig for young singers and dancers despite the privations – but not for the same company. Among many complaints, she is unhappy about the public relations role into which the entertainers have been dragooned: 'We are not allowed to sit in the coffee bar between shows because that would "destroy the illusion", yet it is OK for me to be in my yellow T-shirt showing guests onto their tour buses at 7.30 in the morning. I mean, where's the logic in that?'

I am with her all the way. As a lifelong supporter of labour over management, with a fatal weakness for short, bolshy, northern women – Claire is five foot one and a half inches tall and comes from Formby on Merseyside – it was inevitable she would speak to my depths. I admire her reluctance to play up for the cameras when the TV people were on board: 'They had done some stuff with Penny about her not liking her costume and they wanted me to say something about the costumes on camera. I didn't want to, but they persisted and persisted until I did.'

Interestingly enough, despite her irritation with Penny's camera-hogging, she now speaks quite warmly of her former colleague: 'I got really friendly with her in the end. I think a lot of the ego was just insecurity.' Her recent telephone conversation with Penny may have contributed to her downbeat mood. Penny's father, a fit-looking chap in his fifties, who came to see his daughter perform on the ship, has collapsed and died suddenly at home. In a tearful conversation, Penny, still taking centre stage in the TV docusoap, and having recently appointed an agent to handle the concomitant enquiries, tells Claire she would give it all up to have her dad back. 'She's really down. I feel ever so sorry for her,' says Claire. When I ask her if it has altered her attitude to the pursuit of fame, she says:

> I want to be successful rather than famous. I would like to be like Ruthie Henshall, well respected throughout the profession but not likely to get recognized in the supermarket. My ambition is just to be happy in my professional and personal life. A lot of people in this business are just bitter and twisted.
>
> I had a friend who was in *Cats*, as Gummi Cat, and there was terrible back-stabbing and rivalries in that show, so at the end of the run she gave them a cat litter, and said, 'Here you are, shit in this.'

In fairness, the next time I see Claire she is in a sunnier mood:

> I think you caught me when I was a bit down. I have just been losing patience with the amount of time we waste messing around. I was in an Irish dance show, where we worked, worked, worked, and I much preferred that.
> Don't get me wrong. I don't regret coming on the ship. I am primarily a dancer, so I appreciate the opportunity to do some more singing. I just don't like all the shit [*sic*] that comes with it.

Claire's plan is to rent a bedsit in London and attend more auditions:

> I want to do theatre. I think I can make it now because I have had a year of making real progress, doing really well at opens [open auditions]. I have had about four recalls, so I am beginning to get known.

That's entertainment for you. In any other field of activity, auditioning and then not getting the gig would be viewed as a failure, but for Claire and hundreds of thousands like her, optimism triumphs over despair. It may not unblock toilets but it sure masks the smell.

Claire got her first taste of London bedsit life at the age of nineteen, after three years at the Elmhurst School for Performing Arts:

> It was very strict where I trained, very good for the technical side of dance, but very old-fashioned. It was like a ballet boarding school, really, and did not do anything to prepare you for what the business is all about.
>
> When I moved down to London, I took a waitressing job, and then a job in a holiday park, Great British Holidays in Clacton. This was good for me, teaching me to open up and do the kind of things you need to do to make a living in this business.

Her CV now includes a couple of holiday parks, a P&O cruise ship, and two pantos – at the Birmingham Hippodrome with Brian Conley, and *Aladdin* in Bournemouth with Jeremy Beadle, a show which was beset with technical problems, flopped horribly and got her some publicity in the *Sun*.

A lot of performers would not talk about their flops but Claire has a sense of humour about the business. That *and* a dancer's calves. An unbeatable combination, and if ever I should find myself in the position of casting anything, she will be at the top of my list. As indeed will her friend Danielle Murphy, who is twenty-two and, having not joined the ship until after the TV people had departed, and many of the teething troubles had been dealt with, is a little less world-weary than Claire. In fact, to be honest, she loves it to bits.

Toilets, schmoilets. Danielle gives every thing she does full eyes and teeth: Abba numbers, Beatles, standards, and it doesn't hurt that she has the flawless complexion and sweet smile to make Humbert Humberts of us all. No lonely bedsit for Danielle. She has remained at home in what seems to be a cosy family unit in St Ives in Cambridgeshire, and has been studying at Bodywork Dance Studios in Cambridge. Theresa, the principal of the college, has been acting as her agent and a sort of surrogate mum. 'I auditioned for this, and in the meantime two other job offers came through,' says Danielle, 'but Theresa told me not to jump at them as this would be better experience, and I am really glad I took her advice.'

Danielle is the third of four children. There is an eleven-year and a seventeen-year age gap between her and her two older siblings and she seems to have the same sunny, untroubled nature that I see in my youngest child, who also has the security of an older brother and sisters to look after her. After the *Island Escape*, Danielle breezes into pantomime: *Dick Whittington* in Chatham, playing Alice Fitzwarren, Dick's girlfriend, opposite Trevor from *EastEnders*. I wonder if her open, trusting nature is more conducive to success than Claire's slightly more suspicious battle-scarred attitude. Time will tell, I suppose. Remember their names: Danielle Murphy and Claire Phillips.

In the end, is it not just luck, anyway? If it had not been young Priscilla White taking coats in the Cavern Club all those years ago, but some other gobby Scouse teenager who could shout out a pop tune, would we have been spared decades of Cilla Black? Or does Cilla have the kind of innate ability to communicate with the hoi polloi that makes her indispensable in the modern television age? Don't ask me, I'm only the author.

I hope Danielle and Claire both achieve what they want to because they kept Martha and me and our friends Kate and Jane entertained, and knowing that backstage they did not have, in one of my late father's favourite expressions, a pot to piss in, makes their efforts seem even more admirable.

A middle-aged couple from Leicester who we spoke to over breakfast – well-dressed, tanned, silver-haired and smug, another pair who seemed to have stepped straight out of one of those pensions ads on the TV – were insistent that the shows on the *Island Escape* were 'not a patch' on those on some other cruise ships. But that kind of thing is always happening on holiday. You are constantly having these pointless conversations with people who insist on telling you about other holidays they have been on, how the food was much better, how they got two flights to Las Vegas for sixpence; if you are very lucky you can get away before they tell you how much their house is worth.

It is difficult to avoid this kind of interface on board the inaptly named *Island Escape* because the buffet dining system means shared tables, so however antisocial and miserable you have planned to be, the chances are you will find yourself cornered by someone whose reading matter seems to begin and end with the personal finance section of the *Sunday Times*.

One evening Martha and I are at the end of a table for eight, where some chap is holding court on the subject of Captain Bowie's missed stop in Malta, which he happens to know is because of a cock-up and nothing to do with the weather. 'Mind you, all the food we've been eating (ho, ho) could be slowing the ship down.' He is in his early forties, I guess, quite slim, clean-shaven, bespectacled, neat hair, and is wearing smart khaki shorts, with a crisp white polo shirt tucked into them, sports socks and a decent pair of trainers. He has the confident delivery and vowel sounds of classless, meritocratic, southern England. His normal habitat is in an office, addressing fellow middle managers. I know this before he even opens his mouth.

Sometimes, he says, he and his wife go for the waiter service, which is 'a little more convivial' but sometimes, he says, we just 'go to the buffet and mix 'n' match'. At which point I leap up, grab him by the lapels, and hold a steak knife to his throat, saying, 'You're confusing me, pal, with someone who gives a flying fuck.' Or at least I would have done if I had not been busy making notes under the table.

'I'm on my second marriage,' he says, with what seems like a degree of uncalled-for self-satisfaction. I have never heard anybody say this of himself before. Especially with the lucky second wife sitting there at the table. It is normally something other people say *about* you, when you are out of earshot. Turns out the first wife was half-Maltese so he is not sorry to have missed Malta, as he has been there before lots of times to visit the kids' grandparents. This prompts a deal of unnecessary family detail. Apparently 'gjopskl knleins wifp utkol kids'. (Have you ever tried simultaneously smiling, eating soup and scrawling in a notepad perched on your knee under the table?)

His children, I gathered, are in Aberdeen with wife number one. Wife number two looks exactly like him, except a little chubbier, and wearing women's clothing. She is bespectacled, well scrubbed and shiny, and so on – think a young Pam Ayres without the accent – and is terribly impressed with him, gazing lovingly at him as he speaks, drinking in every word, and pretending not to notice that he is talking bollocks. She is not at all concerned by his public airing of the family linen.

The two are on honeymoon, believe it or not, which might account for her eager beaver attitude. They work together, unsurprisingly – guess where? – in an insurance office in Kent, in wills and estates, planning and trusts. He likes working in that field 'because it's people'. Another bloody people person.

These, then, are the voyages of the *Island Escape*. Palma, to Naples, Livorno, Toulon, Mahon, Palma again, eating, drinking, Rome, Nice, Tunis, eating, drinking, eating, and back to Palma once more, until the last dregs of Mediterranean summer have been drained; and then some proper old-fashioned ocean-going, to Brazil, where the ship will winter.

Bruce and his entertainment team all leave the ship before it crosses the Atlantic and go their separate ways, to their bedsits, auditions, and in some cases other ships. A different company is providing the shows for the Brazilian cruisers, who tend to be younger and with more of a capacity for livin' la vida loca. For one thing, when the ship is in port, they prefer to stay on board and party rather than spend the time in a frenzy of sightseeing.

Maybe they are more comfortable than us with the inescapable truth that cruising is a glorious waste of time, nothing more, nothing less. All that seafaring expertise and a crew from 32 different countries slaving away on subsistence wages, so that I, a bunch of retired people and a honeymooning chartered accountant and his wife from Worthing can drink our vodka and tonics off the coast of Sicily.

Frankly, I find all holidays more or less a waste of time, which is probably not ideal for someone who earns part of his living as a travel writer. Then again, the fact that I am not slack-jawed in awestruck wonder at the Taj Mahal or the Grand Canyon maybe gives my work a different focus. If you need someone to keep an eye on the snack-sellers and the tourists' questionable leisurewear in the face of the Wonders of the World, I may be your guy. I am not saying I don't enjoy having the time to read a novel, and the opportunity to drink my coffee in a different place, preferably somewhere where the sun is shining, but beyond that I fail to see the point of holidays. On the *Island Escape*, though, there is a point. I am collecting material.

On Friday night, after we leave Naples, the show in the Ocean Theatre is stand-up comedy from guest artist Gerry Graham, a full-time professional comedian, who has the audience eating out of his hand with venerable material that must have seen action in working men's clubs the length and breadth of Britain. I mean, 'Goldberg dead: Volvo for sale.' Is there anyone in Britain who has not heard that joke a hundred times? 'I think they're putting female hormones in the beer. After six pints I can't drive and I start talking bollocks.' Nothing for me to steal there. Gerry has a box of wigs and stuff and does a few impersonations in the style of the old TV show *Who Do You Do?* He puts on a curly wig and pretends to be a West Indian for a couple of gags. Honest.

While not for a second wishing to impugn Gerry's professionalism – he tells a gag as well as anyone I came across on my travels – I have to report the reaction of my new friend Jane. I have never met anyone who laughs more readily than she does. Example one: Kate and Jane are trying to persuade me to enter Island Star, the ship's own version of TV's Pop Idol contest. 'But,' I protested, 'I can't remember the words of any song.' 'Don't worry,' says Kate. 'There are people on this boat who can't even remember their names, let alone the words to a song' A twenty-three-second uninterrupted giggle, followed by some gasping for breath. Example two: I leave my shorts out on my balcony to dry and at the height of the storm they are blown into the sea. 'You mean there's some poor old trout tangled up in your shorts?' says Kate. 'Not for the first time,' is my predictable response. Paramedics are called in to revive Jane, who is helpless in paroxysms of mirth. And so it went. She giggled constantly throughout the cruise. In fact, the only time she stopped laughing all week was during Gerry Graham's act.

Gerry is fifty-two, but looks younger. He has that seventies northern club entertainer look, unfashionable in some non-specific way. When I see him a few days after his gig at the seventies disco around the pool on the top deck, he is unmistakable as the stand-up comic: standing alone, miserable, as if his toilet has been blocked for the last six days, and rather morosely eyeing up the ladies. I have found that if you ever see anybody who actually looks cheery like a comedian should, they will almost certainly turn out to be a chartered accountant.

The cruise ships have been good for Gerry. He has been doing them for twenty-odd years and knows exactly what is required. Before he found he could tell a gag he was in pop groups, his shining moment being when he played guitar in the sixties band Love Affair, who had a big hit with 'Everlasting Love'. When the seventies came in he diversified into the style of comedy popular in that era – and judging by the response in the Ocean Theatre still with its supporters today. Good luck to him, I say. As I am about to find, keeping a room full of people laughing is no easy business.

For myself, I would sooner spend half an hour buffing my fingernails than watch his act again but he has carved out a niche for himself and the tour operators know he is a reliable act. A few hundred quid and a free holiday is a good deal for Gerry for very little work. Alongside some corporate gigs and club work, the cruise ships have helped finance a nice house in Derbyshire with several standard lamps, and a college education for his kids.

Gerry's act chimes in with the innate conservatism of cruise ship entertainment. It is as if people want to visit strange places in far-off lands but to have a comfort blanket waiting in the ship's theatre. The names of the acts performing on some of the ships will be familiar to you from TV in the seventies – Norman Collier, Bernie Clifton, those sort of people – and they all do similar material. Go on enough cruises, and you will almost certainly hear the following joke: 'I bought my wife a pair of tortoiseshell shoes. They looked great but it took her two hours to walk out of the shop.'

For performers who would otherwise reside in the file marked 'Where Are They Now?' the ships have been an unexpected bonus. And for the young girls and boys who sing and dance they are an invaluable stepping stone between holiday camp work and theatres, with the added incentive of the possibility of discovery by reality TV, which seems to spend much of its time these days following British holidaymakers abroad.

Were I not writing a book on the subject, it is unlikely I should have gone to see any of their shows, but I am glad I did. Maybe it is because my fifteen-year-old daughter is in a youth theatre group and is currently driving us mad rehearsing her part in *Fame* that I empathize with the young performers. Maybe it is because their youth and enthusiasm is such a refreshing contrast to the cynicism of a hack like Gerry Graham, and my own, of course. Or maybe there is something rather splendid about the way they bend their youth, beauty and energy to the entertainment of middle-class, middle-aged, middle England and in the process keeping dozens of ships afloat and hundreds of people in work.

It's a rotten job but someone has to do it.

8

SPICE OF LIFE

Of all the ridiculous things, how about this? It is a Thursday evening in late November and I am in an upmarket curry restaurant in the City of London, where a man is farting popular tunes for an audience of insurance brokers and oil industry bigwigs. He is making rather a good stab at the Spice Girls' debut hit, 'Wannabe', reworked as a duet for mouth and bottom: 'I'll tell you what I want, what I really really want, I wanna (fart), I wanna (fart), I wanna ziggafarta, ziggafarta ...' (and so on, repeat till fade).

Mr Methane is to the best of my knowledge the only performer in the world making a living out of flatulism, or 'controlled anal voicing', as he rather quaintly puts it. Quite a good living, too. Those lads – and I mean lads – who work in the cut-throat world of high finance like to show they have a sense of humour, and being unable or unwilling to put their mobile phones down long enough to think of their own material, will demonstrate this humorous hinterland by booking acts like Mr Methane for office functions.

This is what is known as corporate work, highly sought after by entertainers at all levels of the business, not particularly because of a desire to oil the wheels of commerce and industry, nor to lighten the load of those who toil to keep Britain at the forefront of world trade, but because where fees are normally negotiated in hundreds, for corporate work you start in the thousands.

Since September 2001 and the terrorist attack on the World Trade Center in New York these kind of bookings have tapered off for Mr Methane:

Two reasons really. A lot of people with connections to the City of London died in the attacks, so many

Christmas parties and so on were cancelled altogether, and where they were held they were low-key affairs. In the circumstances, I think a display of comedy farting would have been considered in rather bad taste.

Then there was the recession that came about partly in the aftermath of the attacks, which meant the money just wasn't there to book people like me. What used to happen was, you would perform at one City function and someone from another firm would see you there and book you for his firm's do as well. But if you are not being seen at all you miss out on that kind of booking.

Mr M explains this to me in an empty side room at Café Spice Namaste, which is in a converted old chapel or some such, and is clearly a cut above the dismal-looking curry houses plying their trade nearby, in amongst the corporate concrete just north of the Tower of London. He talks while changing into his superhero outfit: a green Lycra body suit with a big purple 'M' on the front, and a pair of bright purple crimplene shorts, which he puts on over the Lycra, ready for the big reveal at the climax of his act.

One year on from the World Trade Center outrage, corporate work has been slow to pick up, he tells me. 'It's bizarre really,' he says. 'There's this chap with a beard sitting in a cave somewhere, planning his campaign of terror, not realizing for one moment the damaging effect it might have on the comedy farting business.' He makes this point with deadpan solemnity. What makes his act funny is his absolute seriousness at all times. He always begins by explaining to his audience the mechanics of controlled anal voicing, which is a kind of yogic thing.

For people of a certain age, his flat northern vowels as he runs through the principles of sphincter control, and details his method of taking in and expelling air through the anus, will be reminiscent of the sixties 'TV personality' Farmer Ted Moult, explaining the benefits of double glazing. It helps that he is a bit of a trainspotter, anyway. Long before there was a Mr Methane, there was a Paul Oldfield, who left school at eighteen to work on the railways. He had discovered his unique gift a few years previously when, encouraged by an elder sister, who was a yoga enthusiast, he adopted the lotus position and inadvertently found both ends of the young Oldfield able to inhale and exhale.

The comic possibilities of this skill were not lost on the fifth-form boys at Ryles Park County High School in Macclesfield and young Paul was soon encouraged into his first public performance: 20 rapid-fire rasping farts in under a minute in the squash courts during the lunch break. Although he performed variations on this act for appreciative school audiences on a fairly regular basis, there was no suggestion at this stage that a career as a full-time flatulist beckoned, so when he left school he took a proper job in an industry that interested him, the railways.

He takes up the story on his website, www.mrmethane.com:

I was on a course, learning the finer points of the Brush Type 4 Locomotive, latterly referred to as a Class 47. This is a 2580hp, Mixed Traffic, Diesel Electric Locomotive of 1960's vintage. The course was thorough and comprehensive with schematic diagrams of all the locomotive's component parts and systems.

We had just broken off for a quick cup of tea mid-way through the fuel system. I think we'd just had an overspeed situation and the fuel rack had moved the helix into a no fuel position causing the engine to shut down, or something like that. Whatever, I remember feeling that I had not had so much fun since the last time I cleaned the oven.

With that in mind I decided to inject a little humour into the proceedings with my long forgotten – but thankfully just remembered – trouser trumpet. Needless to say, it was a runaway sensation and the source of much needed light relief among the group on that day. More significantly, word of my ability went before me around the national railway system and 'Lay Over' periods at far flung mess rooms would result in requests for a quick tune on my anal organ from fellow traincrews.

This is more or less how Mr M talks all the time. Dry, I think, is the word. His habit of peppering his conversation with unnecessary tangential detail is quite charming but makes him a bugger to interview. He is not a man to call a spade a spade. He is a man more likely to call it the Broomfield tungsten-coated DB7 garden and domestic.

When I make what I fondly imagine will be a quick check call to find out what material his shorts are made from (I know this is the kind of detail you crave), he tells me it needs to be a weave wide enough to accommodate his talcum powder routine, when he powders his bottom cheeks and then proceeds to parp the powder into the air in comic little puffs, as a kind of visual representation of the fart. 'It's that stuff they use quite a lot in the theatre. What's it called? crimplene, I think. Or is it Crimp'o'lene, like Windolene. You're probably going to have to check it on the internet, or somewhere.'

Somehow we move on from that to his nephew, who plays in a soul band, but occasionally does some highly paid guest spots with a band called the Jamm, a 'tribute', it will hardly startle you to learn, to the Jam. 'The lead singer is going out with Paul Weller's ex-girlfriend,' he says. 'Really. I mean, does that not strike you as strange? I mean, I don't think I could handle that. You can take a tribute too far.' I agree there is probably an interesting story to be written about that, or at the very least a short afternoon play on Radio 4. For the moment, though, the priority is making sense of Mr Methane's own story.

His bottom has been his sole source of income for the past 11 years. As far as he knows, he has no competition in the commercial farting field, although that isn't to say other people couldn't do it. Some years ago Channel 5, in keeping with its reputation as a market leader in the field of factual television, commissioned an in-depth investigation into Mr Methane's act.

Dr Peter Whorwell, an internationally renowned bowel specialist from Withington Hospital in Manchester, explained how, by raising the diaphragm, Mr M would suck air into the colon through an open sphincter, then close the sphincter before discharging the air, causing the farting noises, in much the same way as a child might make a funny noise by letting air gradually out of a balloon. By moving the buttock cheeks, the pitch and tone of the fart is altered. 'The programme was never transmitted,' Paul tells me mournfully. Too many sphincters, I expect, even for Channel 5.

Mr M's bottom has fallen foul of the censor's blue pencil on a number of occasions (I was trying to avoid any *double entendres* – honest – but I feel the spirit of the late Kenneth Williams guiding my hand. I believe there may even have been a mention of hinterland earlier).

A barnstorming performance on the *Frank Skinner Show*, where the comedian joined him for a rendition of 'Da Doo Ron Ron', was felt to be a little edgy for the BBC audience, as was his adaptation of 'Silent Night' for the *Mark Radcliffe Show* on Radio 1. 'Two weeks before the Skinner show I performed at a private party for the BBC's head of light entertainment,' Paul tells me, 'and went down a storm. That's an example of double standards for you.'

In discussing Mr Methane it is impossible to avoid mention of the French variety artiste Joseph Pujol (1857–1945), better known as Le Pétomane, whose act broke box office records at theatres throughout Paris between 1892 and 1914, and whose *modus operandi* was identical to his. Le Pétomane is probably best known through a short film made in 1979, in which he was impersonated by the excellent Leonard Rossiter, working from a very witty script written by Hancock writers Ray Galton and Alan Simpson.

Like Mr M, Le Pétomane would extinguish candles and produce a variety of noises and tunes, using his rear end in the particular way outlined by Dr Worrall. But between Le Pétomane and Mr M, nobody. Two world wars and numerous royal variety shows, yet no candidate stepped forward to exploit the commercial potential of anally exhaled wind. Mr M has looked into it:

There is a book, now out of print, called *Fireproof Pigs and Flameproof Women,* in which there is mention of a chap in Japan in a business suit firing darts with his bottom into a dartboard but I've never been able to find out any more about his act.

Also, there was an article in the *Stage* years ago about a guy called Gaseous Gary. He was a milkman, who apparently used to break wind in various Mediterranean resorts for the entertainment of holidaymakers but there's no mention of him on the net. In fact, it's impossible to find anyone who has actually ever seen Gaseous Gary.

Mr M, you will have gathered, has a lively interest in the theory as well as the practice of his art. His website includes a section on the literature of farting, which turns out to be quite a fertile area of cultural histories, cartoon books and so on. His particular recommendation is a biography of Le Pétomane by Jean Nohain and F Caradec. He writes: 'If you only buy one book about farting, then it should be this one!!!' I have to say that is one more farting book than I had considered buying. In fact, I should probably not even have been discussing the subject, had the worldwide recession in the comedy farting industry not brought Mr M and me together.

Let me explain: the producers of *Showcall* (the publication that is the inevitable starting point for all my journeys into the outer reaches of show business) hold an annual showcase allowing the artistes featured in their directory to perform a version of their act before interested parties – managers, agents, bookers from cruise ships, holiday camps and so on.

Over five days in Leicestershire in early November, 155 acts perform. It is a kind of alternative Edinburgh Festival, although here you will not find any thrusting young TV producers, eating escalope of line-caught sea bass on a ragout of linguini, while seeking out hot new talent, and you will scour in vain the arts pages of the *Guardian* looking for reviews.

Mr Methane, whom I had originally spotted in *Showcall*, has not done the showcase for ten years but the shortfall in bookings from the financial community means he is back seeking alternative areas of employment, although – call me old-fashioned – I do not see him doing cruise ships.

The showcase is held at Barry Young's Stardust in Coalville, Leicestershire, not a place with which I am too familiar. All I know about Coalville is that my friend Tina Baker, a regular broadcaster on breakfast television, was born there. I remember her telling me a story some years ago about how she went for a job with a small independent TV company making hard-line feminist programmes for Channel 4, in the channel's early days when it did that kind of stuff. 'They were happy enough with my TV experience,' Tina told me, 'but they said what they were really looking for was a woman from a disadvantaged background, maybe an Asian single parent, or a disabled woman. I told them, "I'm from bloody Coalville. How disadvantaged do you want?"'

Harsh, I think. It is not the most inspiring place in the world but you could find worse. If you looked really hard. When I tell Tina of my plans to spend a few days there watching the acts, she expresses deep sympathy, but that's provincials who settle in London for you. They end up thinking the centre of the universe is Crouch bloody End. Far from it. Leicestershire is at the heart of England, both literally and metaphorically. If Kent, with its apples and hops and general greenery, is the Garden of England, then Leicester is the Pantry of England.

Apart from a few coal mines, now obsolete or turned into 'heritage sites', to the northwest – hence Coalville – the county is largely agricultural. It is the home of two famous English food products: the Melton Mowbray pork pie and Stilton cheese, the kind of traditional high cholesterol comfort food Pip sneaks out for Magwitch in *Great Expectations*, which I grant you was set nowhere near Leicestershire, but you get the point. There is something quintessentially English, Dickensian even, about the place.

A new museum planned for the county will be dedicated – I am not making this up – to pork pies and fox-hunting. The ever so English place names you see as you leave the M1 tell their own story: Newbold Verdon, Woodhouse Eaves, Kirby Muxloe, the names of baritone-voiced actors in touring theatre companies, with messy private lives, and a middle-of-the-afternoon thirst.

As I leave the motorway on the way to Barry Young's Stardust – one exit too early to make things interesting for myself – it occurs to me that in several thousand trips up and down the M1, only twice previously have I ever departed this great thrusting arterial route (copyright: A Peebles) in Leicestershire; once to watch West Ham in the seventies at Filbert Street, Leicester City's old ground, a ramshackle collection of huts quite unlike any other in the league, and quite threatening (as many grounds were in those days), and once to abandon my broken-down car in a place called Shepshed.

I sometimes feel nostalgic for the days when cars used to break down. When I first started work as a reporter, I drove a succession of fairly hopeless vehicles that from November to March more or less pleased themselves whether they started or not. Fortunately, I lived in Bristol at the time, and was able to rent bedsits in places like Clifton, Redland and Bishopston, where you could enjoy a thrilling freewheel downhill in the hope that you might be able to bump-start the blighter before reaching town.

When you were stuck at the side of the road with a recalcitrant vehicle, though, you would form new friendships, or at least casual acquaintanceships as men – proper men who carried things like maps and a spare tyre in their car, and propelling pencils in their inside pocket – would stop to peer inside your engine and offer free advice and sometimes a squirt of WD40, whatever that is.

I was once stuck at the side of the road with an old Mini for two hours. Some chap got out his jump leads and tried to start it off his battery, another took the distributor cap off and dried it out inside, but the thing would not go, so mostly there was an awful lot of head-scratching, tutting and tooth-sucking. As afternoon turned into evening the tooth-suckers, some of whom had been with me from the start, and I evolved into a little all-male community. Some of the chaps, I think, bought property in the area and telephoned wives and loved ones to say, in the style of Gene Pitney in '24 Hours From Tulsa', that they wouldn't be home any more. A shop selling exclusively male items, like aftershave, power screwdrivers and progressive rock albums, opened up in the area and made a killing.

One comment I shall never forget. A chap, hurrying past on his way to the bus, but who nevertheless felt obliged to exercise his franchise, said, 'Maybe your bendix has jammed.' To this day I have no idea who or what a bendix is and what part it might play in the functioning of a 1969 Mini but I introduce the word into conversation whenever possible.

Given that most cars these days are free of bendix problems, they will mostly follow my lead and merely pass through

Leicestershire on their way either up or down the M1. It is, after all, not the North, it is not London, it is not even the Midlands, really. That is not to say the place does not have its interesting points. It is the home of the Quorn, the biggest fox hunt in the world, as mentioned in the books of the cherishable P G Wodehouse; also of Rosemary Conley, millionairess and inventor of the hip and thigh diet, which I believe requires adherents to eat no part of any animal other than hips and thighs.

According to the council's promotions department, Leicester is 'a city of contrasts', which comes as no big surprise. Is there a city in the world that isn't a city of bloody contrasts? What they mean, I think, is that this traditional English market town – biggest outdoor market in Europe, apparently – is ethnically diverse, thanks, I suspect, to Leicester's traditional industries of hosiery and footwear, now, of course in decline and certainly no longer dependent on floods of cheap labour from overseas.

Shoes and socks have been replaced in the local economy by potato crisps. (There is a point to be made here about modern life, I expect, but I shall leave it to you. I merely say, 'Humph'.) Walkers and Golden Wonder, who between them make pretty well every damned crisp we eat – and I include tortilla chips, kettle chips and hip and thigh flavoured corn fries in that – are both based in Leicester. Walkers, in fact, are a big deal in Leicester. At huge cost they moved the football team out of its higgledy-piggledy old ground to the brand new Walkers Stadium and they pay local football hero Gary Lineker around half a million pounds to advertise their crisps on TV.

Lineker gets pride of place on the council's list of famous people from Leicester. In fact, a friend of mine who worked for the local evening paper, the Leicester *Mercury* – a paper which has somehow managed to retain a masthead that looks like it belongs in the thirties – tells me that in the soccer star's early days each new success was marked by a reporter being despatched to Leicester market to interview his father, Barry Lineker, at the family's fruit and veg stall.

To underline the relative lack of sophistication of the local press, she tells me also that the *Mercury* once had a story on its front page headlined 'Melton Pensioner Injured in Snatch'.

If that headline did appear – and journalists are occasionally inclined to exaggerate such solecisms – I think it is rather encouraging, since it proves there is at least one corner of England where the argot of the New York streets has still not penetrated.

Although there is a hotel in Coalville, it is full, presumably because of the showcase, and the internet suggests the Smisby Manor Hotel in Smisby village, about seven miles away. It is not a manor in the sense of a country hotel run by a multinational leisure combine, featuring a heated swimming pool, shiatsu massage and in-house manicurist, nor is it one bought by a couple of posh Londoners offering gourmet dinners and four-poster beds. This is a manor in the sense of a collection of old farm buildings permanently in need of repairs, owned by a middle-aged local chap, who manages to keep cheerful despite seemingly running the place single-handed.

To complete the retro feel of the room, the TV has an indoor aerial, one of those two-pronged affairs I haven't seen for years, the kind you put on your head and say, 'I am from the planet Tharg ... Take me to your leader ... Nyip, nyip, nyip.' Unusually, a couple of the channels are working perfectly well, even without my standing behind the TV and thrusting the space helmet two feet into the air, as I had to to receive any coverage at all of the 1972 European Cup Final.

Don't ask me why I am watching the TV. At home I would never switch it on for the evening news but in hotel rooms it is almost always the first thing I do, even before checking out the free biscuits. I like to know in which fine hotels CNN is available. None of that, of course, in the Smisby Manor. Just the local news. Trading standards officers are warning people to watch out for bootleg whisky being flogged in Wolverhampton. They say it can cause retching or even blindness. Well, nothing is without risk, I suppose.

Nick Owen, who used to be a famous national TV personality, is presenting the local news show. Now there is a lesson for some of the performers I am about to see, hoping to make it big in the business. One minute it is glittering awards dinners at the Park Lane Hilton, a couple of years down the line you are warning people to watch out for cheap grog in Wolverhampton.

I am unable to find Barry Young's Stardust, and Coalville's main street seems entirely bereft of people to ask – post-nuclear bereft in the way small towns in England are at the *Coronation Street* hour – so I pop into the pizza place, where the chap kindly draws a map for me. The Stardust, it transpires, is not in Coalville at all, but at a place called Bardon, just off the next roundabout up the road.

Approaching the club is like stepping back two decades. It is an aircraft hangar of a place in a huge car park. There used to be lots of venues like the Stardust, especially in the North, where a thousand people a night could enjoy chicken and chips, pints of lager (and a Babycham for the little lady), while watching the biggest names in showbiz: Shirley Bassey, Louis Armstrong, Tom Jones, names of that calibre. But somehow, to paraphrase Gloria Swanson in *Sunset Boulevard*, showbiz got small. The big entertainers did not go away, but their fees became prohibitive and the performers that could be booked were just not special enough for Northerners to get all dressed up for. Bobby Davro is no Satchmo. So it was something of an act of faith 14 years ago when Barry Young, a former dancer – Barry Young and Les Girls, you may have seen them in summer season on the Isle of Man back in the seventies – plunged £1.8 million into this custom-built monster of a cabaret theatre on some spare land between the A50 and junction 22 of the M1.

I had telephoned the club a few days earlier to ask if Barry would object to being interviewed and having his picture taken. A cheerful local-sounding lady I later identified as Mandy Loweth, in charge of reception and bookings, laughed heartily at this suggestion, from which I deduced that Barry was not shy of publicity. This much becomes apparent on stepping into the reception area, the walls of which are decorated with group photographs of big nights in the Stardust's history, in most of which a smiling Barry takes centre stage among the dignitaries and minor show-business personalities. Mandy, a former dancer herself, who now 'teaches a little', had laughed even more heartily when I had asked her over the phone if she and Barry were an item at all.

Chatting to Barry, who is quite charming, I discover the only woman he talks about is his late mother. He is a diminutive chap, about five foot six inches tall, and if he weren't a former dancer you would put him down as an ex-jockey, or even a former flyweight boxer, because his face looks a little battered, with red puffy areas around the eyes. All this is topped off with a fairly impressive silver thatch coordinating with his dark suit and silver tie.

Barry seems quite frail, and when he totters onto the stage to take a bow at the end of the evening, you fear a blast on the snare drum could easily knock him over. He is well into his sixties, I should say. If he were not Mr Showbiz, he would be an old age pensioner, sitting in bus shelters moaning about the weather or asylum seekers. Forever young. That is the secret of show business.

We sit in his little office, a jumble of papers, and on the wall a picture of a long ago beauty queen with her sash and tiara. The scene is familiar from a hundred television dramas about small-time entertainment. He tells me about his career:

> I started dancing when I was about seven. I was lucky enough to be working when all the theatres were still open. You could work 52 weeks of the year in variety and revue. Then one day I just said I didn't want to go around dancing any more. I had just done 16 weeks on the Isle of Man with Les Girls. It was raining all the time, I got bronchitis because of the damp and I had to work through it. That was 21 years ago. I was in my forties when I quit and was probably ready to try something else, anyway.

He came back home and bought a small hotel 'just over the other side of the forest', where he introduced a floor show in the ballroom, which proved a roaring success. 'Two shows a night. It was a 350-seater, so we soon outgrew it.' Which is why he started building Barry Young's Stardust. It took ten months to complete, during which time his mother, who looms large in all his conversations, was diagnosed with a terminal disease. But she lived to see the opening night – and here he goes a little dewy-eyed – starring 'my dear friend Larry Grayson'.

His mission is to bring a little bit of Las Vegas to

Leicestershire. He always employs a troupe of dancers and the large stage is designed to accommodate them. The centre part of the stage drops down 20 feet, and there are 'dancing waters and all sorts'. But the *Showcall* showcase is not Barry's gig. The *Stage* newspaper, more rooted in the realities of today's entertainment business, is in charge. The dancing waters will not be needed.

A Basil Fawlty lookalike meets and greets, setting the tone for three days – I couldn't manage the full five – of tribute acts, tributes to tributes and acts that looked like they might have been tributes if it were a little clearer to whom or what their tribute was intended. I ask Marcus Collingbourne, the *Stage*'s events manager, a chap with big glasses and a brisk, rather self-important manner, what the performers hoped to get out of their showcase. 'Forty-five per cent of them are acts you book direct. Obviously, they have their advert in *Showcall* but by doing the showcase they can get onto the books of agencies and get more work,' says Marcus, who for some reason is wearing a long black frockcoat, an item of clothing more suited to a spaghetti western than Wednesday afternoon at a cabaret club in Leicestershire.

There's another secret of show business. You can wear the most ridiculous clothes and nobody raises an eyebrow.

Marcus points to successes from previous *Showcall* showcases: 'Lee Evans did a showcase and Chris Bylett, a ventriloquist who is here tonight, got a part in *Casualty*, as a ventriloquist. Also, when the James Whale TV show was on, 70 per cent of the guests came from *Showcall*.' Ah yes, but Whale was taking the piss. It seems to me that the immediate aim of many of the acts is to get off the dreaded working men's club treadmill and get some work at Haven Holiday parks, or even better, some corporate gigs.

About halfway through my stint watching these acts, I am reminded of a P G Wodehouse story, in which Jeeves chooses to sing Al Jolson's sentimental song 'Climb up on my knee sonny boy' at a social evening for deprived youngsters in the East End, where his fiancée has persuaded him to appear. For reasons which escape me – probably because Jeeves was trying to extricate the young master from the unsuitable engagement –

several of the acts preceding Wooster decide to perform this same song. When the piano picks out the opening bars once more, and Wooster, who is supposed to be the headline act, opens his mouth, there is uproar. He is pelted with fruit. Jeeves observes, with typical Wodehousian understatement, something like: 'I got the impression, sir, that the audience had lost its appetite for that particular song.' Which is exactly how I felt about Shania Twain's 'Man I Feel Like a Woman' (four times), the O'Jays' 'Love Train' (four times), that Kylie Minogue thing about spinning around (lost count) and Dusty's 'You Don't Have to Say You Love Me' (three times).

A typical act was Sammi Jaye, no worse nor better than many others, but who had the misfortune to show up late in the day when I was in fruit-hurling mood. Like most of the acts, she sang to backing tapes, despite the presence of a perfectly acceptable house band. The tape began in traditional manner with a voice intoning, 'Layzengenmen, Sammi Jaye *is* Kylie Minogue', prompting the rather uncharitable response, 'No she's not. She's some skinny bird from Rotherham.'

I ask a chap sitting at my table, a booker, if he does not feel the tribute act business is getting out of hand. He does. There is apparently a Beatles copy with just two members in it and there's a Robbie Williams tribute that has the chutzpah to put on its publicity 'Accept No Imitations'. Er, hang on a minute.

You can imagine what a breath of fresh air Mr Methane was (yes, yes, I know) in amongst all this Minoguery and Shania nonsense. I am inclined to say – oh, what the hell, I'll say it – he blew me away. It was the dry way with patter and his almost anti-showbiz manner more than anything he did with his bottom that impressed me.

Tufty Gordon, who has hosted the showcase for the last ten years, was the other star. Clearly in the veteran stage of his career, he ambles onto the stage after each act, and helps them tout for work. So, an act called Antonius and the Driftettes, a solo singer with a couple of girls indistinguishable from any number of other soft soul outfits, is encouraged to point out what a fine booking it would be 'for people who can't afford all the Drifters', by which he means one of the fully staffed Drifters tribute acts.

These short conversations between Tufty and the would-be stars are often less to do with the performance than the performer's capacity to drive around the country to all the bookings they hoped they were going to get.

Steve Barclay, a cheeky chappy comedian who performed a song containing the line 'I've burnt out three Ford Sierras searching for fame' was clearly something of a veteran of both show business and driving from one end of the country to the other. He looked mid-forties, possibly fifty. According to the review in the *Stage*, Steve 'will pardon us for suggesting that he is a seasoned trouper'. Why should that be considered a disadvantage? Steve has used his years doing variety, summer shows and pantomime to develop a showbizzy walk, which is more than some of the younger acts had.

It is a big stage at Barry Young's Stardust for just one chap but Steve made use of it, strolling around it in his comedy half-red, half-yellow, suit – a kind of jaunty roll – delivering ancient one-liners with confidence and panache:

I got this suit from a catalogue ... hell of a shock when it arrived ... I'd ordered a greenhouse.
My underpants are from Tupperware ... doesn't do anything for you ... but keeps everything fresh.
The band, layzegenmen, the band ... keyboard player out of *Baywatch* ... drummer out of *Crimewatch*.
My uncle's so unlucky, he bought a box of After Eight, then died at half past seven ...

And so on. Steve even reprised a line I had not heard since Benidorm. As I took a snap, he said, 'No photographs please for security reasons. Social Security.' And he rounded it all off by getting his ukulele out and doing a George Formby number. How seasoned can you get?

Like Mr Methane, Steve was doing the showcase, he told Tufty, because he was looking for new avenues of employment. 'So, you're looking for nice quality work,' said Tufty, 'and you've got the car, haven't you? You've got the car, and you will travel?' He's got the car all right. The Toyota Wotsit, with the comedy suit in one of those waterproof zip-up suit carriers draped over the back seats, and on the front seat the remains of a chicken and stuffing sandwich in its triangular plastic packet, and the wrapper from a king-size chunky Kit Kat.

When there is a lull in the proceedings, Tufty, a short, balding chap with the air of having been there and done it many times before, grabs his clarinet and rips the place apart with a medley of pub stompers like 'Roll Out the Barrel', which I have never heard on a clarinet before and which must require some heavy-duty tonguing, and then takes the mickey mercilessly out of Acker Bilk's 'Stranger on the Shore'. He performs with the house band, of course, gently sending them up, and the old-time managers and agents in the room love it. It is show business before it went all Pop Idols.

I reckon I saw about 50 acts in all. The showcases went on from about one in the afternoon till around midnight each day with a break for what we in the North call tea. I have pages of notes covering the acts I saw at Barry Young's Stardust, from which it would be nice to give you something in the nature of a tip for the top, but no-one bar Mr Methane really inspired me. There were lots of female vocalists, some younger than others, some prettier. Next to one name I have written, 'Walks like a prize-fighter.' A little unfair, possibly, but those would be the kind of judgements my fellow audience members – gimlet-eyed agents and bookers looking for a meal ticket – would have been making, too.

Roger Davis, my own showbiz representative, is not at the showcase, having dismissed it as 'a piss-up for agents', although there is evidence that a fair amount of business is being done between pints. Dean Treleaven, who seems younger and certainly more eager than some of his fellow impresarios, is up in Leicestershire for the whole week representing his firm, Starlite Nights and Productions, from Fairhaven in Hampshire. Within 20 minutes of arriving, he took on an act, he tells me.

For some, finding an agency will be a career move, a step towards the fame and fortune they crave. For others – the more experienced acts – the contacts they make at the showcase are merely a means towards staying in a business that offers unique opportunities to sample motorway cuisine, and happens to be more fun than being a cost accountant.

As Ricky Lavazza, a young crooner, who sang Tom Jones's 'Sex Bomb' and a song from *Les Misérables*, told Tufty: 'I am not bothered where I go. I just want to get more work in the book.' 'I like your honesty,' said Tufty, momentarily struggling to come to terms with a quality that is not altogether customary in our business – especially not when you are looking for work. Even for realists like Ricky, though, there is the belief that the next time the phone rings it could be the big one. In this business hope only stops springing eternal about 10 to 15 minutes after the death certificate has been issued.

Years ago, when I was a radio reporter, I worked alongside someone who progressed quickly onto local TV, did loads of stuff on screen and appeared to be making something of a local name for himself. Then one day he gave it all up 'because there was no future in it'. He went back to college instead and got a law degree, became a successful lawyer, a partner in his firm, invested in property, and is now a millionaire who could retire tomorrow if he wanted.

Tuh! The fool. The complete fool. Does he ever get asked for his autograph? Does he ever open a school fête? No. And when he wakes up tomorrow, what will he be? The same boring old millionaire. 'Because there is no future in it' is not a concept that show business people are overly familiar with. If it were, we should all have been away from the showcase and back on the motorway by Tuesday afternoon.

I take up this prickly topic, the future and all that, with Mr Methane as, with the greatest respect in the world, I do not see him farting into his fifties. 'I am thirty-six now,' he tells me, 'although my showbiz age is only thirty. I don't think it matters myself, but Barry, my manager, reckons everybody in the business knocks a few years off. I think it is probably more important if you are a singer.' Good point. We like to think of our love songs being issued from a moist young mouth, whereas with Mr M's music issuing from where it does, well, I think you know where I'm heading …

This manager, by the way, so wise in the wiles of show business, is Barry Barlow, an old rock 'n' roller, who runs a recording studio in Henley-on-Thames. He has produced three Mr Methane CDs, plus he runs his very entertaining website, full of moving pictures and downloadable bottom noises. 'We get around 3,000 visitors a week from all over the world,' he tells me. 'Flatulence is very much an international language.' He also tells me the anal voicing appeals 'across all stratas of society. We have done gigs for royalty but we had to sign letters of confidentiality. I can't tell you which royals, but you will know them.' As I don't know any royals I assume he means I will know *of* them. We are probably talking middle-ranking members of the family, the younger ones, although I rather like the thought of the late Queen Mother in the front row, occupying one of what Mr M insists on calling 'the ringside seats'.

Barry first met Mr M eight years ago. 'I was managing a band – Kiss of the Gypsy, they were called, they had a record deal with Atlantic – and I booked him in for a private show. We got a room in St David's Hall, Cardiff, and he did the gig, which went really well, and then asked me to help him find work.' Despite his laid-back rock 'n' roll lifestyle – he is a former drummer – Barry has been quite successful in managing Mr M's career. As well as the corporate work, there have been tours of America. 'He's been on Howard Stern four times. Stern thinks he's a god,' Barry tells me. 'The Americans love his accent. They think he sounds like the Beatles.' There certainly is a touch of Lennon, or Ringo maybe, about Mr M's laconic delivery.

When I speak to Barry, he and his protégé are about to leave for Phoenix, Arizona, for two shows at a theatre called the Improv, sponsored by a radio station on which Mr M is a regular guest. The booking later falls through, which is a shame as I thought I might skip Leicester and join them in Phoenix instead. Still, none of this is important when we have Mr M's future to consider. I am actually quite good at giving people career advice, which is ironic, as I am utterly hopeless at managing my own. To Mr M I suggest he gradually increases the ratio of patter to farting, until eventually he can pretty well give an after-dinner speech about his life as a professional flatulist, rounding it off with a demonstration if required.

He is certainly funny enough when he talks about himself. He lives with his eighty-two-year-old father, just the two of them, a life he describes as a bit like Steptoe and Son, describing the old man, with no little affection, as 'manipulative'. On the occasion of one of my phone calls he is cooking chops for the two of them. He even took his dad with him when he went over to Japan for a TV appearance: 'The Tokyo Broadcasting System booked the pair of us. They had Dad lighting a cigarette and me blowing his match out with my rear end.'

At the Café Spice I act as a sort of replacement for Mr M's dad. I had not expected, frankly, to be part of his act, but in time-honoured rock 'n' roll fashion Barry, despite several mobile phone calls and assurances that he was on his way, fails to turn up to the gig, so I help Mr M move a trestle table into the restaurant's main room. He performs his act lying on this, on his back with his legs raised in the air, so that his axe, as it were, faces the audience, or at least those in those so-called ringside seats.

I am also Mr M's DJ for the evening, taking my cues and playing in his backing tracks. This is not as easy as it sounds, as I have to use the restaurant's own system, which is more suited to constant low-level sitar-based mood music, the kind that normally accompanies the enquiry 'Any poppadoms?' rather than stirring tunes to augment displays of comedy flatulence for practitioners of risk management.

I remember some of Mr M's lines from the edited version of his act at the showcase. I know that when he says it is time to 'put the art into fart' he is going into his classical routine and I should play tracks three, four and five, which run into each other. I know that he puts a little talc between his buttocks to raise the pitch a little, when he pretends to be trying to catch a bumble bee. 'And while I'm up there,' he will say, 'I will do a little bit of Tchaikovsky's *Swan Lake* if anyone's in the mood.'
He likes to do a little Madness, whose tunes he describes as 'very fart friendly', especially 'Driving in My Car' (track 16). Try it yourself at home: 'I've been driving in my car/Parp, parp, parp, parp, parp, parp, parp.'

While I am trying to keep a handle on all this, the waiters and kitchen staff, who have all knocked off now the meal is over, cluster around bombarding me with questions, assuming I am the evil genius behind Mr M. They think – as I did at first – that his act is based on some kind of trick. They are what Mr M calls 'sphincter sceptics'. Part of his act is to invite a sphincter sceptic from the audience to place his or her left earhole on his anus to confirm it as an act of nature. 'They won't let us do this in the States,' he tells me, an example of the strange prudery of the country that produces the hardest core pornography in the world. Or so I have been told.

Questions of taste are clearly important when you are performing anally. 'Middle-class people sometimes say to me sniffily, "I expect they really like your act up North," but that has never been true,' Mr M tells me. 'I don't fit well into the traditional Northern club scene. I've never been big in Barnsley. They're a little uncomfortable with a guy in a green Lycra body suit.'

What the working men's club crowd finds particularly off-putting is the big finish, when Mr M lowers his purple shorts. 'I suppose you would call these audiences a bit sort of old Labour, really. They see the climax to the act and think "maybe he's homosexual". It breaks a taboo, if you like. Even though it's funny, it somehow does not seem quite right.'

Mr M is not homosexual, as it happens. Not, of course, that there would be anything wrong if he were. No sirree. Just wanted to make that clear. We sort of touch on the subject of girlfriends in discussing his height. I had not noticed before how tall he is, probably because I had mostly seen him lying on his back, but he tells me he is six foot seven inches and therefore has difficulty meeting girls able to stare meaningfully into his eyes, or into his chin at least.

Coincidentally, I have a friend who is six foot eight, so I am able to tell Mr M about the tall people's club, who hold social evenings so that tall folk can maybe find romance, or at least someone with whom to share experiences of being asked, 'What's the weather like up there?' He's heard them all:

The other one you always get is that complete strangers will come up to you in pubs and say, 'How tall are you, exactly?' and when you tell them, they say, 'Six foot seven, eh? I thought so. We've just had a bit of a bet and I said six foot seven.' I feel like saying to them, 'Me and my friends have had a bit of a bet about you as well. Exactly how fat are you?'

In theory, being in entertainment should be a good way to meet girls, but as Mr M and I sit in a deserted restaurant at one in the morning eating chicken curry it doesn't feel like it. Admittedly, getting on stage and singing will always be sexier than lying on a table with your legs in the air, farting. On the other hand, I find that if you can get a girl to put her ear on your anus you are more or less halfway there.

Interestingly, Mr Methane was not the only performer at the *Showcall* showcase who was uncommonly tall. A singer called Carol Angel – 'Get Happy', You Don't Have to Say You Love Me' and 'Somebody to Love' – towered over Tufty as he stood on a box, comedy-style, to interview her. She was actually rather good, very flirty, and got me thinking how the more you stand out from the crowd, the more difficulty you have blending in with the other kids at school, the more likely you are to go into show business. You don't spend your life seeking the love and approval of complete strangers unless something is awry somewhere.

Mr M, I suppose, is just show business writ large. He is just that bit more unusual than the rest of us: an extremely tall heterosexual with the unique capacity for breathing through his bottom. Also, he is very funny. His big finish, by the way, is to 'fart the dart' (track 21). He drops his purple shorts to reveal a sort of back to front split crotch arrangement in his Lycra leggings, exposing his bare buttocks. He then inserts a tube into his bottom hole – quite quickly and tastefully, believe it or not – and places a small dart in the tube, which he propels via anally expelled wind into a balloon, which pops. Usually to a satisfying accompaniment of gales of laughter and hearty applause.

Because that, ladies and gentlemen, despite anything they might say in Barnsley, is entertainment.

9

LAUGH?

No getting out of it now. I am going to do a stand-up comedy act. I think I have given this broadcasting and journalism business a fair crack of the whip and it is time to try something else.

'But,' whispers a cautionary voice in my ear, 'is the audience for stand-up not made up mostly of kids in their twenties? Those kids are not going to be interested in anything you have to say. It will be a disaster, a humiliation. They don't want to listen to a routine about Viagra and liver spots. They will chew you up and spit you out.'

My instinct is to swat this little doubting Thomas from my shoulder and go ahead and do it anyway. Except it is not an imaginary doubting Thomas whispering in my ear. It is my real wife and she knows how old I am. She has seen my passport. And she bases her somewhat depressing view of my comedic potential on the very sound foundation of having seen me do it.

Five or six years ago I used to present a little strand for our local TV news programme called *Kelner's Choice*, which involved my going along to some event in the region and trying my hand at whatever they were doing: circus skills, Chinese cookery classes, paintballing, that kind of thing. One of the places I visited was the Last Laugh Comedy Club at the Lescar Inn in Sheffield, and for the purposes of the piece I had to go on stage and do a ten-minute set.

I had some fantastic material, even if I say so myself. I stole from the best. I can only remember one joke, one of Steven Wright's, about fitting a skylight in our bedroom ceiling, the punchline being that the people in the flat upstairs were furious. See, good stuff. And, I must say, nobody seemed to object too strongly to me. There was no physical violence or anything, not even any heckling. It is a very friendly club. It was just that people carried on doing what they do in pubs – drinking, talking, smoking, laughing (not at me) – all of which was rather off-putting and had the effect of making my delivery sound increasingly desperate.

What I had not realized was that it would be so difficult to stop people from talking during your act. I had imagined a sort of low-level murmur for the first minute or two, and then someone saying, 'Hey, wait a minute, this kid's good,' and by the end of the act the audience, as one, cheering me to the rafters. That is how it happens for Tom Hanks in that film he did about stand-up comedy with Sally Field, and his material was even worse than mine – some bollocks about being a comedy stylist.

The way my act appeared on the programme, of course, you would never have guessed it was less than a triumph. It looked like Bob Hope in Vietnam. They filmed people laughing heartily at the other acts and cut that footage into mercifully short extracts of my routine. But my wife knew the truth. That is the trouble with wives. They always know. If it weren't for my wife, I could try all sorts of things. I would go for that pilot's licence if she didn't keep reminding me of my inability to reverse out of Sainsbury's car park without hitting something. I could try a *ménage à trois*, except she would ask, what is the point of two women if you are going to fall asleep during *Match of the Day*?

But, sod it. I am going to give the stand-up another go. How hard can it be? I shall watch other stand-ups, take a little advice, have my suit dry-cleaned, possibly even think up some new jokes, and then go for it. Speaking of dry-cleaners, by the way, why is it that in every survey of attitudes to people's professions, journalists, lawyers and estate agents find themselves least liked and respected, whilst dry-cleaners never feature? They continue to move around quite happily in polite society, free from the fear of being spat upon or shunned at parties.

My local dry-cleaners is called Johnson's and I hate them. I'm sorry, but I do. It is not enough that they behaved like Blockbusters, taking over all the little dry-cleaners in my area, virtually forcing me through their doors; now they have to try and recruit me for their 'Privilege Club' every time I go in there. Apparently, if I pay them an annual fee, I will get a discount card and 'priority' in the shop. In other words, my card will ensure I get served before some other poor bastard waiting there. Well, excuse me, but is it not the function of a shop, as part of the deal for our spending our money with them, that they serve all of us, whether we are in their pathetic club or not? This is not transatlantic travel, for God's sake. We are all equal, I believe, in the sight of the dry-cleaners. Dirty trousers recognize no first and second class. So, nothing personal, but you can stick your privilege club up your chemically cleaned corporate arse.

The other thing that annoys me is they always ask if you want to pay the extra £2 for the 'guaranteed crease'. Well, excuse me again, but is pressing clothes not what dry-cleaners are supposed to do? Is that, in fact, not just about all they bloody do? Or are we paying them simply for the joy of standing around in the shop and sniffing the chemicals? Are they so zapped in there that they can't get round to ironing your pants without you lay some extra bread on them, man? Not for the act, I think, but it needed saying.

You will have noticed that I substituted the American usage 'pants' for 'trousers' in that last paragraph. That is because it is a better word for punchlines, being, well, punchier. That is how deep my understanding of comedy runs, so who says I cannot do stand-up? Well, my wife, for one, most of my friends, and me, actually, in my more sober moments. I mean, I understand comedy, I think. I do it on the radio and in my newspaper column to an extent. In many ways, comedy has ruled my life for 45 years. I have sought out laughs at every possible opportunity. If I had a coat of arms it would include the motto 'Anything for a Laugh'. It is my creed.

I shall give you an example. In 1974, or thereabouts, when I was a newspaper reporter and keen to move into radio, I was boarded for a job as a journalist with BBC Radio London. One of the board asked me to imagine I was on a day off, had switched on the radio for a little light music, and instead heard a news flash about the Moorgate tube disaster (an underground railway crash during the rush hour, involving a number of fatalities). What, he asked, would be my reaction? 'Well,' I said, 'my first reaction would be, "Thank Christ it's my day off."'

Wrong crowd, I think. Faces have been stonier, I am sure – I have seen photographs of the funeral of King George VI – but I got the distinct impression I may have lost them at that point. Maybe I should have just pressed on: 'Anyway, there was this Irish lesbian ...' The only consolation was that back at the *Western Daily Press* social club the story played rather well.

I do love getting laughs. And I like laughing at other people's stories, too. I am actually quite a cheap date for a comedian, being very, very easily amused. My father used to say, 'You'd laugh if the cat's arse caught fire,' which has always seemed to me a perfectly reasonable position to adopt. As far as I am concerned, anyone who fails to see the comic potential of a cat with a combustible rear end has no idea what comedy is all about.

Apart from burning cats, a short list of other things that make me laugh like a hyena that has just seen a very funny cartoon in that morning's newspaper would include Monty Python (*The Holy Grail* rather than *The Life of Brian*), Spinal Tap, the Marx Brothers, Jacques Tati, the novels of P G Wodehouse – who once described one of Wooster's fiancées as having 'a laugh like a platoon of cavalry charging over a tin bridge' – the marvellous, cherishable Laurel and Hardy, the Simpsons, Seinfeld, Eddie Izzard, and ... no, this is no good, even cutting the list down to the barest of bones, we are going to be here all day.

Even if I were to restrict myself to a list of things called, say, Peter, that make me laugh, it would be a long one: Peter Sellers, Peter Cook, Peter Kay, Peter Stringfellow, Peter Snow, Peter Sissons ... Knock, knock, who's there? Peter. Peter who? Peter Nightbeforeyougotobed (playground jokes, I love 'em). Oh, and countless more, probably.

As far as I can recall, the first person ever to get a laugh out of me was Charlie Chaplin. I dare say my dad made me giggle once or twice by pulling a funny face or tickling me when I was a baby but Charlie was the first time I paid for it. Or, to be more accurate, my Auntie Rosie did. I must have been about six years old when she took me to town shopping. At the end of the afternoon we dived into the Manchester News Theatre so she could rest her feet while we watched a newsreel and a couple of funny short films. In the Chaplin short, Charlie was strap-hanging in a crowded streetcar, being nudged and jostled down the car. Eventually he gets shoved out of the back door and into a delicatessen. He thinks he's still on the bus, of course, and ends up strap-hanging from a stick of salami with what I believe are usually described as hilarious consequences. They were to me anyway. I was helpless. On the floor. It was the most rapturous experience of my short life and I suppose the story of the forty-odd subsequent years has been an attempt to recapture that delicious feeling.

Would it be too fanciful to describe sitting with my Auntie Rosie watching Charlie Chaplin as my Rosebud? Well, yes, it probably would, but it does explain why on a suffocatingly warm Wednesday evening in midsummer I was trudging through London's heat and dust to the upstairs room of a pub in Camden Town, craving laughter.

August was my month for total immersion in comedy of all sorts – watching, learning, stealing – before relaunching myself on the comedy circuit, though not particularly by popular demand, despite my record-breaking one-night engagement at the Last Laugh, Sheffield, as seen on TV. Everything had to be committed to imperfect memory, though. Sitting in a comedy club, taking notes, more or less guarantees you will become an unwilling participant in one of the acts, which is not my idea of fun. I had already been picked on once, the previous Thursday at the Comedy Store, when I arrived late and was ushered to the one remaining seat, right at the end of the front row.

The Comedy Sore – as I just typed, in a rare example of the word-processor Freudian slip – in Piccadilly Circus, is London's most famous comedy venue, having been the birthplace of a new boom in stand-up in the early eighties. But these days it is, I suppose, what we have to call a brand or a franchise; it now manages many artistes and has opened new branches in Britain and abroad into which its own performers are booked. Corporate comedy, as proprietors of smaller, less successful, clubs like to sneer.

The night I wander in, it is a typical Comedy Store crowd: fairly squiffy hen parties and gangs of braying work colleagues. My seat at the front makes me easy meat for the MC, a chap called Simon Bligh, who grabs off me the two magazines I have in my hand and proceeds to share the contents with the audience. Fortunately, there is nothing too embarrassing. Just *Time Out* and the *Weekly World News*, an American supermarket tabloid I have bought for the wacky headlines – 'Overworked Horse Bites Owner's Penis', 'I See Jesus's Face in the Rust on My Car', that kind of thing, the sort of story you tend not to see in the *Daily Telegraph*.

Bligh is not vicious at all. He is a tall, good-looking chap, with a classless, vaguely east Midlands accent, and a permanent cheeky smile that signals he has no intention of savaging you. His job as MC is to weld the audience into a loved-up laughing machine for the other acts, and this he does very well, although I reckon alcohol may have beaten him to it. He makes me laugh, not immoderately, not as much as I might at a burning cat, for instance, but he is clearly skilled at his job, as are the other comedians, John Moloney, and a woman called Jo Caulfield, both experienced stand-ups who have been on the London comedy circuit for years and have done a fair bit of TV.

Disappointingly, afterwards I am unable to recall a single joke. There was a lot of material about masturbation, and breaking up with your girl/boyfriend, which seemed to hit the spot with the audience – nobody asked for their 13 quid back, as far as I know – but was not particularly relevant to someone like me, turned fifty, married for 18 years, with four children and a Marks and Spencer's storecard. I am not saying that fifty-year-old men do not occasionally bash the bishop – how else are you expected to get to sleep in strange hotel rooms? – but as a burning topic of conversation it does tend to lose its appeal in middle age.

Thirty-odd years ago, gags about bodily self abuse (or BSA, as we used to call it, in tribute to the Birmingham Small Arms company) would have caught me right where I live. As teenagers in an all-boys school we spoke of little else. My friend Jonathan Rosenfield was particularly forthcoming on the subject. Jonathan was frighteningly priapic, which I think caused a certain amount of tension at home, as his parents were fiercely religious Jews who believed sex of any sort was a wicked abomination, almost as bad as buying retail (Woody Allen gag, but irresistible). They must have seen Jon – with some justification – as a kind of walking penis, constantly on the point of eruption, so he stayed out of the house as much as possible. I would get off the bus with him and we would hang around for hours on the corner of his street – Bishop's Avenue, ironically enough – talking about wanking and the Beach Boys.

I think I may have been a little bit in love with him. He was good-looking in a simian kind of way, with a sallow complexion that tanned rather nicely, a very wide nose, and Jaggeresque lips. When he laughed, he showed a lot of big white teeth, apart from one at the front which was grey because the nerve had died, and which added to his strangeness. There was a definite touch of the *enfant sauvage* about Jon.

I am not exactly sure where it came from. His mother was a tall, imperious, very correct Eastern-European type who spoke thickly accented English and seemed to be permanently angry. She only looked like Jon when she smiled, which was not often when I was around. Jon's father was a small, bald, podgy, harassed Jewish businessman, two or three years away from his first heart attack in my estimation, whose role in the home seemed entirely peripheral.

On Saturdays the Rosenfields switched on no lights, or televisions, or cookers. In the morning they walked to the synagogue and prayed and in the afternoon they just sat there and seethed. It was what God would have wanted. But not according to their second son, who took great delight in placing his own interpretation on God's will. God would not have created this build-up of pressure in between his legs, he reasoned, if He had not wanted the young Rosenfield to open the escape valve from time to time. Jon claimed to open the valve so often he was expecting a little notice to appear – like one of those 'Bang, Bang' flags that come out of joke guns in pantomimes – saying, 'That's it. None left. Take up stamp collecting.'

Interestingly enough, my friend the fire-eater, Tony De La Fou, sends me a short story he has written about two clowns who go to perform at a rave weekend. Talking to each other in the van, they pursue a similar theme. The theory of one of them is that we are each allocated a bucket and a half at birth, and once that has gone, the well is dry. Maybe this is one of those subjects chaps will talk about, whatever their age.

Should space permit, and should it appear relevant at any point in this volume, I will tell you more of the Rosenfields, and Jon's tragic end, but for the moment I am not sure any of it contributes greatly to my devising a credible stand-up act.

I don't know though. Jon and I were great fans of a book I found lying around at home called *The Code of Jewish Law* by Rabbi Solomon Ganzfried, out of which we got some big laughs. In Solly, we had pulled off (I know, I know) the difficult trick of finding someone as interested in masturbation as we were. He was, it will hardly surprise you to learn, against it. And pretty well everything else as it happens. Ganzfried's argument, as I read it, is that if you are Jewish and you are thinking of doing anything, forget it.

Here is one of my favourite Ganzfried gags:

Semen is the vitality of man's body and the light of his eyes, and when it issues in abundance, the body weakens and life is shortened. He who indulges in having intercourse, ages quickly, his strength ebbs, his eyes grow dim, his breath becomes foul, the hair of his head, eyelashes and brows fall out, the hair of his beard, armpits and feet increase, his teeth fall out, and many other aches besides those befall him.

I wondered what was causing it.

Too few stand-ups, I feel, bother with this aspect of bodily self abuse. You know, stuff about the body weakening and aches befalling and all that. I suppose it is considered too depressing, although comedians who have grown rich and old in the job, like Billy Connolly and Victoria Wood, will sometimes essay supposedly daring observations about their own experiences of ageing. I never feel that means quite as much, though, as hearing some guy who is just some guy going on about it. When you live in a mansion in the Hollywood hills, the fact that your pubic hair is turning grey does not seem to me to be a major tragedy. Thankfully, I discover Kevin McCarron, a forty-eight-year-old New Zealander so keen to find a platform for his comic view of the world that he has opened his own comedy club, the Laughing Horse, in Camden Town.

I have been doing a guest spot at Talksport Radio, near Waterloo, and if I want to catch Kevin's act I have two choices: I can dash over to Camden, watch him, and then whiz back to King's Cross for the last train to Leeds, the 11.30, which, if all goes to plan, will have me tucked up in my own bed for around two in the morning; or I can find somewhere in London to stay.

As I cross Waterloo Bridge, en route to the Laughing Horse, the late afternoon sun is lending even more lustre to the finest view in London. In Covent Garden, the bars are beginning to fill with office workers, the smell of flirting and fashionable bottled beer heavy in the air. The heat is getting to me, and I am beginning to regret my policy of walking everywhere. My shoes do not feel as comfortable, nor my laptop as portable, as they did in Leeds, so I decide to find a flophouse in which to flop.

The Gresham Hotel in Bloomsbury Street is a handsome Georgian townhouse fallen on rather hard times. A basic single room can cost as little as £40 but I pay £55 for a few extra luxuries – like a shower, a private toilet and a bed. My accommodation is in what they call the annexe, a house three or four doors down the road, and I have to climb three flights of stairs to reach my spartan room. Despite the fact that I am now sweating bullets, as the Americans like to say, I do not risk the shower as it appears to have been designed for a person much smaller than me: Danny DeVito, say, or my twelve-year-old daughter. Also, I am travelling without my shampoo or moisturizing body wash and I do not trust the single tablet of soap provided, which smells as though manufactured from a cocktail of napalm and Domestos. My skin has reached the age where it needs a little pampering.

Cheap hotels in Britain, I find, are nowhere near as interesting as they used to be. When I was in my twenties I used to work for the Central Office of Information, producing propaganda about British business successes for the foreign media. This involved a lot of travelling around the country bilking the government out of expenses by charging for expensive hotels and staying in cheap ones.

Each of these establishments had its own unique horrors, from elaborate sets of rules and regulations regarding the taking of a bath, to little pink candlewick overcoats with frilly lace edges on to cover the spare toilet roll, to sheets and pillowcases so inescapably and defiantly nylon you could power your electric razor in the morning from the static electricity. But then along came the French to spoil the fun, with their chains of hotels, the Campaniles and Ibises, pursuing their shameful policy of providing decent, clean rooms at reasonable prices.

Our shambolic British shit-holes were forced to compete and now, in the major towns at least, there are no surprises any more. Your room will be cleaned to an acceptable standard, the bed will be at a level of comfort stipulated by some Euro regulation somewhere and your towels will be just sufficient – and absolutely no more – in quantity and thickness to deal with whatever you might need them for in an economy-priced hotel room many miles from home. This is bottom-line Britain, where you are never more than a minute away from an accountant.

When you go somewhere like the Comedy Store you feel comedy might be going the same way. You pay a reasonable price for a night out in the West End and schooled professionals hit enough of the right buttons to amuse you to a level consistent with all the latest European standards for comedy. You don't feel cheated, but then again you don't feel inspired. The Laughing Horse is a refreshing departure from all this. It is in an upstairs room at a fairly soulless bar called Liberties in Camden High Street, halfway between Mornington Crescent tube station and Camden Town. Kevin McCarron himself is at the top of the stairs to take your three quid off you.

Kevin is unusual among stand-up comics, in that he is a doctor of philosophy. When he is not slinging your pound coins into a tin and stamping the back of your hand, he is Reader in American Literature at the University of Surrey. His PhD thesis was on religion and spiritualism in the later fiction of William Golding, while his MA covered the same author's early work, with particular reference to human sacrifice and cannibalism, an understanding of which, some would say, is ideal preparation for a career in stand-up comedy.

Although I do not tell him immediately, I have decided Kevin will be my mentor. I shall enlist him as a guide through the comedy minefield, my insurance policy against the flesh wounds I suffered last time. He is of the same generation as me, so should have some sort of insight into how we more mature types can connect with the pissed-up twenty-somethings who hang around comedy clubs.

Actually, that is how he got into the laughter business. As a university lecturer, his working life was spent standing up in front of young people trying to engage and hold their interest, the kind of work experience he felt would equip him for a future in comedy:

> I watched stand-up on the TV, and occasionally when we went out for the evening, and I just thought, 'I could do that. I'm an experienced public speaker.' Fortunately, I didn't appreciate the difference between stand-up comedy and lecturing until I started doing it, otherwise I would never have bothered.

Kevin was forty-four years old when he first ventured on to a stage armed with nothing but jokes. He did not want to go through the long and tortuous process of try-out nights and open-mike spots in pubs and clubs all over London, so he opened his own club, in Kingston-upon-Thames, and immediately booked himself. He has the confidence and self-belief to do that kind of thing, which may be half the battle. For someone who left school at seventeen, travelled halfway round the world before starting in further education at the age of twenty-seven, and then sat down and produced two weighty tomes on the work of William Golding, the prospect of a bunch of unruly twenty-somethings should hold few terrors. Anyone with Kevin's intimate knowledge of *Lord of the Flies* should feel capable of surviving the Laughing Horse comedy club, Camden.

Tonight he is trying out a new hour-long routine intended for Edinburgh, where he will travel for the last weekend of the festival. Watching him work, I get some clues as to where I went wrong last time; I should talk about what I know. I seem to remember doing jokes I had stolen from other comedians, about getting drunk, and living in flats, despite the fact that my drunken, flat-dwelling days were far behind me. Kevin, who has two young children, Ella, eight, and Max, six, does a routine about watching the adventures of Pingu the penguin on children's television. The joke is the thinness of the plots in these programmes. In one episode, invented by Kevin, Pingu loses his trousers and looks for them. They turn up in the fridge. End of story. 'What's a penguin doing with a fucking fridge?' is Kevin's pay-off.

There cannot be more than about 30 people in the club, several of whom seem to be known personally to our host, so he is clearly not making much money out of his jokes. But that has not stopped him opening – with Alex, his friend and business partner – eight Laughing Horse clubs around London. All operate on the same basis: Kevin and Alex pay nothing for the hire of the rooms, and they trouser all the money taken at the door, while the pubs get the bar. 'It's a way for pubs to sell a bit more booze,' Kevin tells me. 'We're like a quiz night or a karaoke night. We run midweek, so that pubs can get a few more people in on quiet nights.'

Kevin mostly acts as MC, shuttling around the outer reaches of the *A–Z* – Hounslow, Greenwich, Richmond – introducing on stage a selection of first-timers and acts relatively new to the circuit who will be performing for free. If my experience in Camden is anything to go by, most of them will be fairly awful so I should not have to hit any great comedic heights to blend in.

Rob and Colin were a mildly amusing village-idiot-style act, who worked very hard, shouting quite a lot. One of them, I remember, appeared at one point with clothes pegs attached to his face, which must have been quite painful, and asked his partner to guess which character from *EastEnders* he was supposed to be. Turned out to be Peggy (geddit?). Oh, how we must suffer for our art.

Another comedian, Dave Miles, a pleasant young chap I was chatting to before the gig, and who was really interested in my book, froze. I had never seen anyone lose it completely before. He was doing some gag about Diogenes being visited by the *Changing Rooms* people, and understandably lost track of where he was heading, so he just jacked it in, just like that.

The bill was completed by a big-boned, ponytailed young man from Yorkshire called Garth Wilson. Garth talked about getting into fights, but not very convincingly as he looked like the sort of softie who would run a mile from any threat of physical violence; not a Leeds hard man but a rosy-cheeked, outdoor type from good solid rural stock, by the look of him.

I cannot say I laughed a great deal but it did only cost three quid. One of the wonders of life in Britain in these early years of the twenty-first century is the number of people, who are not even remotely amusing, who think they can get up and make an audience laugh.

On this one Wednesday night in the dog days of August, when the comedy establishment has more or less decamped to Edinburgh for the festival, there are still, according to my *Time Out*, 92 different comedians performing somewhere in London. That is on just one night. Most of them will be as funny as an impacted wisdom tooth. How did these people express themselves before the craze for stand-up? I suppose they joined pop groups, or recited Monty Python sketches word for word.

But Kevin, while some way short of a burning cat or Charlie Chaplin gripping a charcutier's sausage, does make me chuckle. I actually manage to commit two of his gags to memory. British prisoner-of-war movies, he said, were essentially unrealistic, because the prisoners usually put on some kind of pantomime as cover for their escape, whereas in reality there was no way any Englishman would leave the camp if there were the slightest chance he might get to dress up in women's clothing. And girls, he said – this was memorable gag number two – sometimes ask if you want to come in for coffee and then put a cautionary hand up and say, 'Just coffee, mind you.' '"Yeah, that's great," I say. "Perfect. I'd love a cup of coffee. Normally I've got to fuck somebody to get one."'

Fairly original material, but not exactly ground-breaking, so why the burning desire to share it with a handful of students in the upstairs room of a Camden Town pub? Kevin explains:

Sheer enjoyment. I enjoy running the comedy nights. I actually prefer being the MC to doing my own stuff. Then you have to work with what you've got, react to the audience, think on your feet. Your role, in a way, is sacrificial. You are the ringmaster and you have to create the atmosphere in which the other comedians can survive. I enjoy that. It is much harder to find people to MC than it is to find comedians who want to do their own set, so mostly I do it myself.

He is good at commanding an audience. Possibly it is his teaching experience, or maybe his appearance. He is a grizzled, weather-beaten Antipodean, quite tall, bespectacled, and what little hair remains is close shaven. He looks the sort of chap you would expect to see hunting crocodiles on a satellite TV channel. He is a pussycat when you get to know him but on stage you would not want to mess with him.

Kevin was actually born in Stockport but his parents emigrated to New Zealand when he was two, and he grew up there. After leaving school at seventeen, he worked in theatres in a variety of backstage jobs. He came to England in his early twenties and discovered – after three years or so of various odd jobs – that his birthplace qualified him for a grant for further education. He completed a degree in English literature, which led him into his glittering academic career. 'The fact that I am unquestionably better educated than my audience may give me the arrogance you need to stand up and do comedy,' he says. 'I am a doctor of philosophy with 50 academic articles to my name and there won't be many in the audience who can say that.'

He seems fairly content with his position in the comedy hierarchy, running his clubs, nurturing young talent – during the breaks the try-out acts gravitate towards him to discuss comedy business, almost an extension of his teaching career – although he must once have hankered for greater fame. He entered a *Daily Telegraph* stand-up contest three years ago, sailed through the early rounds and then froze in the semi-final in a cavernous club in Birmingham. 'Basically, I was ill prepared,' he remembers. 'I was writing a book at the time, trying to meet a deadline, and I didn't know what I was doing on the night. The heat, the noise, the lights, it all got to me, and I died on my arse.'

Spending a certain amount of time metaphorically on your backside is a rite of passage in the comedy business and has not discouraged Kevin from occasionally seeking a wider audience for his material. In fact, despite his protestations, and notwithstanding his comfortable life in academia, my suspicion is that if fame turned up on his doorstep he would not exactly slam the door on it. He claims the comedy is 'just a hobby that pays for itself', adding, 'Some guys play five-a-side football. My release is standing up and doing jokes. My academic career is

reasonably assured, so maybe I need a little danger in my life.'
We decide to meet up in Edinburgh, where he is performing in 'a
mate's pub'. He is vague about the details but he gives me his
mobile number and I give him mine to ensure that we don't miss
each other.

We miss each other. Two days of playing answerphone
tennis, during which he seems to be partying a good deal harder
than me, gets us nowhere. He is asleep when I am awake and
vice versa. Still, it is an excuse to visit the Edinburgh Festival,
which remarkably I find I have never done before.

I am constantly shocked by all the things I have failed to do
in my life. It has got so I have stopped reading those checklists
they print in men's mags of 50 things you should have done by
the time you are thirty, forty or fifty – woken up in a complete
stranger's bed with no idea how you got there; got locked into a
flaming Lamborghini session with Russell Crowe and a ladies'
hockey team; sniffed cocaine from the breasts of an
international supermodel – because I know I will never have
done any of them, except the cocaine thing, obviously. I expect
we've all done that.

It is the last weekend of the festival and Edinburgh is
packed. Only an idiot would leave it until the Friday afternoon
to start trying to book a hotel room. Eventually I am offered a
rather spartan room at Herriot Watt University, which does not
sound like the ticket at all. I am beginning to ponder the
possibility of kipping in the car – being fellated in a moving
vehicle, there's another thing *Loaded* says I should have done,
which I haven't – when I get a call from an agency offering me a
cancellation, pretty well the best hotel room in Edinburgh, and
it is only going to cost me about three times as much as I had
been planning to spend.

After all the bargain basement places I have been staying in,
a posh hotel should be a treat, and by employing the old Navajo
Indian trick of getting my mother-in-law to babysit, I am able to
go up to Edinburgh with my wife. She appreciates things like
heavy curtains and towelling bathrobes far more than I do.

Let me explain the Navajo Indian thing. Some years ago I
had a hugely enjoyable time hosting a series of Radio 2
roadshows in resorts along the south coast in the company of a

producer called Keith Loxam. Keith's favourite joke was the Woody Allen routine about being set upon by bullies, and saving himself 'by lapsing into the old Navajo Indian trick ... of screaming and begging for mercy'. Keith loved this line and peppered his conversation with variations on it. He would take the crew into a restaurant and say something like, 'Why don't we lapse into the old Navajo Indian trick of ordering garlic bread for starters?' or you'd be driving along, and he would say, 'At the next junction, do the old Navajo Indian trick of turning left.' Eventually this was shortened to, 'Take the main road for about 200 yards just past the hospital, then do a Navajo.'

Keith's father, Arnold, used to play one of those big theatre organs in Blackpool and he had a hugely popular show on Radio Leeds called *Dial-a-Hymn* where listeners phoned in and Arnold played their favourite hymn live. Keith is a proficient player himself and has a huge collection of all sorts of keyboards he is constantly adding to. You just don't find radio producers with that kind of hinterland these days.

Keith was going through a marriage break-up during our tour so was a little hysterical a lot of the time, as a result of which he enjoyed my act immensely. I say 'act' but that is rather a grand word for getting a few people on stage, making personal remarks about their clothes, and telling a joke, which was a favourite of mine at the time, about a chap in his car running over a cat. What this did for the image of Radio 2 does not bear thinking about but it was around this time that the station's listening figures began to rise so I think Keith and I are entitled to pull the old Navajo Indian trick of taking some of the credit.

Anyway, early on Saturday morning, my wife, Janet, and I – me driving, she telling me I am too close to the car in front – hit the road disc jockey Andy Peebles once called 'that great highway to the North we know as the A1'. (If you have not got into the cult of Andy Peebles yet, I recommend it. Andy never uses one word where 126 will do, all perfectly modulated. I nominate him as Britain's number one radio presenter of the past 30 years, a man capable of talking absolute utter unmitigated bollocks and making it sound convincing.)

Our room is perfect, overlooking the Royal Mile. From our window we can see white-painted mime artistes, oblivious to the fact that their art has become a standing joke in most parts of the civilized world, students handing out flyers for shows no-one will go to see, and numerous people outside bars having discovered that while live entertainment may be uplifting, at times even life-enhancing, there are other times when only beer will do.

Having the little lady with me, the temptation is to make the most of the hotel room and romp wildly like show business personalities, making liberal use of the free shower caps and towelling dressing gowns; but for the benefit of the volume you are currently enjoying, and in order to pick up some hints for my own forthcoming live performance, we behave like culture vultures, diving straight down to the Pleasance Downstairs, a stuffy cellar, where Gavin and Gavin are presenting *The Full English Breakfast*.

It's two girls showing off. They are sisters Lauretta and Sharon Gavin, who sit on stools pretending to be various characters in an airport waiting for a flight back home from Portugal. They are very good at the voices but some jokes might have helped. 'Have you noticed, you never make cup-a-soup in a bowl?' was about the best they had. It's an observation of sorts, I suppose, but it doesn't bring us that much closer to an understanding of the human condition.

Here's another observation. In Edinburgh during the festival you will probably not meet up with the person you want to – Kevin McCarron in my case – but you will bump into all sorts of other people you were not expecting to see.

On Sunday morning in Waterstone's, for instance, I spot someone I take to be a contestant in an Alan Rusbridger lookalike contest. Turns out it *is* Alan Rusbridger, editor of the paper for which I write. I engage him in conversation and he appears to know who I am, which I think is a very positive sign. The *Guardian* is sponsoring a debate at the TV Festival, which is why Alan, as I feel I can now call him, is there.

I get the impression that half the people in town this weekend, possibly more, are media types living high on the hog (no idea what that means but I have heard the expression used) on expenses, signing up for a TV pilot the Perrier award winner, or some fringe act that gets a few half-decent reviews, and spending the rest of the time in eating, drinking, snorting and other hog-like activities. Actually paying to go and see lots of shows is for the mugs, like me and Mrs Kelner.

We are diverted from this plan, however, by another chance encounter, this time with a friend of mine called Darren who works for BBC radio's comedy department and who has recently smuggled me onto an edition of Radio 4's *Quote, Unquote*, where I was able to leaven the parade of G K Chestertons and Oscar Wildes with wisdom from the world of football – including the former international who said playing in Europe was 'very much the carrot at the end of the tunnel'.

Clearly, gung-ho though I was for the idea of more live entertainment, Darren needed to be rewarded with food and drink. So, while the big beasts of the media jungle stalked the agreeable seafood restaurants of Leith, our little party made for the World's End, one of many packed bars on the Royal Mile where, after a wait of, oh, I don't know, no more than an hour and a half, we were served nachos, ciabattas and other wholesome Scottish treats, by a New Zealander.

Is it my imagination or is New Zealand systematically emptying? The compere at the evening of stand-up comedy we went to was another Kiwi, Al Pitcher, who fulfilled all the requirements of a good MC, as outlined by Kevin, his compatriot. In this he was helped by the presence near the front of the audience of a fairly mature Yorkshireman ('What, three quid for a bloody sandwich?'), who seemed perfectly happy with his role as the butt of some good-natured humour.

There were three comics on the bill, all experienced pros who convinced me that my misgivings about getting up on stage and doing stand-up were not at all ill-placed.

Hal Cruttenden trades on the fact that he is rather short and a little ordinary-looking, with curly brown hair and a shy smile, and talks a little like Tony Blair, soft and middle class. He is a repository of typically English male insecurities and the audience warms to him. There is no way, without several years practice – which I assume Hal has had – that I could connect with a crowd the way he does and it is an insult to suggest otherwise. It is odd that when the big names in comedy were Ken Dodd, Frankie Howerd and so on, nobody thought they could just get up and do stand-up, but now everybody thinks they can, and the brutal truth is that most people are just not funny. Kevin McCarron tells me he has 1,600 comedians on his database. I guarantee you that approximately 1,568 of them will not even be mildly amusing.

Hal's best joke is about how as a shy single bloke he used to get annoyed by married couples who got all self-satisfied just because they were having regular sex. 'I used to live with a married couple once,' he says, 'and the guy would come down to breakfast with a smug grin on his face, saying, "Sorry if we kept you awake last night, got a bit … ha, ha … carried away, I'm afraid," and I would say, 'Dad, should you be telling me all this?"'

Rohan Agalawatta is a short Asian guy with unfeasibly long hair. His style is similar to that of American comedians Steven Wright and Emo Philips: one-liners and ridiculous puns, delivered at the kind of deliberate pace which demands supreme confidence. Best joke: 'If … you're … having … sex … on … a … bed … of … nails, try and get on top.'

The line-up is completed by Jim Jeffries, a foul-mouthed Aussie who claims to have been voted Australia's Caravan Park Comic of the Year. His material, none of which I can recall, certainly has a trailer trash flavour, and is delivered at speed and with tremendous brio. He steamrollers the audience into liking him. Jeffries looks about fourteen years old, and of the three, he is the one with real star quality in my view. Filth delivered with cheek and real warmth can be a winning formula, as Max Miller and, more recently, Frank Skinner have found.

It is our first time at the festival, so we take in two more shows and quite a lot of drink before the evening is over. We feel we should.

I have known of Dana Gillespie since about 1978, when I was doing a late-night radio show, and in amongst the newly released pop stuff the record companies sent me I found an album of hers called *Blue Job*. I was playing mostly New Wave and heavy rock at the time but Dana's album was full of rude blues, originally performed by concupiscent males; classics like 'Big Ten Inch Record', 'Sailors Delight', and 'Play With Your Poodle', whose joyous obscenity seemed to chime in perfectly with the tenor of my programme.

As luck would have it, she is doing a late-night cabaret in the Crowne Plaza right opposite our hotel, which we find hugely enjoyable. Dana is a chunky lady, in her mid-fifties, perfect for singing the blues. There is no substitute for experience and after all that comedy it is a relief to be offered a little misery in the shape of songs of lost love and no-good men.

At the Edinburgh Festival, however, post-modern irony is the preferred flavour. The titles of the shows nudge and wink at you from every fringe programme: *The Cat Must Die!*; *Miranda Hart – Throbs*; *Lesbian Launderette – St Kylie's Love Hospital*; *Artificial Hip-Hop*; *My Old Man's a Dustman – a Deconstruction*. As our nod to this trend we go to see *Elvis the Girl*, which does exactly what it says on the packet. It is a girl, and she sings Elvis songs, to backing tapes. Very badly, as it happens. I assume some lesbian chic or post-modern whatsit is intended, but really, any half-decent tribute act in a working men's club could do it better and they wouldn't charge you £7.50. ('Seven pounds fifty for a bloody Elvis tribute act? Daylight bloody robbery.')

Here is a game you can play at home. Invent your own fringe show. You can decide on content later. Maybe a few trenchant observations: you never make cup-a-soup in a bowl, that kind of thing. But what is really important is the title, which should be a little like a tabloid headline, and preferably include the name of a vaguely laughable figure from popular culture. I have already booked a room for my show next year: *Chesney Hawkes Stole My Bike.*

The Seinfeld Conspiracy is a title that catches my eye, which is why on Sunday lunchtime, instead of eating or drinking – culture vultures or what? – we make for one of the lesser known but handsome festival venues, the Hill Street Theatre, in among the striking Victorian terraces and squares behind Princes Street.

Jerry Seinfeld is my comedy hero. He does not have a whole lot of warmth but he makes up for it by being very clever indeed. His television show, with its four amoral self-obsessed Manhattanites fretting over the minutiae of their meaningless lives, is a work of genius. Brave is not a word I like to use in connection with works of art – brave in my book is pulling someone out of a burning building – but, within the context of the world of American sitcoms, it must have taken some balls to make Seinfeld and his chums such thoroughly dislikeable characters. There are no cuddles in *Seinfeld*. Name another prime time American sitcom of which you can say that. So *The Seinfeld Conspiracy: The Official Unauthorised and Scandalous Truth*, a one-man show written and performed by Joey West, with its promise of maybe adopting the style of my favourite TV show to uncover dark truths, was something I was looking forward to more than lunch. When we get to the theatre, though, it is cancelled. Turns out there have been 'artistic differences' between West and the theatre and he has thrown all his toys out of the pram and upped sticks.

If the review of the show I later read on the internet is anything to go by, I didn't miss much. West, apparently, was a student of politics in the USSR, where he lived for a while. He wrote speeches for US vice-president Dan Quayle for three years before branching out into comedy writing, producing books like – wait for it – *101 Things Not to Say During Sex* and *The Dumb Blonde Joke Book*. Now there's a CV you could not make up.

Disappointingly, his show revolves round the claim that he thought of the idea for *Seinfeld*, and some gags, and introduced Jerry to his collaborator, Larry David, for all of which he got no credit. And that's it. Just another show business hard luck story. The reviewer complains that West is 'whiney and bitter'. Well, of course he is, you fool. This is show business.

I shall always be grateful for West's hissy fit, however, which had the effect of diverting me to an absolutely entrancing afternoon at the Assembly Rooms: *Filler Up!*, a one-woman show written and performed by Deb Filler. This may have been the best hour and a half I have ever spent in the theatre.

Filler is an overweight, Jewish, forty-four-year-old lesbian from New Zealand (enough already with the New Zealanders) and I am sure she will not mind my saying that. Her late father, a concentration camp survivor, was a baker in Auckland, her mother is – well – a Jewish mother. Deb's brilliant monologue deals with her relationships with her family and lovers, her family's very complex and very Jewish relationship with food, her therapy, her acting and everything that has made her into a manifestly funny, warm and attractive performer.

The show manages to be witty – 'My mother's gone organic now. Her chickens are so healthy, each bird has a personal trainer.' – and moving, without being sentimental. Gavin and Gavin should watch this performance and know that it is not enough just to do the voices. The twist is that while Deb talks, she bakes: two loaves of *challah*, the soft, sweet Jewish white bread that turns us all into the lean, mean fighting machines that we are (joke). At the end of the show she invites the audience to tuck into the bread, a useful pointer for me as I prepare for my own one-man performance.

If I can invent a bit of business for myself, a prop or two, I reason, it might distract the audience from the paucity of my material, and if I can give them a free gift at the end, so much the better. A crazy idea but it might just work. Unfortunately, I appear to have left it a little late to learn to bake bread, and since I cannot pick up a guitar or a ukulele in anything like a convincing manner, it begins to look as though I might have to win the audience over through wit and charm alone, a high-risk strategy I think.

When I finally find Kevin McCarron in Soho a couple of weekends later he is generous with his advice and admirably direct on the approach I should take. 'Try not to look like a c**t,' is his first tip. I point out to him that I recently got rave reviews for a best man speech at my friend Paul's wedding, getting big laughs, and attracting almost no comment on how much like the female private parts I looked. The bride's mother, I think, was the only one.

'A best man's speech is completely different,' says Kevin. 'They're not expecting you to be funny, and if you are, it's a bonus. But when you walk out on stage in front of a room full of people, you are making a statement: "Hey, look at me, I'm funny" and if you are not, they can be very unforgiving. An audience has got tremendous power over you and five minutes is a hell of a long time.'

We are downstairs in the Coach and Horses, not the famous one of *Jeffrey Bernard is Unwell* fame, but a fairly characterless pub in Poland Street, not far off Oxford Street, the sort of place tourists might pop into after a hard day's shopping, thinking they were venturing into a typical English pub. They might even be unwise enough to hazard a steak-and-ale pie or 'traditional' English fish and chips.

It is 6.30 on a Saturday evening. At the bar is a sallow-skinned chap with a frayed shirt collar, and the weary, resigned look of someone who has been let down by a few favourites that afternoon. He is being served Scotch by a surly, crop-haired guy in his thirties who looks like he could handle any trouble that might break out. Unusually for a London pub he appears to be from the northern hemisphere.

Our company is completed by two young, fresh-faced chaps in Tottenham Hotspur shirts, carrying little rucksacks, and eagerly swapping statistics and Spurs-related anecdotes; some streetwise-looking friends of the barman who look like they might be hiding some pretty useful muscles under their sports gear; and one or two shoppers in need of a livener before facing the tube home. It is quite a small pub so it appears fairly full. Its upstairs room is a relatively recent addition to Kevin's roster of Laughing Horse comedy clubs but prospects do not look good for tonight's session. The barman and his mates have failed to put up posters and that means Kevin has lost any passing trade, shoppers or tourists who might see the poster and decide to come back to check out the famous English sense of humour.

The evening starts at 8.30 so it is a little late to try and whip up interest now but Kevin enlists the grudging help of the barman to put up a few posters outside the pub and a rather sad little sign at the side of the bar with an arrow on it, pointing upstairs, decorated with the simple legend: 'Comedy'. There are five or six comedians booked to appear, Kevin tells me, of whom only one is being paid enough to cover his tube fare, possibly, and maybe a curry and a pint next door.

As previously indicated, there are around 1,600 people on this circuit, the beginners' circuit if you like, prepared to work for fees of between nothing and £50, a similar number of more experienced but still relatively unknown comics going out for around £100 a time, and then a third circuit, the inner circle as it were, of comedians who do it for a living, the Hal Cruttendens and Jo Caulfields of this world, earning reasonable money, as they wait to pick up their own TV show, or a series of beer commercials.

These concentric circles of comedy were described to me as 'the circles of hell from Dante's *Inferno*', by Robin Cousins (not the skater but one of the comedians on the same bill as me in Camden Town). Kevin takes a similar line. 'The process is Darwinian and ruthless,' he says, when I ask him how long would-be comedians might last before they and the audiences decide their future might lie elsewhere.

I am only looking to last for one night, upstairs at Liberties in Camden a week on Wednesday, and Kevin gives me some advice:

> Your first five-minute open spot is the hardest you'll ever do. You have to remember your material, which can be quite a feat in itself – five minutes eats up more stuff than you think – and also learn some performing skills at the same time. Never forget that it's a performance. You have to look at the audience, engage them confidently, but don't catch anyone's eye in particular. But if you do, don't look away, that would be fatal. What you are trying to do is sort of look through them rather than straight at them. You must direct your material at the audience as a whole.

He also tells me to stick to observations rather than gags: 'You must have ownership of your material or the circuit will not give you bookings. There is a market for gag-based comedy but it's mainly at strip shows, stag nights, gentlemen's evenings, that sort of thing, not in London's comedy clubs.'

I have some good stuff, I tell Kevin. Does he think there's any chance I could have a future on the London comedy circuit, maybe progress from the losers' circle to one where some real money changes hands? 'A lot of people have got a good five minutes in them,' he tells me, 'but they are unable to expand it into a longer set. Also, there is a massive amount of luck involved. Finally, it doesn't hurt to be young and attractive.'

What are you saying, Kevin? 'Ironically, the so-called alternative comedy circuit is far more ageist and sexist than old-fashioned showbiz.'

I consider Kevin's words of wisdom as I stroll down to Soho to meet a friend for supper. When I return to the pub and contribute my £3 to what looks like a paltry haul, the scene is a familiar one: a parade of hopeless hopefuls who show no evidence of having taken any advice from Kevin, especially not his first and most important tip.

Kevin tries to gee them up by laughing wildly at stuff that is only marginally amusing and then rounds the evening off with ten minutes of his own, which, notwithstanding the advice he gave me not two hours earlier, includes a gag. A real actual gag. Dressed up, maybe, but still a gag, of the type you might hear at a gentlemen's evening.

It's about young Kevin getting a job in a remote mining area of Australia and being told by the boss how grim it would be. 'But don't worry, every Friday, hundreds of barrels of beer get flown in and we all get slaughtered,' says the boss. 'I don't drink,' replies young Kevin. 'That's all right,' says the boss, 'every Saturday two planeloads of prossies fly in and you can shag yourself stupid.' 'I don't think I'd be interested in that,' says young Kevin. 'Wait a minute,' says the manager, 'you're not one of those prancing, mincing, lily-livered, handbag-carrying, lipstick-wearing pooftahs, are you?' 'What me, a homosexual? Certainly not,' says Kevin. 'Well, you're not gonna enjoy Sundays either,' came the reply.

Old as the hills, but the way Kevin told it – and I have edited it mercilessly – it dovetailed nicely into his life story; and the list of insults the manager slings at so-called pooftahs, of which there were about four more, is reeled off at machine-gun speed with deadly accuracy, leading me to believe I could get away with gags myself if delivered with Kevin's confidence.

So I consulted the classified ads at the back of the *Stage* and answered both ads offering gags for sale, as a result of which, Alan Austin, of 23 Western Road, Torquay, sends me '90 pages packed with a wealth of one-liners/ audience gags/ routines etc. etc.' for £9 – sample gag: What's the difference between an oral and a rectal thermometer? Answer: the taste – while Tim Maloney, of 2a Woodfield Avenue, Flint, Flintshire, despatches by return of post '700 NEW GAGS!!!!' for only £8' – sample: As the plane took off, one man went hysterical. You might think that's not bad out of 250 on board. But he was the pilot!

As well as the gags, Tim sends me a cutting from his local paper, headlined 'Joker Tim – An Ace in the Comedy Pack' from which I learn that Tim is forty-six and single, and that his parents, Maeve, seventy-eight, and Ted, seventy-nine, have been very supportive and have been backstage at many shows with him. 'Comedy has become Tim's life,' reports the newspaper, 'and he believes the best thing about his job is the laughter.' Easy for him to say. He does not have to face a possibly hostile crowd in the upstairs room of a pub in Camden Town.

In the event, I take one joke from Tim's selection, one of Alan's, and a few that I remember myself, and weave them into what I believe is a thoroughly modern comedy set, including some topical stuff about TV personalities Angus Deayton and John Leslie, who are in the news for drug-related misdemeanours. Centrepiece is a rant, naming market research, Bird's Eye potato waffles and John Peel as three particular horrors of modern life.

I discuss my routine with my friend Jayne Tunnicliffe, who did stand-up for a number of years as the character Mary Unfaithful, is a regular member of Lily Savage's team and has appeared on TV with Peter Kay. She takes out all the stuff about Bird's Eye potato waffles, and my more abstruse observations about market research, and in direct contrast to Kevin, she points up the actual gags. But then, like me, she's from the North.

I plan to end my routine by reading out an agency report which arrived at the BBC, covering the trial of a man in Goole accused of outraging public decency by approaching a couple of grazing horses and performing on them the act of which Rabbi Solomon Ganzfried so heartily disapproved. The report, I believe, is hilarious, partly because of the unintended *double entendres*, but mostly for its po-faced seriousness, and the unnecessary detail it goes into, all of which, incidentally, is reprinted verbatim in the *Goole Times*, together with an interview with the horse masturbator himself.

I try my set out on my wife on the eve of performance, and while she is generally approving of my own material, she absolutely refuses to see what is funny about a man dispensing equine relief on a river bank in East Yorkshire. She makes great play of surfing the TV channels looking for a late-night movie on Sky TV while I amend the horse report and read it to her again and again, adding my own 'humorous' observations. Eventually, she loses patience and says, 'No more horses. The horse just isn't funny. I'm going to bed. Don't do the horse.' I compromise by cutting the piece savagely, and I have to say it goes down a storm, a fitting climax to what is, if not a triumph, at least a qualified success.

Judge for yourself. Here is the horse masturbation story, as performed, with my asides in brackets. I explained to the audience that the story had been sent to the BBC by a news agency, and proceeded to read, as follows:

'A JOBLESS painter masturbated two horses on a busy Yorkshire riverbank in front of two pub doorways and a public bridge as people walked past, a court heard today (18 October 2002).

'The horses –' (And this is the bit I like.) – 'which cannot be named –' (Why not? Were they under age? Was it likely to affect their TV career? I mean, one of them apparently had a gig lined up on *Grandstand*.) '– were eating grass next to a river in Goole, East Yorkshire.

'He had his arm underneath the horse and was making a forward and backward motion with his right hand, the court heard.

'Now at this point a woman walked past, and –' (Wait for it.) '– Mr Baker verbally acknowledged the woman as she walked past.' (What do you reckon he said to her? 'Evening, lovely weather. Are you watching *Celebrity Big Brother*? Do you think Gary Neville's worth his place?')

– All the time, while relating this imaginary conversation, I continue to make the forward and backward masturbation motions. – (The report continues:)

'The following evening around the same time Mr Baker was seen with a horse in the same area by the same lady again.' (Two nights on the run – and he didn't take those horses out to the pictures, for a meal, anything?)

'Under interview with detectives Mr Baker confessed.

He said: "I grabbed its penis, and that, as normally a man would do –" (Normal for Goole, that is.) "– and I worked the horse off."

'His solicitor Mr Geoff Ellis said: "Mr Baker accepts that he masturbated the horse. But the basis of his plea is he does not accept, as the Crown have suggested in their opening –" (Opening? Geddit? These guys are doing their own bloody jokes.) "– that he put his hand in the anus of the horse."' (I mean, you wouldn't do that, not on a second date, not even in Goole.)

'Magistrate, Brian Kitson said: "We believe the crime is at least as serious enough to warrant more than a fine or a discharge."' (Discharge, geddit? I told you they were doing their own jokes.)

'Mr Baker left court with his hands in his pockets to laughter from other defendants who made horse noises.

'He stood outside the court house and said: "I don't know why I did it. I really don't. This is an absolute nightmare. What are people going to think?"' (Mmm, I wonder ...)

'Mr Baker denied any animal lust but admitted: "I haven't got a girlfriend."' (And I'm sure some of you know what that's like ... you know, no girlfriend – what should I do? Stay at home, watch a video and eat an entire box of Cadbury's miniature heroes or go out and jerk off some horses? Tough call ...)

My *coup de théâtre* – because there just wasn't the space to be baking bread – is to give everybody in the audience a copy of the original agency story to 'take home and share with your loved ones, as a memento of a very special evening'. 'It's the gift that goes on giving,' I tell them, as I hand out the photocopies, the effect of which is spoiled somewhat by the fact that several of them are personal friends, and have already received the story from me by email.

I may have neglected to mention, in trumpeting the qualified success of my stand-up, that I was on first-name terms with at least 60 per cent of the audience. I had taken the precaution of alerting a number of interested parties of my forthcoming personal appearance in the hope that they might act as my supporters' club and pitch in should anyone in the audience threaten physical violence.

My best and oldest friend, Paul, made a camcorder record of the event; Kate from the *Daily Express* was there; Darren from the BBC showed up; Asha, also from the BBC, came along with her friends; top London PR man Eugen Beer turned up with a small party. The problem was it had been raining solidly all day – one of those days when London comes to a standstill – so there was pretty well nobody else.

None of the other comedians brought along any friends, and Liz Stephens, the MC and host, a tall, slim, fresh-faced young woman, who looked like the kind of person who might have been described as gawky as a teenager, said that if the evening went ahead with just my supporters present, it would not be fair to the other comedians. 'Where are all your friends?' I asked my co-performers. 'We haven't got any friends, we're comedians,' said one. Many a true word. The only way I managed to persuade Liz to proceed with the evening was by getting two late-arriving chums to pretend not to know me.

There is a touch of the Joyce Grenfells about Liz. She would not look out of place in a youth hostel common room, not exactly jolly hockey sticks, but hearty. She laughs exaggeratedly at some fairly desperate material, doing her best to lighten up what could turn into a rather grim evening.

First performer on is a chubby forty-five year old who calls herself Mary Hail and does Catholic stuff and menopausal woman stuff. 'I've become a stalker,' she says. 'Some people say it's wrong but it's a great way to meet people.' According to my friend Kate, 'she looks like she's dropped in on her way from the Co-op', which does not make a lot of sense but I think I know what she means.

Most of the acts have one or two half-good lines but they don't have funny bones, any of them. Well, look who's talking. But I do take the precaution of including in my set more of what you might describe as jokes, lines that at least sound as though they might be funny.

I start with some topical observations about celebrities in the news for various sexual misdemeanours, which I spoil slightly by fluffing the first line. But I recover with a line imagining a situation in which a teenage girl might go for both the Blue Peter badge *and* the Jim'll Fix It badge.

I acknowledge Kevin's comedy check list, starting with the advice about not looking like a c**t and say, 'Tut, there's always one thing you forget.' I say I am going to do observational comedy, but as I am slightly older than the average comedy audience, some of my observations might be slightly different from theirs:

> Have you noticed how we're all getting liver spots on our hands these days? (Small titter.)
> But I'm not one of those older people who says everything was better in my day. Children's television, for instance. That's much better now. *The Tweenies*, for instance. We never had anything half as good as that. My daughter actually stands in front of the TV when the Tweenies are on, lost in wonderment, eyes all dilated, joining in with all the songs and dances ... She's twenty-six. We're a bit worried about her.' (Medium-sized guffaw.)

I explain that I have broken Kevin's rule by telling gags. but as I had sent £8 to a man in Flint for these jokes, I was damn well going to use them. This is a running joke through the act. Every time I tell a joke, which gets a sort of half-groan of recognition from my fellow comedians, I turn to them and plead, 'Eight quid, come on.' I make fun of Flint a little, but:

> I don't know why I am taking the piss out of Flint, because I'm from an impoverished coal mining area in the North, and proud of it. Every evening my dad would come home from work black as the ace of spades, hawking up coal dust from his lungs, spitting great black globules of it into the hearth ... I don't know why. He worked in a fucking bank.

And then a little bit about the internet, quoting two genuine sites whose wares I have lately been made aware of: *Grandmas Who Take it up the Ass* and *Extreme Adult Farmyard Action*. This leads fairly naturally into the horse masturbation story, its rapturous reception, and my being chaired up Camden High Street.

All this is how it happens (apart from the bit about being chaired up Camden High Street). The following morning I telephone my friends to thank them for their support. 'I bet not many comedians telephone each member of the audience individually and thank them for turning up,' I say to Paul. 'And do the whole job in under five minutes,' counters Paul, a little harshly, I think.

The bizarre thing is, I want to do it again, this time in a room full of strangers. I know I have little to offer in the way of originality, and I am way too old to consider stand-up as an alternative career, or even as a hobby like Kevin. But it is like learning to drive. It is quite a heady feeling when you first find you are able to change gear smoothly, synchronizing your feet on the clutch and accelerator pedals. You want the lesson to go on forever. There were brief moments during my short set when it felt like I was ready to remove the L-plates, and I would like to test myself once more. The famous comedy club Jongleurs is opening a branch in Leeds so I may try it out there.

Ah, the intoxicating drug of laughter – as I meant to say during my act – so often these days followed by the even more intoxicating drug of cocaine.

I have now seen more comedians than can possibly be good for your health, in Benidorm, in Edinburgh, in miserable upstairs rooms of pubs, but it was only when I gave it a try myself that I got some idea of what drives them on, even the dreadful ones. Basically, it is the knowledge that you have the power to get a response from complete strangers. Not unlike the chap with the horses.

It's not an analogy I would want to push too far but it does give me the opportunity to tell you what happened to my friend Jon. I mentioned that we shared an interest in Californian pop music, but whereas I diversified into soul music, he went the whole way with the West Coast movement, especially the psychedelic bands, and threw himself into it, with all the attendant intake of hallucinogenic drugs.

It was clearly not easy to pursue these hobbies in a strictly orthodox Jewish household (although it would make an interesting experiment) so, either because he was thrown out, or chose to leave, he began to spend much of his time in various hippy colonies in North Africa. We had lost touch by this time – apart from anything else I couldn't take the music he liked – and as he hit the hippy trail, I went to university in Glasgow and then started work as a journalist in Bristol. It was only when I got a call from an old Manchester friend, when I was in my early twenties, that I discovered Jon had had a brain haemorrhage, possibly drug-related, and was now in a mental hospital.

I didn't see him again before he died, and really it is only writing about laughter that has brought him suddenly so vividly to life. We laughed a lot. I am not sure you ever abandon yourself to laughter quite as readily as you do with a childhood friend. Certainly, masturbation and pop music have never seemed quite as funny since those days.

Only twice in my search for comedy did I witness an audience putting up the white flag and surrendering to the forces of laughter in this childlike way; Gerry Graham on the cruise ship, with his ancient gags about henpecked husbands and so on, had the crowd in raptures, while the paying customers at *Night Collar*, the play I went to see in Liverpool, were similarly enraptured, on their feet, shouting responses to the actors, and generally behaving in a very non-Royal-Court way.

The only reason I can present for this is that the crowd's own lives, particularly their frustrations and prejudices, were being reflected back to them, enveloping them in the kind of warm feeling of shared experience you normally only find with a childhood chum when you suffer Mr Backhouse's French class together or when you share the fear that your mum might catch you in an act of auto-eroticism.

Beyond that, no analysis. As someone once said, analysing comedy is like removing the entrails of a frog and studying them, and about as funny. Ken Dodd was once asked on the Parkinson show if there were regional differences in comedy. 'Sure,' he said, 'you can tell a joke in Glasgow and get a big laugh. In Manchester, though, they don't laugh at all. Same joke.' 'Why's that?' asked Parky. 'They can't hear it,' replied Doddy.

Having criss-crossed Europe in search of laughs, I wish

I could offer something a little deeper than the great Ken Dodd's analysis. Failing that, of course, it would be great to end what I like to think of as my comedy odyssey with a joke. Really great.

10

TRIBUTE

I think we have established that when Ethel Merman said there was no business like show business she knew what she was talking about.

An example: I telephoned the hypnotist Andrew Newton to check on his progress since we last met and we got to chatting about the string of high-profile entertainment figures whose careers had recently been blighted by scandals, arrests, and so on, which I reckoned might be a little depressing for those striving so hard for fame and fortune. 'Not at all,' said Andrew. 'I was discussing this with a stand-up comic I know and he reckons it's marvellous news. Every time one of them falls off, we all move one rung up the ladder.' It's true, you see, there *are* no people like show people. Always look on the bright side of life. The sun will come out tomorrow.

Andrew is certainly upbeat about his act, despite councils in some areas continuing to take a dim view of stage hypnotism. 'In Aberdeen and Halifax, nobody under twenty-one is allowed to attend the show. How stupid is that?' he asks. So he has been staying out of Aberdeen and Halifax. 'I had some splendid results in the summer, in Jersey, Guernsey and Alderney, where I packed out the theatres,' he tells me. 'Then again, Torquay turned out to be a bit of a flop. You win some, you lose some, but you press on.'

Well, up to a point. Freddie has jacked it in. All those Saturday nights in damp back rooms in working men's clubs with concert secretaries telling him to keep the noise down have clearly got to him. The appeal of a job that enables you to sit around in your armchair watching daytime television only goes so far. 'We don't handle him any more,' I am told when I telephone his manager Mike Allen's office. 'He flitted to Tenerife at the beginning of January.' But Freddie has taken his PA with him, so there is every chance he will be performing out there, and in the balmy evenings with the holiday spirit abroad, they will probably let him turn it up to 11.

Not that Freddie's disappearance from these shores leaves us with a desperate shortage of tribute acts. The directory at the back of the *Stage* is still full of them: Kylie Likely, the Cheatles, Killer Queen, the Village Peeple, with a double 'e'. The market for people – or peeple even – pretending to be other people seems as vibrant as ever. Colin Cross, manager and technical guru to Abbagirls, claims to have 'a fantastic year booked'. Japan, Hong Kong, the Czech Republic and Dubai are on the itinerary as he and his girls continue to spread the international language of Benny and Björn worldwide. 'We are already fully booked right up to Christmas and into 2004,' he says.

Tony Blackburn, of course, is the ultimate tribute act. He is going out as a kind of tribute to himself and, since his success in reality TV, bookers cannot get enough of him. His price is now probably double what it was when I saw him in Newcastle; he has a new radio show and is rarely off our television screens. I happened to catch him in a *Celebrity Stars in Their Eyes* special recently, 'doing' Cliff Richard, an act I expect the TV types would define as post-modern irony, although taking the piss is the way we like to put it round our way.

I confess, when I embarked upon my year of travels in showbiz, starting with Tony in Newcastle, I was fully prepared to indulge in a little irony myself. What fun I was going to have with these small-time acts on the road to nowhere, or even – with people like Tony – on the road back. As it turned out, that was not the story. For a start, the kind of unusual acts you see over the credits at the end of *Phoenix Nights* on TV – the one-legged Elvis, the elderly lady conjurer producing doves from unlikely places ('spesh acts' as they used to be known) – have all but vanished (notwithstanding Sticky Vicky in Benidorm), driven from the business by lookalikes and tributes.

But more important than that, I enjoyed myself so much I forgot to sneer. The acts I spoke to were unvaryingly friendly, helpful and eager to please, and when you spend much of your working life trying to wheedle something half-interesting out of professional footballers and their managers, that comes as rather a pleasant surprise. Their performances were not all to my taste but what they had in common was that they all gave what in the football world is often calculated as 110 per cent. There was nobody out there trying to get away with 108. These people work hard for the money.

When you work in radio, you can coast, be lazy, under-prepared, and no-one will notice. There are people I know in radio – household names – who have been freewheeling for years and getting away with it. But when you appear before a live audience, however sparse, you will soon be found out if you try and short-change them. Strange thing is, despite having had ample opportunity to digest this lesson, I gave two talks recently, disregarding – through pressure of work – Andrew Newton's six 'P's (Prior Planning Prevents Piss-Poor Performance), and on both occasions I floundered somewhat. After one of my appearances I was even bad-mouthed on a website message board, where an attendee complained that I 'looked uncomfortable'. 'So would you after a bottle and a half of cheap red wine,' I was inclined to reply, but didn't.

The point is, it takes a certain kind of ridiculous dedication to be a performer. Dreaming up new stuff, costume changes, altering the inflection in a gag, smiling, projecting yourself to the audience, attention to detail, always attention to detail, even before the least appreciative of audiences; at a wedding party, where you will be barely noticed, or a barmitzvah, where the chopped liver may get better reviews than you.

Then there are the jobsworths you have to deal with at the business end who think you are a prima donna if you ask for a stage on which you can be seen and a microphone that enables you to be heard. Not to mention the managers and agents who will rip you off if you are not careful. And at the end of it all, a twist of fate, a stroke of luck, and it's some other lucky bastard who gets the Roller, the drug habit and the place in Tarby's celebrity golf tournament, while you're left with the Allegro and the chunky Kit Kat.

So, why bother? I will tell you why. Because how many other jobs are there where a single phone call can be your passport to fame, fortune and Britain's finest bedrooms? It happened to Tony Blackburn. And even if the call is not from the TV show that will pitchfork your name before a celebrity hungry nation, every now and then it will be a gig involving first-class travel, free quality food and a sum of money not unadjacent to a big wedge. I was once flown over to Holland to stand on a bridge in Delft in the pouring rain to present a programme about antiques for a satellite channel nobody watches. We bought a lovely dining room table and four chairs with the money. When you get those gigs, it sort of makes up for not having a decent pension scheme, and having about the same level of job security as Mussolini in April 1945.

When I phone Tony De La Fou, he has just returned from one of those good gigs: a corporate event at the Belfry, the famous golf course in the Midlands. 'They were a firm of surveyors, having a big posh piss-up to celebrate ten years at the top in surveying or something,' he tells me. Given the ludicrous obsession with property in Britain, they are probably about the only people who still have money to splash out on acts, so Tony had been booked to hang around the entrance eating a bit of fire. 'Ironic, really,' he says, 'because it was a non-smoking venue, so people kept on coming out to smoke, giving me a sort of captive audience.'

Tony is still available for children's parties but – partly inspired by my example, I am proud to say – he is branching out into other areas. He has been doing a radio show on Phoenix FM, the independent voice of Billericay (it really exists, I have been a guest on Tony's show), and has sent me a football-based sitcom he has written which he thinks we might work on together.

The thought that the business can send you pinging off like a pinball in lots of different directions is what makes it so attractive. In a way, I suppose, it is what makes show business people appear younger than they are. They never really lose that just-out-of-college feeling that anything is possible. (The other sure-fire way of retaining your youth, by the way – and it is often disregarded in the search for miracle elixirs – is to lie about your age, and I write as someone who has been thirty-eight for the past 14 years.) The big drawback of the business is that your life is controlled by the whims and fancies of the public. If the public do not want what you do – and the public are almost always wrong, as any entertainer will tell you – you will not be working. At this particular point in time they want tribute bands feeding them a facsimile of their youth, so-called surreal comedians (laughter without a point, basically) and people who have been on television for any reason whatsoever.

I think my friend Mr Methane could be a star, though, if he adopted my suggestion and reinvented himself in a post-modern way. Maybe he could interest someone in a television documentary about a very tall man who is alone in the world in having mastered the art of controlled anal voicing. For the moment he continues as a novelty at sportsmen's dinners and the like. When I phone him he has just returned from a gig in Workington, where he has been appearing alongside the old-style comedian Mick Miller. He has split from his manager, Barry, he tells me. 'He kept getting flooded out. His house got flooded at Christmas, so he decided to jack it in,' he explains, in one of his typical non sequiturs, made extra dry by those flat northern vowels.

Mr M is now represented by Mike Malley, who has a reputation as something of a showbiz shark. Malley's other main act is Stevie Starr, the Regurgitator, a chap who swallows Rubik's cubes, live goldfish, light bulbs and the like, and then brings them up again, so there is a certain synchronicity there. Malley could be said to have both ends covered. 'I tried representing myself for a while,' says Mr M, 'but bookers are like second-hand car dealers. They hammer you down on price. The beauty of Mike is, you know you've got somebody who is constantly on it. He's going to build me a diary, so I think it's going to be a good year.'

Crissy Rock is also bullish about the future. She is testing for a new character in *Coronation Street*, and they like her. But she has to be Mancunian and not Scouse, so she is having elocution lessons. 'It's 20 quid an hour with this posh lady in Liverpool, but she's told me first of all before I do Manc I've got to learn the Queen's English. You know, to speak posh like her. I thought "fuckin' 'ell", pardon my French, but she's so far back and la-di-da …' at which point she slides effortlessly from her native Scouse – about the thickest I've heard – into something that sounds like Diana Rigg's classier sister. I think she would be great in *Coronation Street*, but then again, what do I know? Maybe I just got too involved with the people I met on the lower rungs of the show business ladder, but I liked them all, almost without exception.

Hey: here's a question. Is it because these people are charming and open and likeable that they are not higher up the ladder? Or is it that when you get to the top of the ladder the instinct is to stamp on the hands of those climbing up behind, and that is when you are transformed into a complete arsehole? Who knows?

For the moment it is a question I have no time to address. I am busy working on a format for a show involving a hypnotist, a fire-eater, a very tall farter and a gritty Scouse actress that will make us all famous.